Dyslexia in the Foreign Language Classroom

SECOND LANGUAGE ACQUISITION
Series Editor: **Professor David Singleton,** *Trinity College, Dublin, Ireland*

This series brings together titles dealing with a variety of aspects of language acquisition and processing in situations where a language or languages other than the native language is involved. Second language is thus interpreted in its broadest possible sense. The volumes included in the series all offer in their different ways, on the one hand, exposition and discussion of empirical findings and, on the other, some degree of theoretical reflection. In this latter connection, no particular theoretical stance is privileged in the series; nor is any relevant perspective – sociolinguistic, psycholinguistic, neurolinguistic, etc. – deemed out of place. The intended readership of the series includes final-year undergraduates working on second language acquisition projects, postgraduate students involved in second language acquisition research, and researchers and teachers in general whose interests include a second language acquisition component.

Full details of all the books in this series and of all our other publications can be found on http://www.multilingual-matters.com, or by writing to Multilingual Matters, St Nicholas House, 31-34 High Street, Bristol BS1 2AW, UK.

SECOND LANGUAGE ACQUISITION
Series Editor: David Singleton, *Trinity College, Dublin, Ireland*

Dyslexia in the Foreign Language Classroom

Joanna Nijakowska

MULTILINGUAL MATTERS
Bristol • Buffalo • Toronto

Library of Congress Cataloging in Publication Data
A catalog record for this book is available from the Library of Congress.
Nijakowska, Joanna.
Dyslexia in the Foreign Language Classroom/Joanna Nijakowska.
Second Language Acquisition
Includes bibliographical references and index.
1. Dyslexia. 2. Second language acquisition. 3. Dyslexic children–Education. 4. English language–Study and teaching–Foreign speakers. I. Title. II. Series: Second language acquisition (Clevedon, England)
[DNLM: 1. Dyslexia–etiology. 2. Dyslexia–therapy. 3. Language. 4. Learning. WL 340.6 N691d 2010]
RJ496.A5N55 2010
616.85'53–dc22 2010018314

British Library Cataloguing in Publication Data
A catalogue entry for this book is available from the British Library.

ISBN-13: 978-1-84769-280-1 (hbk)
ISBN-13: 978-1-84769-279-5 (pbk)

Multilingual Matters
UK: St Nicholas House, 31-34 High Street, Bristol BS1 2AW, UK.
USA: UTP, 2250 Military Road, Tonawanda, NY 14150, USA.
Canada: UTP, 5201 Dufferin Street, North York, Ontario M3H 5T8, Canada.

Copyright © 2010 Joanna Nijakowska.

All rights reserved. No part of this work may be reproduced in any form or by any means without permission in writing from the publisher.

The policy of Multilingual Matters/Channel View Publications is to use papers that are natural, renewable and recyclable products, made from wood grown in sustainable forests. In the manufacturing process of our books, and to further support our policy, preference is given to printers that have FSC and PEFC Chain of Custody certification. The FSC and/or PEFC logos will appear on those books where full certification has been granted to the printer concerned.

Typeset by Datapage International Ltd.
Printed and bound in Great Britain by Short Run Press Ltd.

Contents

Introduction vii

1 Becoming Literate 1
   Defining Dyslexia 1
   Getting Ready for Reading and Spelling 10
   Reading Strategies and Stages of Reading Development 15
   Orthographic Depth and Grain Size: A Cross-language
   Perspective on Reading and Dyslexia 21

2 Causes of Dyslexia 33
   Introduction 33
   Genetic Mechanisms in Dyslexia 35
   Brain Mechanisms in Dyslexia 37
   Phonological Coding Deficit Hypothesis 43
   Double-deficit Hypothesis 54
   Magnocellular Deficit Hypothesis 56
   Cerebellar Deficit Hypothesis 61

3 Dyslexia and Foreign Language Learning 66
   Native Language-based Foreign Language
   Learning Difficulties 66
   Foreign Language Learning Disability versus Continuum
   Notion of Language Learning Differences 70
   Review of Research in Support of Linguistic Coding
   Differences Hypothesis 74

4 Symptoms and Identification of Dyslexia 85
   Lifelong Nature of Dyslexia 85
   Emotional-motivational Disorders in Dyslexia 97
   Identification of Dyslexia 100
   Identification of Dyslexia: Bilingual/Multilingual
   Perspective 106

5 Treatment and Teaching 115
   Issues in Dyslexia Treatment 115
   Principles of the Multisensory Structured
   Learning Approach 122

Multisensory Structured Learning Approach and
Foreign Language Study 127
Educational Accommodations Towards Learners
with Dyslexia 145

6 Sample Activities for Learners with Dyslexia Learning
English as a Foreign Language 153
Activities for Developing Phonological Awareness and
Awareness of Sound-letter Relations 153
Orthographic Awareness Activities 165
Morphological Awareness Activities 175
Grammatical Awareness Activities 179

Afterword 190
Appendix 1 197
Appendix 2 200
Appendix 3 206
Appendix 4 207
Appendix 5 208
Appendix 6 209
References 210
Index 233

Introduction

Naturally enough, ensuring access to information in various fields of knowledge, literacy skills exert considerable influence on our personal growth and professional development. Thus, researchers have been intensively investigating the phenomenon of reading and spelling disorders and, even more importantly from the practitioner's standpoint, ways of helping reading-impaired individuals.

Perceived as a significant commercial asset as well as a good investment in children, the ability to speak foreign languages constitutes another prerequisite of success in our fast-developing, multilingual society. Not only does it equip a person with a useful tool for international communication, but it also enhances an individual's chances of getting a position on the professional ground. The necessity of possessing the command of a foreign language has been well recognised by the authorities, which resulted in a foreign language requirement becoming a compulsory part of educational systems. Viewed as an advantage, recently bilingualism has become a social necessity, allowing people to face the challenges thrown up by the united, frontier-free Europe.

The foreign language requirement forms an integral and compulsory part of educational systems. Apparently, fulfilling this requirement seems to bring about considerable difficulties in many students with dyslexia. This is because the specific reading and spelling problems they encounter frequently prevent them from accomplishing this social and educational demand. Weaknesses such as poor decoding and remembering, slow processing and retrieving linguistic information, mainly on the phonological level, are believed to be salient features of individuals with dyslexia, leading to educational achievements much below their intellectual potential and requirements posed on them.

Students with dyslexia tend to face difficulties in foreign language learning (FLL) and, in fact, the problem is associated with native language learning. Ganschow and Sparks (Ganschow *et al.*, 1998; Sparks, 1995; Sparks *et al.*, 1989, 1998a) plausibly show that for individuals with dyslexia, native language learning poses variable difficulties, which then translate into similar problems in foreign language learning. It follows that the skills of an individual in the native language components of linguistic coding form the cornerstone of successful foreign language learning. It has been shown that the performance on standard measures of native language skill is related to the level of foreign language proficiency. Namely, higher levels of oral and written foreign language proficiency are achieved by the students who exhibit higher levels of native language skills. Thus, difficulties in reading, writing, listening and speaking, be they subtle or overt, existing in the native language are likely to be responsible for similar difficulties in foreign language learning. The most noticeable deficit concerns the inability to consciously isolate and manipulate the sounds of language and relate them to the appropriate written symbols – letters. Suffice it to say that poor native language skills may significantly impede the process of foreign language learning.

In the modern foreign language classroom, where emphasis is put on authentic situational contexts, the almost-exclusive use of the target language and the inductive acquisition of grammar, pronunciation and spelling, the needs of students with dyslexia are hardly catered for. Learners with dyslexia require explicit and structured instruction. A direct structured multisensory instruction (MSL) in the phonological/ orthographic system of a language has unequivocally proved successful in teaching reading and spelling skills to children with dyslexia, not only in their native language, but also in a foreign language (Crombie & McColl, 2000; Ganschow et al., 1998; Jameson, 2000; Miller & Bussman Gillis, 2000; Nijakowska, 2008; Sparks et al., 1989, 1992b, 1998c; Sparks & Ganschow, 1993).

In the multisensory approach, it is assumed that the more modalities are involved in the learning process, the more effective it is. Multisensory methods utilise simultaneous engagement of several sensory channels and the synthesis of stimuli coming from these channels. Thus, teaching reading and spelling is realised by the integration of visual, auditory, kinaesthetic and tactile stimuli and involves simultaneous presentation of information coming from various senses (Bogdanowicz, 1997a/2000; Ganschow & Sparks, 1995; Jędrzejowska & Jurek, 2003; Sparks & Ganschow, 1993; Sparks et al., 1991, 1998c; Thomson & Watkins, 1990). In order to minimise the literacy problems of children with dyslexia, it is necessary to automatise their skills through carefully designed, monitored and long-term training (Nicolson & Fawcett, 2001). Unfortunately, in many cases, neither special methods of teaching foreign languages during regular teaching hours nor special classes outside school are offered to students with dyslexia. Foreign language teachers' awareness of developmental dyslexia still seems rather poor. Those who are familiar with the problem and want to help their students with dyslexia become discouraged by the lack of materials designed especially for teaching foreign languages to dyslexics.

In most educational systems, the foreign language requirement is compulsory. Many foreign language teachers are likely to be faced with the challenge of teaching learners with dyslexia. It follows from the above that by far the most important issue seems to be raising awareness among pre-service and in-service foreign language teachers of the nature of dyslexic difficulties and effective teaching methods. There exist great social demand and pressure on teachers to be able to understand and help students with special educational needs. Also, foreign language teachers themselves feel the need to broaden their professional knowledge. They repeatedly report being in need of a comprehensible guidance on how to work with children with dyslexia, since these issues rarely constitute a part of curricula realised during teacher training. It seems especially crucial in light of the necessity to create equal educational opportunities for all children. Teachers are expected to accommodate their educational requirements and examination conditions to the individual needs and abilities of students with dyslexia. However, too often, there seems to be a considerable mismatch between the legal educational law concerning individuals with dyslexia and the way it is executed in school practice.

There is a wide spectrum of publications concerning both the theoretical and practical aspects of the phenomenon of dyslexia; however, they are prepared mainly for psychologists, teachers-therapists, native language teachers, kindergarten and elementary education teachers. Very few publications on dyslexia are addressed specifically to foreign language teachers. This book aims to fill this gap and present the problem of dyslexia from a foreign language teacher's and cross-language perspective. It is intended to serve as a reference book for those preoccupied with foreign language teaching, including experienced in-service teachers, novice teachers as well as teacher trainers and trainees. My intention in this work is to provide the reader with a concise overview of the current research, both its theoretical and practical aspects, in the field of specific difficulties in learning to read and spell – developmental dyslexia. Understanding the phenomenon of dyslexia requires interdisciplinary knowledge. Advances in the fields of science such as psychology, pedagogy, neurology, biology and linguistics contribute to the explanation of the nature of this learning disorder. Equipped with greater awareness as well as solid background knowledge of a wide spectrum of the theoretical and practical aspects of the problem, one can more efficiently help children with dyslexia. It is hoped that the book will help teachers to face one of the many challenges that the educational system poses on them nowadays, namely, the organisation of an effective teaching process for students with dyslexia, which is accommodated to their needs and abilities.

Terminological issues related to dyslexia, together with a definition of the disorder are covered in Chapter 1. The potential to develop literacy skills and the need to do likewise are fundamental. Abilities to read and spell are complex and multilevel in character and engage several physical, physiological and psychological phenomena. Chapter 1 discusses the issues of general readiness for learning to read and write and best predictors of reading success. The focus then shifts towards the nature of the reading process, strategies, developmental stages, to finally touch upon the issues of orthographic depth and grain size. Reading and dyslexia are discussed from a cross-language perspective, highlighting the similarities and differences between dyslexia manifestations and literacy acquisition in different languages.

Due to the complex nature of dyslexia, any organised attempt to understand its multiple facets should involve the analysis of its underlying causes. Chapter 2 is devoted to both the neurobiological substrates and cognitive correlates of dyslexia. It familiarises the reader with the major facts and hypotheses and presents selected findings from massive research. As already mentioned, phonological processing impairments responsible for the specific reading disability in the native language may similarly impede the acquisition of foreign languages. Chapter 3 deals with the issue of native language-based foreign language learning difficulties and includes the verification of the notion of a disability for foreign language learning versus continuum notion of language learning differences.

Dyslexia is a lifetime condition, one does not grow out of it, once qualified to have dyslexia a child continues to demonstrate symptoms of the disorder, altering in range and severity, into adulthood (Gregg *et al.*, 2005; Snowling, 2001a). The ways dyslexia leaves its imprint on behaviour varies across individuals. In addition, throughout life, symptoms of dyslexia manifest in a given person are subject to dynamic change. These issues as well as the problem of identifying the cases of dyslexia among the multitude of poor readers are addressed in Chapter 4. There is general agreement that early diagnosis of learning disorders is pivotal to the further educational career of at-risk children, however, various universally applicable but also country- and language-specific factors seem to influence the assessment procedures. There is increasing and widespread sensitivity and concern over the issues of literacy acquisition and assessment of reading disabilities among school children in multicultural and multilingual settings, in particular those who learn English as a second or subsequent language. This issue is also referred to in Chapter 4.

Supporting individuals with dyslexia in their attempts to overcome reading and spelling difficulties, experienced both in their native language as well as in the second or additional language that they frequently struggle to learn, is a standing challenge for teachers. Chapter 5 is concerned with treatment and educational accommodations for children with dyslexia, it revises teaching principles and methods, with special attention given to a multisensory structured approach and its application in the foreign language context.

Chapter 6 comprises a collection of activities, worksheets, games and movable devices that are designed to enhance the sensitivity to and foster the acquisition of phonological, morphological, orthographic and, last but not least, grammatical aspects of the English language. The orthographic awareness section contains a set of sample activities selected from the programme used in the small-scale intervention study described in Chapter 5. The study concerned the effectiveness of direct multisensory instruction for improving word reading and spelling skills in English as a foreign language, through the systematic study of selected grapheme-phoneme relations, spelling patterns and rules. The activities proposed in the book may be used during additional classes conducted with students with dyslexia, either for one-to-one lessons or for group work, however they can equally well be incorporated into the regular classroom routine.

The feeling of success is especially important for students with dyslexia, who frequently experience failure in their educational endeavour because, needless to say, an individual constantly confronted with an unattainable challenge can, eventually, become frustrated and discouraged. In addition, confusion caused by an inadequate teaching approach and by requirements that are impossible to fulfil, deprives individuals with dyslexia of the feeling of joy and satisfaction brought about by learning. Teachers' sensitivity and awareness of the nature of dyslexic difficulties and ways of overcoming them can definitely help to steer clear of such danger.

Chapter 1
Becoming Literate

Defining Dyslexia

Terminological issues

This book is devoted to a developmental cognitive disorder, more precisely, to a specific learning difficulty in reading and spelling – *developmental dyslexia*. To begin with it is important to ensure terminological and definitional clarity, which would be most helpful for appropriate understanding of the described phenomena. Reading disorders are quite intensively studied and several terms have been proposed in different countries to denote reading deficits of various kinds, in children and adults alike. Apparently, such a situation is a consequence of the complex nature of the skill in question as well as the diverse causes and multiple types of reading and spelling disorders.

Let us focus first on the distinction between *acquired* and *developmental disorders*. Acquired reading and spelling deficits result from brain injury or disease and connote either total or partial loss of the already possessed ability to read or spell. The intensity of symptoms largely depends on the size and location of the lesion as well as the age of the person. *Acquired alexia* and *acquired agraphia* are spelled out as a total loss of the faculty of reading and spelling, respectively, while *acquired dyslexia* denotes only a partial disappearance of reading competence, and *dysgraphia* is a partial loss of spelling ability. To stress again, acquired reading and spelling disorders are connected with deficits in qualifications that a given person, be it an adult or a child, had already possessed prior to brain injury (Bogdanowicz, 1989, 1999; Krasowicz, 1997).

Acquired reading disabilities in adult patients are often taken as a model for interpreting and achieving further understanding of the neurological concept of developmental reading impairments (Borkowska, 1997). However, such an approach is rejected by Hulme and Snowling (2009), who advocate investigating developmental reading disorders in children by relating them to patterns of typical reading development in children. Much as adult models usefully specify what normally constitutes a result of development, they do not describe the development itself. Reading development undergoes certain changes over time as children develop, thus, naturally, younger children are less accomplished in this respect than older children. Developmental disorders would typically involve modified – slowed down – rates and patterns of change. Children with dyslexia will learn to read slowly and with difficulty and this delay in the rate of the development of the reading skill is claimed to be the most salient and striking characteristic of this disorder.[1]

Developmental disorders can be divided into *specific (restricted)* and *general difficulties/disorders*. General disorders concern deficits in most, if not all, cognitive functions. By contrast, specific disorders refer to situations where impairment in just one or a limited number of skills is involved, while functioning in other areas remains typical. Krasowicz (1997) suggests further division of specific developmental reading disorder into *specific decoding disorder* and *specific comprehension disorder*.

In the UK, such a specific (restricted) difficulty, which involves a selective (occurring in a restricted domain) impairment in acquiring a skill that must be learned, is referred to as a *specific learning difficulty*; whereas *global learning difficulty* concerns problems in acquiring a wide range of skills and in understanding concepts. In the USA, the terms *learning disorders* and *mental retardation* are used to denote specific and global learning difficulties, respectively. In practice, the results of a standardised IQ test (a measure of general intelligence) are used to distinguish between cases of specific and general learning difficulties.[2] The diagnosis of specific learning difficulties is frequently conditioned by the achievement of IQ score within or near the average range, while general learning difficulties are diagnosed in children with IQ scores below 70.

Specific developmental reading disorder – developmental dyslexia is one of the most intensively researched, best known and understood specific learning difficulties. Specific learning difficulties experienced by children with dyslexia concern acquiring reading and spelling skills, while the ability to understand concepts is normal. In addition, they often demonstrate talents in various areas of study – in science, sport or art (Hulme & Snowling, 2009).

Developmental dyslexia has its place in the international classifications of diseases, mental disorders and related health problems. In the 'International Classification of Diseases and Related Health Problems, Tenth Revision (ICD-10)', specific difficulties in learning to read and spell are classified as follows: general category – *specific developmental disorders of scholastic skills*; specific learning difficulties in reading – *specific reading disorders (developmental dyslexia)*; specific learning difficulties in spelling – *specific spelling disorders*; specific difficulties in acquiring the technique of writing due to lowered motor ability and motor coordination of hands, which is characterised by a very low graphic level of writing – *specific developmental disorder of motor function*. For the sake of comparison, in the 'Diagnostic and Statistic Manual of Mental Disorders, Fourth Revision (DSM-IV)', the following notions have been introduced: general category – *learning disorders*; specific reading problems – *reading disorder (or dyslexia)*; specific writing problems – *disorder of written expression*; specific technical problems in writing – *developmental coordination disorder* (Bogdanowicz, 2007).

The notion *dyslexia* can be understood as a narrow concept, comprising solely of a difficulty in reading or as a whole syndrome of specific difficulties in learning to read and spell, indicating the coexistence of reading difficulties with spelling impairments (pertaining to both poor orthography and graphic level) (Borkowska, 1998; Pętlewska, 1999; Zakrzewska, 1999). Drawing on clinical experience, Bogdanowicz (1999) has suggested that isolated reading and spelling disorders can be diagnosed apart from the whole syndrome of specific difficulties in learning to read and spell. For example, a spelling disorder may arise that coincides with neither a reading disorder nor poor graphic level of writing (developmental coordination disorder). However, according to Szczerbiński (2007), as much as dysorthography (specific spelling disorder) may happen to be dissociated from dyslexia, the reverse case is extremely rare. Most usually, low-level performance of decoding and encoding coexist. Bogdanowicz (1989, 1997b, 1999) uses the term *developmental dyslexia* to signify the syndrome of specific learning difficulties in reading and spelling as a disorder of written communication. Within this syndrome, she identifies three isolated disorders: *dyslexia* – to symbolise specific difficulties in learning to read (poor decoding), *dysorthography* – specific spelling difficulties (poor encoding) and *dysgraphia* – specific difficulties in acquiring the appropriate graphic level of writing. The above terminology has been widely used in Polish publications (Borkowska, 1998; Juszczyk & Zając, 1997; Knobloch-Gala, 1995; Krasowicz, 1997; Miązek, 2001; Pętlewska, 1999; Sawa, 1999; Zakrzewska, 1999; Zelech, 1997 and others). Much as the abovementioned terminology has gained wide acceptance in Poland, the terms may be interpreted differently in other countries. By way of example, according to Smythe and Everatt (2000), in Italy, *dysgraphia* denotes motor difficulties, while *dysorthography* refers to spelling difficulties; however, the term *dysgraphia* is used as synonymous with spelling difficulties as well. Yet, in Russia, *dysgraphia* stands for a spelling disorder characterised by inadequate usage of graphemes or syntactic impairments, whereas *dyslexia* refers exclusively to a reading disorder manifesting itself in a slower rate of reading, paired with numerous persistent errors.

All in all, *dyslexia*, often qualified by the adjective *developmental*, is the most popular and internationally accepted expression denoting specific difficulties in learning to read and spell, specifically with regard to decoding and encoding single words, which come into play in children at the beginning of school education (Critchley, 1964; Krasowicz, 1997; Ott, 1997; Reid, 1998). Additionally, apart from *dyslexia* and *developmental dyslexia*, several descriptive notions, such as *learning difficulties, learning disabilities, specific reading disorders* or *specific learning difficulties/disabilities*, which have been introduced in the international medical, psychological and pedagogical classifications, are internationally recognised as well. Snowling and Caravolas (2007) argue that the characteristics of dyslexia – a delay in reading development – makes us perceive the disorder as dimensional. It means that individuals can suffer from a disorder to varying degrees; children with dyslexia seem to occupy a bottom end of the continuum of normal variation in the skill in the population. However, despite the apparent arbitrariness in putting a cut-off point between dyslexia and normal reading, it is common, and often easier, to use categorical labels such as 'children with dyslexia' rather than dimensional (descriptive) terms – 'children with specific severe difficulty in learning to read and spell'. Such diagnostic categorical labels are found useful in communicating the types and nature of difficulties experienced by children (Hulme & Snowling, 2009).

In this book, the terms *dyslexia, developmental dyslexia,* as well as descriptive notions such as *specific learning difficulties, specific difficulties in learning to read and spell, specific developmental reading disorder and learning disorder/disability,* are used interchangeably. They denote specific difficulties in print processing, with respect to word decoding and encoding, which children experience in learning to read and spell from the beginning of their school education.

Definition of dyslexia

Educational science qualifies children with developmental dyslexia to the special educational needs (SEN) group, together with particularly intelligent and talented children as well as mentally retarded children, children with neurological diseases, deficits in motor and sensory organs, emotional disorders, culturally (environmentally) and didactically neglected children, and, last but not least, those with speech disorders. It is a frequently observed fact that these children invariably function badly in the school environment when following the routine educational programmes. They typically stand in need of: firstly, a pace of work accommodated to their abilities and needs; secondly, individualised teaching programmes and requirements, and, finally, special methods of teaching, put into practice by qualified teachers (Bogdanowicz, 1995, 1997b; Tomaszewska, 2001).

It is widely acknowledged that dyslexia constitutes a neurological condition with genetic traces and is typically designated with phonological processing impairment at the cognitive level. Essentially, the fundamental dyslexic difficulty relates to the below-standard print processing at the level of single words, more precisely, inaccurate and/or slow decoding of attempted words as well as incorrect word encoding (spelling). Children with dyslexia fail to recognise printed words at the level expected for their age. Reading is primarily dependent on phonological processing and visual analysis, and some importance is also attributed to general speed of information processing and the ability to integrate information of various modalities. While morphological, syntactic and semantic factors may play a part in decoding, they are most probably language-specific and their role is rather limited here in comparison to the engagement of these processes in comprehension. Children with dyslexia find accurate and fluent reading truly difficult, while impairment of reading comprehension is quite distinct from dyslexia. A consequence of persistent difficulty in skilful recognition of printed words, not specific to dyslexia but rather constituting its result, gives rise to certain difficulties. Frequently, trouble in understanding written texts and organising thoughts on paper may become apparent, which, in the long run, can intensify, inevitably leading to persistent problems in the general process of gaining knowledge. Importantly, notwithstanding some reading comprehension problems brought about by impaired decoding of written text, individuals with dyslexia would be very unlikely to demonstrate any limitations in understanding complex spoken text and concepts. Last but not least, dyslexia is a life-long condition,[3] whose characteristic features alter with age and development; symptoms are dynamic in nature, they tend to be evident and then diminish at given points in development. Certain deficits are compensated, for example, attainment of customary accurate reading is within reach, however, even in adulthood, spelling remains a painful task and reading speed seems less susceptible to remediation (Snowling, 2001b).

The complex and diverse nature of dyslexia naturally invites multiple attempts at defining the phenomenon in question. There are several competing etiological theories of dyslexia at large (though one might perceive them as actually complementary to one another), hence a natural tendency towards promoting a definition that would aptly reflect the main assumptions of a given theory. Most relevantly, dyslexia is claimed to be the outcome of the influence that various pathogenic factors exert on the central nervous system, leading to disorders of functions underlying the processes of reading and spelling. Beyond doubt though, difficulties encountered by children with dyslexia are specific, narrow and limited in range as opposed to unspecific, global learning difficulties. Generally, reading disorders are claimed to depend on the occurrence of a substantial mismatch between the reading achievement of a child (operationalised as the score on a standardised reading test) and that expected, given the level of intelligence, education and chronological age. Children with dyslexia experience persistent learning difficulties in spite of adequate intelligence, lack of sensory and motor deficits, and absence of environmental and didactic negligence (Bogdanowicz, 1997b, 1997c; Elliot & Place, 2000; Heaton & Winterton, 1996).

The following definition was recommended by the World Federation of Neurology in 1968:

> Specific developmental dyslexia is a disorder manifested by difficulty in learning to read and write despite conventional instruction, adequate intelligence, and socio-cultural opportunity. It depends on fundamental cognitive disabilities that are frequently constitutional in origin. (Bogdanowicz, 2002a: 56; Borkowska, 1998: 41; Krasowicz-Kupis, 2008: 49; Ott, 1997: 3)

The neurobiological, constitutional character of the disorder and limited range of difficulties are highlighted here. However, the feature that earned this definition the unfavourable attitude of practitioners is its clearly exclusionary character (Snowling, 2001b). Exclusionary definitions are described as negative, they are frequently heavily criticised because exclusionary criteria may be ambiguous, which in turn multiplies doubts (Krasowicz-Kupis, 2008). Nevertheless, at least to some extent, exclusionary definitions can be useful for introductory clinical diagnosis, especially when additional explanations with regard to the concepts included are added in order to avoid ambiguity.

For example, on the one hand, rightly enough as one would think, instruction is brought to light in this definition, which potentially conveys crucial implications for diagnosis. More precisely, since inadequate teaching too often produces intense difficulties in print processing of other than a dyslexic character, it is of extreme importance to verify the methods of teaching that a person being assessed towards dyslexia was exposed to in order to escape misclassification (Szczerbiński, 2007). On the other hand, what exactly is 'conventional instruction'? What kinds of methods and techniques do the authors conceive of as conventional? The same holds true for 'adequate intelligence', one might wonder why children with an IQ below average may not qualify for the diagnosis of dyslexia.[4]

'Socio-cultural opportunity' lacks precision as well. There is enough evidence to claim that experience can alter the way genes are expressed in children predisposed to dyslexia. Variable patterns of gene expression can be responsible for differences in health and brain development, which in turn may exert diverse influence on behaviour. Importantly, environmental factors operating at biological, cognitive and behavioural level can add to the risk of developing reading impairments in children. Poor socio-economic background as well as poor literacy environment (literacy-related activities, children interest in books, reading experience opportunities at home, parents' educational level and literacy problems, schooling, print exposure) seem to generate greater chances for the occurrence of reading problems, though with probably greater impact on comprehension than decoding skills (Frith, 2008; Hulme & Snowling, 2009). Nevertheless, as stressed by Hulme and Snowling (2009: 329):

'We are not born with genes that make us dyslexic, nor are we born into the environment that makes us dyslexic. We may, however, be born with genes that give an increased risk of developing dyslexia, but this risk will in turn be moderated by environmental factors'. The influence of both genetic and environmental risk factors as well as their interaction on development seems undeniable.

The discrepancy between IQ level, age and scholastic attainments of children with dyslexia are elucidated in another definition, provided by Thomson and Watkins:

> Developmental dyslexia is a severe difficulty with the written form of language independent of intellectual, cultural, and emotional causation. It is characterized by the individual's reading, writing and spelling attainments being well below the level expected based on intelligence and chronological age. The difficulty is a cognitive one, affecting those language skills associated with the written form, particularly visual-to-verbal coding, short-term memory, order perception and sequencing. (Thomson & Watkins, 1990: 3)

Again, children with dyslexia are claimed to exhibit a typically unexpected, considerable mismatch between the low level of their reading skill, age and generally high intellectual ability. In this definition, a reference is also made to the emotional aspect of dyslexia. Importantly, emotional causation of the disorder is definitely denied. It needs stressing that even though emotional-motivational disturbances frequently accompany dyslexia, they are not responsible for the occurrence of the reading failure, quite the contrary, they may follow from it.[5]

The following, widely cited, definition was compiled in 1994 by the Orton Dyslexia Society Research Committee in conjunction with the National Centre for Learning Disabilities and the National Institute of Child Health and Human Development:

> Dyslexia is one of several distinct learning disabilities. It is a specific language-based disorder of constitutional origin characterized by difficulties in single word decoding, usually reflecting insufficient phonological processing. These difficulties in single word decoding are often unexpected in relation to age and other cognitive and academic abilities; they are not the result of generalized developmental disability or sensory impairment. Dyslexia is manifested by variable difficulty with different forms of language, often including, in addition to problems with reading, a conspicuous problem with acquiring proficiency in writing and spelling. (Bogdanowicz, 1999: 821; Borkowska, 1998: 42; Cieszyńska, 2001: 11; Krasowicz-Kupis, 2008: 53; Lyon, 1995: 9; Ott, 1997: 4; Reid, 1998: 3; Tomaszewska, 2001: 30)

It is an inclusionary definition; it focuses on characterising what dyslexia is rather than what it is not (Schneider, 1999). According to Reid (1998), it is an example of a research-based definition, which means that it draws on the constructs that can be measured directly and clearly indicates when an individual may be diagnosed as dyslexic. Bogdanowicz (1999) states that this definition is clinical in nature, since it pertains to the characteristic symptoms of dyslexia. The definition clarifies that dyslexia is inherited, clearly stresses difficulties in processing linguistic stimuli, and points to insufficient phonological processing skills as the underlying cause of dyslexic reading and spelling difficulties. However, other scholars seem to voice a contradictory opinion on the listing of possible causes of the disorder in its definition. Much as Uppstad and Tønnessen's (2007) postulate that a definition of dyslexia should concentrate on the symptoms, they also advocate not stating the causes, such as phonological deficit, in order to avoid promoting circular arguments and setting limits on the search for causes.

Still, it seems that formulating a definition of dyslexia based on its symptoms indeed poses substantial problems. First of all, we lack unanimous agreement as to the understanding of the phenomenon and specifying its symptoms, and second, it goes without saying that the clinical picture of dyslexia is quite dynamic, symptoms change with time during the course of development and can be influenced, for instance, by methods of teaching, remedial instruction and compensation abilities (depending on the intelligence level, range and severity of deficit). As stressed by Frith (2008), on the one hand, lack of severe problems in acquiring the reading skill does not necessarily exclude dyslexia, on the other hand, frequently, reading difficulties manifest in children are not of a dyslexic nature. Moreover, development is characterised by change, and behavioural signs of dyslexia can reduce with time as a result of education and compensation, however, the underlying cognitive cause, most probably in the form of the phonological deficit, may remain impaired. Thus, to avoid faults and mistakes, diagnosis towards dyslexia cannot be based solely on the outcome of reading tests. In order to distinguish dyslexic difficulties from reading problems of other kinds, dyslexia should be defined as a neurodevelopmental disorder, implying the existence of a complex causal chain embracing biological, cognitive and behavioural factors, present since birth and characterised by a set of behavioural symptoms subject to change over time.

Despite the most noticeable tendencies in dyslexia research concerning the language deficit highlighted in the definition, the fact that all children with dyslexia are said to encounter problems with phonological processing seems an oversimplification since, as clinical experience together with research findings (White *et al.*, 2006) show, there is a group of children with the visual-spatial pathomechanism of dyslexia

(Borkowska, 1998; Cieszyńska, 2001). Nevertheless, beyond doubt, the phonological processing deficit is perceived as a core deficit by the majority of academics and practitioners, which is, as a matter of fact, quite well reflected in intervention programmes.

Determining the approximate number of children with dyslexia is important in order to estimate the scale of the phenomenon. Admittedly, a rough calculation differs strikingly across countries – from 0.1% to as much as 20% or even 30% (Bogdanowicz, 1989; Zakrzewska, 1999). Elliott and Place (2000) quote the following numbers: 10% of children experience mild dyslexic difficulties and 4% experience severe dyslexic problems. Stein (2001) claims that 5–10% of children, mainly boys, are found to suffer from dyslexia. According to Hulme and Snowling (2009), the disorder appears to be quite common and affects about 3–6% of children.

It seems that the apparent inconsistency with regard to estimates of the prevalence of dyslexia, not only in different countries but even across a given country, results from the lack of a commonly accepted definition of the disorder, naturally inviting diverse interpretations of the nature and severity of disorders qualified as dyslexia (Zakrzewska, 1999). As indicated earlier, reading difficulties can be placed on the continuum, ranging from mild to severe, thus defining the disorder is not just stating dyslexia versus its lack, but it involves selecting, quite arbitrarily, the point on the continuum the scores below which denote poor readers (Szczerbiński, 2007). The situation referred to above is conditioned by adopting various, not uniform (apparently not quite reliable and valid) criteria used for identification (Wagner *et al.*, 2005). Last but not least, diverse results of studies on dyslexia in different countries are dependent on the specificity of a given language as well.

Intense scholarly discussions set aside, there seems to be some general agreement mirrored in the proposed definitions, namely, dyslexia has a biological, constitutional basis. Moreover, this developmental disorder is most commonly characterised in terms of inadequate facility in language processing, which is manifested by decoding and encoding difficulties. The most ubiquitous cause of dyslexic reading problems is below-standard word identification ability, which itself is brought about by print decoding impairments. Word identification is heavily dependent on the successful acquisition of the alphabetic principle, allowing comprehension of the phoneme-grapheme conversions, which in turn draws on the acquisition of phonological awareness – defined as the knowledge that spoken words are composed of individual speech sounds. Furthermore, it is explicated that, firstly, dyslexic difficulties do not arise as a result of sight or hearing impairment, secondly, they are not due to emotional problems, environmental or didactic negligence or mental retardation, and finally, that the discrepancy between their potential and scholastic achievement is indisputably tangible. The failure in acquiring reading and spelling skills is incontestable despite conventional teaching methods, understood as those that proved effective as relates to other individuals. At the same time, frequently, individuals with dyslexia prove to be high-achievers in other academic disciplines, which incontrovertibly indicates that dyslexic scholastic difficulties are very specific, concerning the limited range of abilities.

Getting Ready for Reading and Spelling

Reading and spelling skills

Literacy concerns the skills of reading and spelling, learning of which requires intentional and conscious control. They are evidently dynamic, complex and, above all, multilevel in character; both are linguistic activities (forms of communication based on language), metalinguistic activities (grounded in the awareness of the relationship between print and spoken word, phoneme-grapheme relation and the awareness of language resources used to formulate utterances), metacognitive activities (requiring conscious control of the cognitive processes involved – understanding the meaning conveyed in texts), pragmatic and metapragmatic activities (connected with purposeful use of written texts) (Krasowicz-Kupis, 2004). Reading involves decoding the text and interpreting its meaning, while writing is connected with shaping ideas and encoding them with the use of print, both requiring linguistic skills on phonological, morphological, syntactic and semantic levels (Bogdanowicz & Krasowicz-Kupis, 2005a).

As indicated above, reading is concerned with transmitting information in the form of a written text from the author to the reader. Thus, print forms a medium for sending and receiving information via the visual channel (Kaczmarek, 1969). From a rather technical standpoint, reading can be viewed as converting graphemes into phonemes and, consequently, changing written words into spoken words. Even though it actually allows access to higher levels of linguistic processing, mere decoding does not guarantee understanding (Shaywitz, 1997). It is the ability to comprehend the identified symbols that indicates mastery of the reading skill (Brzezińska, 1987; Szempruch, 1997). To recapitulate, there exist three interrelated aspects that are incorporated into the reading process, namely, the technical aspect of matching phonological units to graphic symbols, the semantic aspect – understanding, and the reflexive one, operationalised as critical reading. In other words, the multifactor character of reading involves identifying phonological elements and their corresponding graphic symbols, recognising the meaning of these symbols, as well as understanding and assessing the value of the content in the context of individual experience. Additionally, Velutino *et al.* (2004) stress the fact that words in a text must be identified not only accurately but also fluently enough in order to infer the meanings from the text, within the limits posed by working memory. Altogether, reading as a compound psychological process, consisting of several stages and involving numerous activities, is principally about unlocking the code of printed symbols used to represent speech in a given culture in order to access meaning (Ziegler & Goswami, 2006).

As it stands, the process of reading is frequently presented as a form of communication inseparable from spelling (Kaczmarek, 1969; Szczerbiński, 2007). However, closely interrelated as they are, they still seem to follow slightly differing courses of development. It is a frequent observation that some words that are read correctly tend to be misspelled by children and adults alike. Similarly, children can appropriately write down words that they cannot read easily (Bryant & Bradley, 1980). Frith (1985) proposed not only the existence of qualitative differences in the time-courses of reading and spelling in children, but also a causal relation between the two. More precisely, at the very beginning on their way towards literacy, children tend to break the alphabetic code through spelling and this knowledge of letter-sound conversion rules is then used in their initial reading attempts. However, along the process of becoming literate, certain changes occur with regard to the causal link between the two skills. That is to say, a year or two later, there is a shift of roles; orthographic patterns and rules are first to be recognised in reading and it is the reading experience that promotes subsequent application of new principles in spelling. Let us take the split-digraph rule in English (e.g. 'a-e' in 'fate') as an example. It has been observed that at first, children represent vowel sounds with single letters (e.g. 'o' in 'dog' or 'a' in 'hat'), that is why they find it harder both to read and spell long vowel CVCe words (which involves the orthographic rule) than short vowel monosyllabic CVC words, conforming to simple letter-sound rules (e.g. 'fame' versus 'cat'). Then, over time, they first improve their reading performance of CVCe words before they internalise their spelling, and, finally, this reading upgrade leads to subsequent success in the spelling of these words (Davis & Bryant, 2006).

The educational implication of Frith's claims is that enhancement of children's reading experience is most likely to have a beneficial effect on their learning of spelling choices, letter sequences and orthographic rules because initial acquisition of orthographic regularities and patterns achieved through reading practice is later transferred and applied to spelling.

Readiness for learning to read and spell

Moving on now to the notion of *readiness for learning to read and spell*, let us elaborate on it from a more global perspective and within a wider social context first. School readiness can be understood as a part of the process of bringing up and educating children, whereas in a much narrower scope, it is perceived as a factor conditioning the acquisition of certain specialist skills and abilities, e.g. reading and spelling or mathematics (Krasowicz-Kupis, 2004). Thus, as such, readiness for learning to read and spell constitutes an integral part of a more general notion of school readiness, which is perceived as dependent on the advances in the physical, mental, emotional and social development of a child.

Looking more closely at the issue of readiness for learning to read and spell, Brzezińska (1987) proposes that, firstly, it incorporates the development of psychomotor functions, which enable children to acquire the technique of reading and spelling. Secondly, it comprises the development of linguistic-notional processes, which condition the comprehension of meaning, and, finally, it involves the development of emotional-motivational processes, which allow discovery of written speech as a form of communication. Much as the above description seems to provide an insightful perspective on the notion in question, it is criticised for its apparent lack of a clear and direct reference to the impact of language awareness on the process of learning to read and spell (Krasowicz-Kupis, 2004).

By and large, Krasowicz-Kupis (2004) formulates the concept of readiness for learning to read and spell, aptly defining it as a moment in which a child reaches the level of physical, social and psychological development which makes him/her both sensitive and susceptible to systematic teaching of reading and spelling. Being sensitive refers to being interested in the knowledge provided at school (emotional-motivational aspect of readiness), while susceptibility is connected with an ability to understand, remember and acquire knowledge and skills taught at school. In her model, Krasowicz-Kupis (2004) lists six general components of readiness for learning to read and spell, grouped into two broader sections, namely, factors specific and non-specific to reading and spelling. Among the non-specific components, she classifies attitude and motivation, development of perceptual-motor abilities and intellectual development. To further elaborate on the subcomponent of perceptual-motor development, it comprises visual perception (encompassing visual analysis and synthesis, identifying, comparing, directionality, visual memory); auditory perception (including differentiating between speech and environmental sounds, perceiving and reproducing rhymes as well as auditory memory); motor abilities, settled pattern of lateralisation, spatial orientation (left-right, top-down) and perceptual-motor integration.

The components specific to reading and spelling are as follows: development of speech (understood not in terms of correct articulation but rather as an ability to form and comprehend linguistically correct oral utterances, which most fully reflects the level of language acquisition) and language (basic linguistic abilities – phonological, morphological, syntactic, semantic and verbal memory), language awareness, and, last but not least, awareness of print as a system of signs, with a set of rules and specific reference to speech and the surrounding world. The role of attention and memory is stressed as well.

Predictors of reading success

The study of predictors of reading success has gained substantial interest among researchers. There exists an impressive amount of empirical evidence supporting the claim of the causal link between pre-existing (underlying) early phonological skills (prior to reading instruction) and later reading achievement (Bowey, 2005; Krasowicz-Kupis, 1999). The strength of phonological abilities measured at the beginning of school education significantly predicts later ability to read, which is in accord with the causal theory of development of the ability to read by Bryant and Goswami (Goswami, 1999; Goswami & Bryant, 1990). Apart from phonological awareness, considerable attention was given to letter knowledge, short-term memory, rapid serial naming speed, pseudo-word and expressive vocabulary, all of which qualify as powerful predictors of later reading attainment identified among pre-schoolers (Carroll & Snowling, 2004; Puolakanaho et al., 2008; Snowling et al., 2003). The acquisition of the alphabetic principle (the idea that the individual sounds of spoken words can be represented by letters or letter clusters) is of critical importance for mastering the reading skill in alphabetical scripts. Both phoneme awareness and knowledge of letter-sound correspondences are essential for mastering the alphabetic principle, in addition, both strongly predict reading and spelling achievement in children and influence each other in a reciprocal nature (Hulme et al., 2005; Vellutino et al., 2004).

Ziegler and Goswami (2006) put forward an argument that in all languages studied to date, reading development depends on the children's phonological awareness. They admit that developmental differences in the grain size of lexical representations across languages emerge, brought about by the varying consistency of phonological-orthographic relations, which in turn invites the application of variable developmental reading strategies in different languages. Consequently, the awareness of onsets, rimes and phonemes studied in various languages may not predict reading success to the same extent. Generally, phonological skills and the ability to recognise letters in a pre-literacy period constitute the best predictors of future reading achievement (Adams, 1990; Bradley & Bryant, 1983; Wolf et al., 2005). For instance, phoneme awareness strongly predicts reading success with regard to all the alphabetical orthographies that it has been measured in (Goswami, 2000). Nikolopoulos *et al.*'s (2006) findings with regard to the transparent orthographic system of the Greek language support the existing evidence that phoneme awareness is a strong within-age predictor of variations in reading rate and a unique longitudinal predictor of spelling ability. On the other hand, the strong predictive link between onset-rime awareness and reading development exists in English (Bradley & Bryant, 1983; Bryant *et al.*, 1990), however, it is not as prominent in Norwegian and Swedish (Hoien *et al.*, 1995) or in Polish (Krasowicz-Kupis, 1999), finally, it has not been confirmed for German (Wimmer *et al.*, 1994). Goswami (2000) speculates that these differences might result from the relatively high degree of spelling-sound consistency in English orthography as relates to rimes in comparison to individual phonemes.

Puolakanaho *et al.* (2008) support the claim that the level of reading accuracy is based on very early core phonological abilities. They demonstrated that early pre-reading skills, measured as early as 3.5 years of age, were strong predictors of reading accuracy, however, that did not hold true for fluency. Fluency, on the other hand, could be partially explained by letter knowledge. Substantial doubts have been cast on the presumed equally predictive power of phonological awareness with regard to reading accuracy versus fluency across orthographies. Apparently, the outcome of studies, predominantly concerning regular orthographies, even though there is a growing body of evidence to support the claim with reference to less transparent orthographies as well, indicates that although it prognosticates reading accuracy well, phonological awareness tends not to best predict reading fluency (Aro, 2006; Hogan *et al.*, 2005; Puolakanaho *et al.*, 2008; Seymour, 2005).

In sum, Reid (1998) considers the following subskills crucial in the acquisition of reading: phonemic awareness, segmenting and blending abilities, letter recognition, grapheme-phoneme correspondence, recognition of word patterns and visual memory. Having access to the abovementioned subskills in the pre-literacy stage fosters greater and faster competence in reading. Conversely, children with poor reading subskills tend not to make successful readers and, consequently, lack opportunities to further develop the skills via the reading activity itself. Hence, good readers seem to be in a favourable situation because they can improve the skills they already possess, whereas poor readers become even poorer – the phenomenon described by Stanovich (1986) as the 'Matthew effects'.

Starting school life and becoming a student poses a considerable cognitive burden as well as psychological and social pressure on children, let alone the problems emerging due to poor reading subskills. Thus, to escape the turmoil of reading failure, children require assistance and special training from an early stage, not only when they start formal schooling and reading instruction, but also prior to that. Kindergarten children, in particular those at risk for developmental disorders such as dyslexia, should be given support in order to optimally develop the components of readiness for learning to read and write, which would make their early training in reading and spelling easier. Still, it cannot be denied that arriving at a diagnosis before a child is expected to demonstrate the skills in which difficulties are likely to arise poses problems. What matters most is teachers' sensitivity and awareness of the need to promote success for children from a pre-school stage, however, with the social risk of categorical labelling during the identification process in mind.

Reading Strategies and Stages of Reading Development

Reading strategies

It is undeniable that reading primarily constitutes a linguistic rather than visual activity. Still, the role of visual-orthographic and phonological processing in single-word recognition across languages is intensely debated, especially with reference to the orthographic depth hypothesis (assuming that different word recognition strategies are invited by different levels of grapheme-phoneme transparency). That is why generalising the results of research on reading and spelling with regard to diverse languages and orthographic systems seems problematic. Additionally, the role of context and language awareness in the course of reading acquisition is perceived differently by researchers (Bogdanowicz & Krasowicz-Kupis, 2005a; Goswami, 2005; Miller-Guron & Lundberg, 2004; Ziegler & Goswami, 2006).

Let us now concentrate on reading strategies. When the ability to read single words is taken into consideration, two major strategies to reach the meaning of the printed information can be enumerated, namely, the visual (*whole-word, lexical*) *direct* and *phonological indirect strategy*. During whole-word visual recognition, meaning is attempted directly from the graphic image of a word, thus it is independent of the knowledge of the alphabetic principle. Children lacking awareness of the grapheme-phoneme relationship, quite naturally, are in no way capable of reading words they are not familiar with. By contrast, the holistic lexical approach proves effective with regard to well-known words, which children have already come across and read several times, and it is efficient with homophones as well. Also, skilled readers use the opportunity to rely on the visual strategy for quick and automatic recognition of familiar letter sequences.

On the other hand, during phonological decoding, particular letters in a word are first transposed into their corresponding sounds (or their mental representations), which are then synthesised into a kind of acoustic code that is recognised. In that way, with the use of speech processing mechanisms, the meaning of the word is unlocked. Phonological decoding might seem relatively complicated, however, it is indispensable for reading unknown words and pseudo-words. By contrast, it loses its efficiency with reference to reading homophones and homographs.

Unknown, difficult words and pseudo-words can also be successfully decoded with the use of both the analogy between the well-known and unknown words and contextual cues. When approaching new words, readers are equipped with the ability to recognise familiar sequences of letters, frequently occurring at the beginning or end of other words that they are already capable of reading. A natural tendency that children demonstrate towards identifying subsyllabic elements, such as onsets and rimes, promotes reading through analogy.

The lexical (visual) and sublexical (phonological) strategies for reading constitute the principal components of the *dual route model of reading* (Coltheart et al., 2001). The model assumes that words can be read either via direct orthography-to-phonology mappings or indirect phoneme-to-grapheme correspondences. The former depends on knowledge of how the whole word is pronounced, and the latter involves knowledge of how individual graphemes (sublexical units) are pronounced.

Readers have at their disposal yet another strategy for attempting the meaning of unknown words, namely, anticipation from context. Sentences containing a target word, illustrations accompanying the text and knowledge about the world can be of considerable help in gaining access to meaning. Still, it is not surprising that a lot of guessing is bound to take place when this strategy is employed. Nonetheless, the role of contextual clues in gaining understanding of printed information is highlighted, mainly in reference to text reading strategies. The following is a short discussion of the concept of bottom-up, top-down and interactive ways of text processing.

Let us begin with the *bottom-up model*, which presumes that the reader analyses the visual stimuli, often transforming them into auditory stimuli, and then recognises the meaning of the consecutive elements of the text, until he/she understands the whole phrase or sentence. This model entails two different mechanisms/strategies. The first one – visual – assumes immediate transformation of the information from the eye to the mind. More precisely, a graphic representation (picture) of a fragment of a given text is used as a code, opening the mental lexicon, and in this way the meaning is reached. On the other hand, the second mechanism – phonological – involves a direct transformation of the visual substance of the text (or its image) onto the phonological level or, in other words, visually perceived elements of the text are changed into articulation expectancy (mental representation of pronunciation), which, in turn, opens the mental lexicon, utilising the mechanisms of perception and comprehension of speech. It means that the reader pronounces the words being read, or at least imagines their sounds, and in that way arrives at their meaning. Apparently, these mechanisms do not exclude each other; what is more, both can be used during the process of reading a given text, but with regard to its different elements. The phonological mechanism is used in processing unknown words, whereas the visual mechanism is utilised in reading familiar words (Bogdanowicz & Krasowicz-Kupis, 2005a; Jorm, 1985; Krasowicz, 1997; Krasowicz-Kupis, 1999; Reid, 1998).

By contrast, in the *top-down model* the reader forms hypotheses and predictions about the text and then tries to absorb the meaning from the available clues. The hints concern the syntactic (the structure of the sentence) and semantic (the anticipated meaning) context of the text being read as well as the graphic information, pertaining to what a word or a sentence looks like. Thus, the reader draws on his/her experience and knowledge of the world and language (Bogdanowicz & Krasowicz-Kupis, 2005a; Krasowicz, 1997; Krasowicz-Kupis, 1999; Reid, 1998).

In his *interactive-compensatory model*, Stanovich (1980) describes reading as an interactive process, in which the reader utilises both the bottom-up and the top-down strategies, thus the information from the graphic and contextual levels is used simultaneously. It is implied that some readers may rely more heavily on a given way of processing (e.g. the use of context), depending on the level of development of the reading skill. Interestingly, for the most part, individuals whose decoding (recognition) skills are poor use contextual clues; therefore, quite naturally, children in the beginning stages of learning to read and individuals encountering reading disorders would fall into this category. Furthermore, for poor readers, recognising words requires such a great effort that the cognitive capacities for comprehension are reduced. Unlike poor readers, good readers, armed with efficient word recognition skills (quick and automatic decoding), demonstrate no need to lean on the context. On the contrary, they visually process every word, even highly predictable ones. Therefore, they may concentrate their full cognitive potential on understanding (Adams, 1990; Stanovich, 1980). Nevertheless, a tendency for the partial use of contextual clues may occur in good readers when approaching particularly difficult texts, including complex or unclear information. Moreover, the model proposes that the weaknesses of the reader are compensated for by his/her strengths (Stanovich, 1980).

Reading development

The development of reading is commonly seen to proceed in phases or stages. The way childrens' reading ability changes with age is specified in various phase models of reading, however these models often fail to delineate how exactly the changes take place. In most developmental (phase) models, the acquisition of reading begins with a visual stage followed by a linguistic stage. However, the models differ in the way the stages of reading development are sequenced and in descriptions of the characteristic behaviour of children during particular stages, with the most salient difference regarding when (how early) and how children begin to rely on phonological information in learning to recognise words (Ehri, 2005; Treiman & Kessler, 2007). Still, the fact that the models lack convergence with respect to certain areas, while, at the same time showing certain similarities in other aspects, allows interpretation of a relatively more complete and reliable picture of the process. It needs stressing though that the stages are not discrete, but rather overlapping and reflecting the specific demands of the texts being dealt with.

Generally, when children start learning to read, they use a visual approach and form quite arbitrary connections between printed words and their pronunciation, then they begin to perceive and understand how letters of printed words map onto sounds in a systematic way. As reading skill develops, children consolidate the knowledge of letter-sound correspondences (alphabetic stage), the application of which becomes progressively more automatic and less effortful. Finally, the orthographic representations become fully specified (the orthographic stage).

Models of reading are numerous and diverse (e.g. Sochacka, 2004; Wolf et al., 2005); however, it is not within the scope of this book to discuss them extensively. Let us instead draw the attention of the reader to the general characterisation of the following models: the phase model of word reading proposed by Ehri; the three-stage model of reading by Frith, claiming universality across languages; and the balance model of reading by Bakker, pretending to possess an explanatory power with regard to specific difficulties in learning to read and spell – developmental dyslexia.

Ehri (Ehri, 1995, 2005, 2008; Ehri & McCormick, 1998) distinguishes four phases in the process of learning words – *pre-alphabetic phase* and three *alphabetic stages*, namely, *partial, full* and *consolidated*. The pre-alphabetic stage is characterised by forming connections between selected visual features of words and their pronunciation and meaning, children are not yet capable of making use of systematic letter-sound mappings. There are tight bonds between the following three stages, moving from partial, through full towards consolidated alphabetic phase reflecting the process of development from immature towards mature and automatised reading. During the partial alphabetic stage, beginning readers, who are aware of several letter names and their corresponding sounds, learn how to remember words through creating conventional, though still partial, matches between the letters and sounds in words. Very often, first and last letters leave most lasting traces in their memory. Children become familiar with selected letter-sound relations, they are also capable of performing simple phonological analysis tasks. Equipped with the knowledge of the alphabetic system, children become more advanced in using the powerful tool, enhancing the process of forming and remembering links between printed words and their pronunciations. The strategy of relying on phonological hints is beyond doubt much more efficient and productive than depending on visual clues – specific to pre-alphabetic stage. In full alphabetic phase, beginning readers learn to read words through creating full letter-sound connections, in addition, they gain access to the decoding strategy and the strategy of reading words by analogy. Finally, the consolidated alphabetic phase involves automatic application of grapheme-phoneme conversion rules. Moreover, children learn how to make use of bigger units – syllables and subsyllable spelling patterns (e.g. alliterations, rimes), which they repeatedly come across in different words. Relying on multiletter units in order to decode words reduces memory load.

Frith (Dockrell & McShane, 1993; Frith, 1985; Krasowicz, 1997; Krasowicz-Kupis, 1999; Ott, 1997; Reid, 1998; Sochacka, 2004) identifies three stages in reading acquisition. The first is the *logographic stage*, during which a child visually recognises the overall word patterns. More precisely, words are perceived as units based on the first or last letter, a cluster of letters or a general shape of a word. Thus, recognition depends on the visual memory of words that children are already acquainted with. Therefore, they find it very difficult to read unfamiliar or nonsense words. During this stage, the relations between letters and sounds are not yet integrated, which is why children frequently misspell the words they can already read.

The next stage in Frith's model of reading is the *alphabetic stage*. A child becomes aware of the fact that words can be segmented into phonemes and, further on, that these phonemes can be mapped on letters. The ability to match the sounds to the corresponding symbols – letters – is defined as the alphabetic competence. As such, this competence constitutes a necessary but, in fact, insufficient condition for appropriate reading, as it does not allow differentiating between irregular words. Spelling is believed to enhance the alphabetic stage of reading by virtue of more direct links to the letter-sound relationships. When a child enters the third stage – the *orthographic stage* – his/her reading is a result of an amalgamation of the skills acquired during the previous stages. Words are recognised quickly, automatically and with the use of adequate decoding strategy.

As already mentioned, the course of the three stages differs for the acquisition of reading and spelling. That is to say, the visual, logographic code is used faster during reading, while the alphabetic stage is first observable in spelling, and in fact the reverse is the case as relates to the orthographic code. According to Reid (1998), children with dyslexia may have some difficulties in the visual stage, but they will almost certainly encounter problems in translating the letters into their phonological equivalents.

The physiology of the human brain together with brain functioning as relates to the cognitive processes, form the basis for the *balance model* of learning to read, proposed by Bakker (Bakker, 1984, 1990, 1995; Bakker et al., 1991, 1995; Bednarek, 1999; Bogdanowicz & Krasowicz, 1995, 1996/1997; Dryer et al., 1999; Kappers, 1997; Krasowicz, 1997; Robertson, 2000a, 2000b). The left hemisphere is said to be specialised or dominant for language in the majority of people, whereas the right hemisphere deals with perception of shape, form and direction (visual-spatial information). The balance model of learning to read presumes that both hemispheres are simultaneously involved in the process of reading, though not equally. Furthermore, the level of the right- and left-hemispheric entailment shifts according to both the ability to read and the perceptual features of the text. To be more precise, the right and left hemispheres predominantly mediate beginning and advanced reading, respectively. Greater activity of the right hemisphere is noted when the text includes some perceptually challenging features, for instance, unusual fonts or drawings. In the beginning stages of learning to read, spatial-perceptual analysis of letter shapes and letter strings, identification of letter names and unfamiliar words require greater right hemisphere involvement. On the other hand, advanced reading is characterised by the use of linguistic strategies that are under the control of the left hemisphere. Hence, in successful reading, the visual-spatial processing becomes increasingly automatic and then the linguistic strategies (syntactic and semantic analyses) become superior, thus a shift from right hemisphere dominance to left hemisphere dominance is presupposed and it is claimed to take place at around eight years of age.

In his balance model, Bakker proposes a quite plausible, though not without faults, explanation of specific difficulties in learning to read. Apparently, some children are unable to adopt the appropriate strategies, either perceptual or linguistic, at the right time during the process of learning to read; consequently, some disturbances may emerge. Bakker proposes the existence of two types of dyslexia – the P-type and L-type – which result from the overuse of the perceptual (P) and linguistic (L) strategy, respectively. The difficulties emerge if during the process of learning to read, the shift of dominance from the right to the left hemisphere takes place either too late (P-type dyslexia) or too early (L-type dyslexia). A child with P-type dyslexia fails to utilise the left-hemispheric strategies, necessary to achieve reading fluency, at the same time heavily relying on the visual-spatial features of the texts. That is why reading is slow, fragmented, but still characterised by relatively high accuracy. Conversely, L-type dyslexics are claimed to adopt linguistic (left-hemispheric) strategies from the very beginning of learning to read, they lack the automatic ability to recognise letter shapes and strings. Since they do not focus on the surface (visual-spatial) features of the text, they read relatively quickly, however, they tend to produce numerous substantive mistakes (low accuracy), which in turn may lead to comprehension problems. Thus, L-type and P-type dyslexics may be distinguished by reading speed, accuracy and type of errors they commit. Two types of errors are generally taken into consideration: substantive (omissions, changing the sequence of sounds and other deformations) and time errors (frequent pauses, repetitions, reading letter by letter). Substantive errors indicate the superiority of the left hemisphere and are to be expected in L-type dyslexics. On the other hand, time errors indicate the supremacy of the right hemisphere and their existence is to be assumed in P-type dyslexics. However useful the abovementioned typology may seem, some children with dyslexia cannot be classified in this way. Approximately 60% (Bednarek, 1999; Bogdanowicz & Krasowicz, 1996/1997; Kappers, 1997) to 65% (Bakker *et al.*, 1995) of children with dyslexia fall into either the P-type or L-type group, whereas the remaining 35–40% cannot be classified according to Bakker's typology.[6]

The abovementioned developmental models of reading invited criticism owing to the lack of description of the causal conditions. Bryant and Goswami (Goswami, 1999; Goswami & Bryant, 1990) in their *causal theory of development of the ability to read*, concentrate on specifying factors that condition progress in learning to read rather than on describing the phases of reading acquisition. Causal influence on the process of learning to read has been assigned to several factors. Firstly, to early phonological abilities (e.g. recognising and creating rhymes), secondly, to formal teaching of reading and spelling, with special emphasis placed on the acquisition of grapheme-phoneme conversion rules, and, finally, to the mutual influence that reading and spelling exert on each other.

Orthographic Depth and Grain Size: A Cross-language Perspective on Reading and Dyslexia

Orthographic depth

Alphabetic orthographic systems can be classified according to the consistency of the letter-to-sound relations, defined as *orthographic depth*. Deep orthographies demonstrate considerably unpredictable and unequivocal grapheme-phoneme correspondences and complexities such as, for instance, multiletter graphemes or frequent irregularities.

Conversely, shallow orthographies have simple letter-sound relations. In some languages, a given letter or letter cluster is always pronounced the same way (e.g. Greek, Italian, Spanish), whereas in other languages it can have several distinct pronunciations (e.g. English, Danish). It works similarly in the other direction – a phoneme can be represented with multiple spelling choices (e.g. English, French, Hebrew) or is nearly always spelled the same way (e.g. Italian) (Ziegler & Goswami, 2006; Frost & Ziegler, 2007). Among deep, opaque orthographies there are, for instance, English, French, Danish and Portuguese, while Spanish, Finnish or Turkish fall into the category of shallow, transparent orthographies.

Spencer (2007) sees the need for a less intuitive and more refined definition of the orthographic depth, with adequate attention given to the actual direction of the grapheme-phoneme relation. Highly transparent orthographies, such as Finnish or Turkish, have one-to-one correspondence in both phonology-orthography (spelling) and orthography-phonology (reading). By contrast, English lacks consistency in either direction. German or Greek, however, show highly regular mappings in reading, but they tend to be considerably complex with regard to spelling. Goswami (2000) uses the terms *feedforward* (spelling-to-sound) and *feedback* (sound-to-spelling) *consistency*, both of which can be measured and both exert substantial influence on the phoneme-level restructuring.

In addition, individual words within deep orthographies may be characterised by varying degrees of depth, which has a strong effect on reading and spelling accuracy. Some resemble words from shallow orthographies with simple one-to-one mappings between graphemes and phonemes, whereas other words pose considerable difficulty due to grapheme complexity. Spencer (2007) cites an example of two three-phoneme words – 'might' and 'sly' – which appear to represent different degrees of grapheme complexity, operationalised as word letter-length.

Generally, increased word letter-length was found to correlate with more complex orthographic structures within words. The effects of word letter-length can be modified by word frequency – with high-frequency words being resistant to word letter-length effect. According to Spencer (2007), word orthographic depth, especially the level of individual phonemes transparency, word complexity and frequency, uniquely influence word spelling and reading in young children. Spencer (2007) investigated the comparative strength of both orthography-phonology and phonology-orthography measures of transparency at the fine-grain phoneme-grapheme level in high-frequency English words in predicting young children's difficulty with word spelling. Both orthographic inconsistencies as well as complexities were shown to influence the degree of difficulty with word spelling, with the orthographic complexities (translated simply into the differences between the number of letters and phonemes in a word) having greater effect size.

Still, given that greater or lesser transparency or orthographic depth characterises particular alphabetic languages, it is interesting, whether this varying degree of consistency in mapping graphemes onto phonemes can be responsible for qualitative differences in literacy acquisition and, consequently, for the way reading difficulties manifest themselves in these languages. According to research findings, this indeed is the case (e.g. Davies *et al.*, 2007).

The *orthographic depth hypothesis* (Frost *et al.*, 1987; Katz & Frost, 1992), based on the *dual route model of reading* (Coltheart *et al.*, 2001; Treiman & Kessler, 2007), assumes that differences in literacy acquisition depend on the orthographic system of a language. In shallow orthographies, the process is based mainly on language phonology; readers tend to rely on the sublexical or phonological route, simply due to unambiguous, transparent letter-to-sound relations. Deep orthographies require the application of the logographic strategy, based on the visual-orthographic structure. Shallow orthographies permit greater use of sublexical correspondences because they provide reliable pronunciations, whereas deep orthographies invite mainly lexical mappings or orthographic route because sublexical correspondences repeatedly turn out to be unreliable, thus leading to erroneous pronunciations.

Inasmuch as the orthographic depth hypothesis suggests that, depending on the nature of a given orthography, readers choose to rely on the whole word recognition/orthographic route or phonological one, it does not propose that the varying psycholinguistic units may develop due to differences in orthographic systems (Ziegler & Goswami, 2006). However, it appears that the importance of a type of linguistic chunk (e.g. onset, rime, phoneme) in the process of developing phonological awareness and the ability to read is different across languages. In more transparent or shallow orthographies, the awareness of individual phonemes is seemingly more important for the effects of reading. Children learning to read in these orthographies rapidly form orthographic representations of phoneme-level information. By contrast, in languages with deep, inconsistent orthographies, the awareness of onsets and rimes seems crucial. Grouping words according to the sounds they begin with or common endings, and decoding new words through analogy is rather typical of non-transparent orthographies such as English. For instance, the onset-rime level representations provide a sufficiently effective tool for distinguishing between numerous similar-sounding words. Words like 'cat', 'hat', 'rat', 'bat' or 'hen', 'pen', 'ten', 'men' form similarity neighbourhoods (Bogdanowicz & Krasowicz-Kupis, 2005a; Goswami, 2000; Krasowicz-Kupis & Bryant, 2004; Sochacka, 2004).

Psycholinguistic grain size

The *psycholinguistic grain size theory* (Ziegler & Goswami, 2005, 2006) attempts to explain substantial differences in reading accuracy and speed across languages. These differences are said to reflect both the fundamental disparities in the nature of the system for mapping visual symbols onto phonological segments (units of sound) and reading strategies, whose development is considerably influenced by a given orthography. Davies *et al.* (2007) specify *grain size* as the size of an orthography-to-phonology mapping unit (the number of letters corresponding to a phonological unit). Hence, grain sizes vary from grapheme-phoneme, through rime to lexical level. Individual sounds are represented by graphemes (consisting of one or more letters). Single syllable words comprise onset (initial consonant or a consonant cluster) and rime (the remaining part). Finally, lexical mappings relate to complete phonology to orthography representations of a word.

The proponents of the psycholinguistic grain size theory argue that learning to read in more transparent orthographies (e.g. Finnish, Italian or Greek) involves heavy reliance on the grapheme-phoneme correspondences for word recognition because these grapheme-phoneme mappings are relatively consistent. Still, it is not denied that larger grain size representations may successfully develop in mature readers of orthographies with a high degree of consistency (Goswami & Ziegler, 2006). Unlike in the case of transparent orthographies, while learning to read in languages that lack substantial regularity as relates to grapheme-phoneme conversion, like English or unvowelled Hebrew, children cannot resort to smaller grain sizes as easily because such languages are characterised by greater inconsistency with regard to smaller (single letters or letter clusters representing individual phonemes) than larger reading units (rimes or syllables). As a consequence, English-speaking children may face the need to master mapping strategies at more than one grain size (multiple grain size strategy). Hence employing, apart from the grapheme-phoneme conversion strategy, which does not seem to be sufficiently effective, the strategy of recognition of letter patterns for rimes and the whole word recognition strategy. However, the bigger the grain size, the more orthographic units to learn. Some implications for instructional practices can be drawn from the above discussion, with probably the most obvious suggestion that small grain size units should be given special attention in teaching reading in consistent orthographies. On the other hand, children learning to read in less consistent orthographies could possibly benefit more from a combination of teaching the small and large grain size units and whole-word approach ('look and say').

Interestingly, Vousden (2008), in order to form a rationale for choosing the amount and types of spelling-to-sound units for reading instruction, views differently sized unit knowledge from an environmental rather than a developmental perspective. She reports evidence on the potential usefulness of English sound-to-symbol relations with regard to whole words, onsets, rimes and phonemes in monosyllabic text reading. In fact, the most frequently occurring mappings at each level allow reading of a large proportion of monosyllabic text, with small-size (grapheme-phoneme) units seemingly being more effective than onset/rime correspondences. This potentially bears some important implications for reading instruction as long as support is provided to generalise the findings to multisyllabic text as well.

Much as the evidence in favour of the larger grain size effects on reading in less transparent orthographies is striking (e.g. Ziegler et al., 2003), it is worth considering a view that is alternative to the strong version of the psycholinguistic grain size theory and the orthographic depth hypothesis, assuming heavy reliance on grapheme-phoneme correspondences in transparent orthographic systems. Davies et al. (2007) highlight that resorting to sublexical mappings can be characteristic of early reading, followed by the establishment of larger grain size mappings. Furthermore, they propose that large grain size correspondences may well be formed quite early in reading development as can be the case, for instance, in Italian, where lexical and morphological properties exert considerable influence on print (Burani et al., 2002; Barca et al., 2007). Davies et al. (2007) aptly explain that such a phenomenon may depend on the relative frequency of multisyllabic (between two and four) words in transparent orthographies such as Italian or Spanish. Approaching these words armed with a grapheme-to-phoneme conversion strategy may turn out ineffective in terms of time. Hence inviting the strategy of large grain size mapping (e.g. lexical level), which enhances reading efficiency by allowing the pronouncing of larger groups of graphemes at a time.

In addition, factors such as word frequency, word length and orthographic neighbourhood size may modify reading speed and accuracy gains (Davies et al., 2007). Across languages varying in orthographic consistency, longer words in comparison to shorter words are typically read more slowly, and less accurately at times. This length size effect is especially manifest in younger and less able readers (Burani et al., 2002; Ziegler et al., 2003). Greater length effects are more evident with regard to reading low-frequency words than high-frequency words, which usually remain unaffected. The latter are also, more often than not, read quite accurately and fast, at least in some languages (e.g. Italian; Barca et al., 2007; Burani et al., 2002), a fact probably attributable to experience. Finally, orthographic neighbourhood size, defined as the number of words that can possibly be formed by changing a single letter of a word or non-word, with letter positions preserved, reflects the facilitating impact of the large grain size mappings. Words with numerous orthographic neighbours are repeatedly read more accurately and with greater speed, by children and adults alike, in comparison to words from sparse orthographic neighbourhoods. Importantly, orthographic neighbourhood size effect, being greater for younger and less-skilled readers, is also more evident in reading low rather than high-frequency words (Davies et al., 2007). For example, 'marsh' has two neighbours, 'harsh' and 'march', while 'cover' has as many as 13, including 'coven', 'cower', 'hover', 'lover', 'mover' and 'rover' (Lavidor et al., 2006).

Lavidor et al. (2006) present a case study of developmental dyslexia where orthographic neighbourhood was tested. They observed larger reliance on right hemisphere orthographic processing strategies in dyslexics when compared to normal readers. It appears that dyslexics, because of their preference towards more global processing, which can be traced back to the absence of clear phonological representations and fine-grained orthography-to-phonology coding, demonstrate considerable skill in processing words that belong to a given neighbourhood, and thus share certain letter strings. Generally, it is argued that, in the face of the apparent failure in achieving phonology-based left hemisphere word recognition processing, some individuals with dyslexia can be characterised by an increased sensitivity to orthographic cues. All in all, while it is not argued that the right hemisphere holds an absolute advantage over the left one in orthographic processing, it seems that even though the phonological, orthographic and semantic representations of words are processed in the two hemispheres in varying proportions, these proportions may be different in dyslexia.

There is growing evidence that orthography, in particular the grapheme-phoneme consistency concerning vowels, exerts considerable influence on the word reading strategies used by readers in a given language. In cross-linguistic comparisons, readers of English typically commit more errors with regard to both word and pseudo-word reading than readers of more regular orthographies. This situation may be the result of the strategy choice, namely, grapheme-phoneme assembly is apparently more heavily relied on by readers of shallow orthographies. Seymour et al. (2003) report the results of a cross-language reading comparison. Children from 14 European countries, in their first year of reading instruction, were given a matched set of items of simple real words and non-words. Strikingly, the children learning to read in consistent orthographies demonstrated excellent skill in reading both familiar real words and pseudo-words by the middle of the first grade (Greek: 98 and 92% correct real words and non-words, respectively, Finnish: 98 and 95%, German: 98 and 94%, Italian: 95 and 89%, Spanish: 95

and 89%). By contrast, the gains of children learning to read English almost reached floor levels (real words: 34% correct, non-words: 29% correct); slightly reduced results were also found for Danish (71 and 54% correct real words and non-words, respectively), Portuguese (73 and 77%) and French (79 and 85%).

Miller-Guron and Lundberg's (2004) comparative investigation of word reading efficiency involving the analysis of frequency and types of errors committed by early readers of English and Swedish indicates that they adopt differing strategies. The findings suggest that English children were faster on the task because they attempted more task items, however, they made significantly more errors (mainly skipping items) than the more careful Swedish readers, for whom it took longer to complete the task but they corrected their errors more often. The differences apparently follow from the strategies adopted in approaching the task, more precisely, whole-word recognition in the cases of English-speaking children and grapheme-to-phoneme conversion in Swedish readers. Similar pattern holds true for poor readers.

The general finding that it seems easier to learn to read in a transparent rather than in a deep orthography is interestingly extended and strengthened by Spencer and Hanley (2003), who compare the acquisition of reading in transparent Welsh and deep English orthographies, both of which constitute a part of the same educational system in Wales, where some children are taught to read in Welsh and some in English. They are typically, though not necessarily, the native speakers of these languages, which makes possible the comparison between Welsh children learning to read English and children learning to read Welsh. The findings of the study appear to support the view that the degree of orthographic transparency substantially influences the initial choice of reading strategies. Children learning to read Welsh showed a preference towards phonological strategies while attempting unfamiliar words, unlike those learning to read in English, who preferred visual, logographic strategies.

Hanley et al. (2004) verified the facilitating effects of the transparent Welsh orthography on early reading ability. They re-examined the children from the abovementioned study three years later and found that children learning to read English remained behind in reading low and medium frequency irregular words but, apparently, had caught up with those learning to read in Welsh with respect to reading regular words and non-words. The findings demonstrate that the slowed down acquisition of reading in English can be traced back to the effects of its non-transparent deep orthography.

In addition to reading skill, the acquisition of spelling ability also seems to be influenced by the type of orthographic depth of a language. Juul and Sigurdsson (2005) demonstrated a detrimental effect of the opaque Danish orthography on slower development of encoding skills in comparison to the transparent Icelandic orthography. They compared a deep orthography to a handicap for children learning to spell in it and specifically showed that Icelandic children markedly outperformed Danish-speaking children on word medial consonant doublets and on word initial consonant clusters.

There is no denying that, as it stands, the psychological grain size theory is attractive and rich in potential to explain variations in reading accuracy and speed across languages, but it has not escaped some criticism. It has been pointed out that greater attention should be devoted to the role of morphology in predicting the degree of sensitivity to smaller grain sizes and explaining sound units sizes preferred for decoding in particular languages. This observation seems especially valid with reference to Turkish, an agglutinative language in which morphemes occupy a predefined order of attachment and a single phoneme in a suffix can alter the meaning (Durgunoğlu, 2006). Furthermore, the particular choice of certain grain sizes for decoding may be determined, for example, by unavailability of other sizes, not necessarily by orthographic consistency. Frost (2006) claims that the Hebrew unpointed print consonant string is ambiguous because different vowels may be inserted into it, thus forming different words. Consequently, root and word pattern morphemes (large grain size) have to be used to provide information about the missing vowels. In fact, this missing phonemic information about vowels is responsible for the opaqueness of Hebrew orthography. Interestingly, even though Hebrew and English are irregular orthographies, their nature is apparently different. In English, unlike in Hebrew, the perceived orthographic depth results from inconsistency of letter clusters used to represent sounds. However, inserting diacritical marks ('points') representing vowels into the text converts deep Hebrew orthography into a shallow one. Frost's (2006) conclusion as to the character of the reading process in Hebrew is that readers activate both letter-by-letter units and morphemic units in parallel.

It seems that, indeed, the differences in the orthographic mapping on phonological elements across languages can be responsible for the discrepancies in the word recognition strategies adopted by children, as well as the incidence and types of errors. However, it would be simplistic to assign the responsibility for these differences to the orthographic depth only. Other factors, such as morphemic complexity, apparently play a role as well.

Grain size and dyslexia

As may be expected, especially in view of the propositions posed by psycholinguistic grain size theory, the intensity of dyslexic difficulties depends on the nature of a language and the range of skills required for reading in that language. Reliability of the letter-sound mappings is crucial: it seems that the more transparent or shallow the orthography of a given language, the fewer the difficulties encountered by dyslexics learning to read in it (Miles, 2000; Snowling & Caravolas, 2007). As indicated by Wimmer (1993), it applies mainly with regard to accuracy. The effect of phonological impairment on reading speed in children with dyslexia is apparently evident even in highly consistent orthographies, however, poor word and non-word reading fluency remains the primary behavioural marker for dyslexia in more transparent orthographies. In a similar vein, Hanley *et al.* (2004) proved that reading is very slow in poor Welsh readers. Ziegler *et al.* (2003) observed that German children routinely outperformed their English counterparts in terms of accuracy and fluency alike in both languages, while children with dyslexia did not differ in accuracy; they were significantly poorer with respect to reading speed in comparison to reading ability-matched controls.

Opaque, deep, inconsistent orthographies such as English or French tend to pose much more pronounced problems on individuals with dyslexia than transparent languages such as Italian, Spanish or Greek (Goswami, 2000; Lundberg, 2002; Reid & Fawcett, 2004). Let us take English spelling as an example: firstly, a single sound may be written down with one letter or a combination of letters, secondly, a single sound may be noted down with different letters or combinations of letters, and, finally, a given letter or a combination of letters may represent more than one sound, let alone irregular words (Payne, 1995). Thus, unsurprisingly, while attempting to write a word in English, several potentially correct spelling patterns for certain phonemes may be taken into consideration (e.g. 'rane' instead of 'rain') (Lundberg & Hoien, 2001). However, Kessler and Treiman (2003) make a successful attempt to reject some misconceptions about the irregularity and chaotic nature of the English orthographic system, pointing to several useful patterns and principles capable of reducing the complexity of the system.

Davies *et al.* (2007) investigated reading development and dyslexia in a relatively transparent Spanish orthography, their sample comprising of normally developing (both chronological age-matched and ability-matched controls) and dyslexic children. Reading accuracy was considerably high for all children, including dyslexics, which was an anticipated result given the orthographic consistency level of Spanish. Dyslexics and ability-matched controls committed significantly more errors than older age-matched controls, importantly though, the types of errors (mainly substitutions, additions and deletions) were similar across groups. With regard to speed, dyslexic and ability-matched control groups appeared to read slower than age-matched controls. The significant modifying effects of word frequency, length and orthographic neighbourhood size on reading times were observed. Altogether, the findings indicate delayed rather than abnormal reading development in Spanish-speaking dyslexic children.

Interestingly, Oren and Breznitz (2005) analysed reading processes in Hebrew (L1) and English (L2) in dyslexics and chronological age-matched regular bilingual readers. The behavioural and electrophysiological evidence collected in this study seems to support the proposition of a universal basis of dyslexia in the brain, however, at the same time the observed manifestations of dyslexia in reading activity turned out to be orthography-specific. Dyslexics performed consistently better in the shallow orthography of a pointed Hebrew than in the deep English orthographic system, where their difficulties were considerably aggravated.

In the study by Spencer and Hanley (2003), even the least-skilled, under-achieving Welsh young readers were anything but close to the low-performing English readers, a finding indicative of less pronounced dyslexic difficulties present in children learning to read in Welsh than in English. The differences remained valid three years later, when the same children were re-examined by Hanley *et al.* (2004), suggesting that in the long run the most harmful and damaging effects of a deep orthography on reading development are evident in the poorest readers.

All in all, there is a greater prominence of the causal relationship between problems in word identification and deficits in phonological skills in dyslexics learning to read in opaque orthographies such as English (Vellutino *et al.*, 2004). On the other hand, the core phonological deficit in dyslexics is harder to detect and not so persevering in more transparent orthographies with regular relationships between letters and sounds (Snowling, 2001a). Impaired fluency and speed in word identification and text processing that lead to reading comprehension difficulties are claimed to be the key markers for dyslexia in such languages (Vellutino *et al.*, 2004). Several potential areas of difficulty for students with dyslexia might be enumerated even in highly transparent and regular orthographies. Hungarian, for example, may pose problems connected with visual processing (diacritical marks) and with auditory short-term memory due to its agglutinative nature. Theoretically, given enough time, a child should be able to read a particular word by translating each of the graphemes into the corresponding sounds. However, in the case of Hungarian, very slow speed of processing, responsible for poor access to meaning, seems to be a better predictor of a reading failure (Smythe & Everatt, 2000).

As mentioned above, orthographic features may be conducive to diverse occurrence and manifestations of dyslexia in different scripts. Interestingly, Chinese children with dyslexia, apart from a visual-orthographic deficit, considered to be more specific to reading problems in Chinese, encounter phonological processing deficits similar to their alphabetic counterparts. Furthermore, bearing in mind the peculiar characteristics of the two scripts, Chinese children learning English as a second language (L2) demonstrate generally low-grade phonological processing in both languages. What follows from these facts is the presumed existence of multiple factors contributing to dyslexic difficulties in Chinese children, additionally, both common and specific causes responsible for reading difficulties in Chinese and English can be enumerated (Ho et al., 2000; Ho & Fong, 2005).

Given the vital importance of phonemic awareness in reading acquisition, another crucial issue to be addressed is its cross-language transfer. Phonological processing skills are consistently found to be critically related to word recognition faculty across languages. This means that phonological processing abilities in one language, no matter whether first language (L1) or L2, can predict individual differences in word recognition skills within and cross-linguistically, which gains special importance in the context of assessment in multilingual settings (see Chapter 4) (Geva, 2000).

Atwill et al. (2007) investigated the effect that L1 proficiency has on cross-language transfer of phonemic awareness in Spanish-speaking children in the USA, entering kindergarten classrooms with instruction in English. They found that sufficient L1 skills determine the successful transfer of phonemic awareness from L1 to L2 and, in the long run, the L2 reading ability in young children. In fact, children with below-average L1 faculty showed no evidence of cross-language transfer of phonemic awareness from L1 to L2.

Petrus and Bogdanowicz (2004) suggest that the simultaneous acquisition of both native (Polish) and foreign (English) language could have a supplementary effect on the development of particular skills making up phonological awareness, especially the awareness of onsets and rimes. This assumption is based on the abovementioned claim that there exists a relation between phonological competence in the native and foreign language, more specifically, that there occurs a positive transfer of a well-developed phonological competence, at least as pertains to the initial stage of its acquisition, from L1 to consecutive languages. It is concluded then that since phonological awareness is reflected in all languages acquired by a given child, one does not have to develop it separately in each language. It is further argued that the intervention programmes for children who, for various reasons, fail to properly develop phonological skills, could be equally well provided in a foreign language, on condition that a child understands and uses it confidently. The outcome of the research conducted on Polish kindergarten children by Petrus and Bogdanowicz (2004) implies strong positive correlation between the phonological skills measured in Polish (L1) and in English (L2). Additionally, the greater the intensity of learning a foreign language, the more pronounced the transfer of phonological skills from Polish to English and vice versa.

In sum, it appears that the phonological processing impairments responsible for the specific reading disability in the native language may similarly impede the acquisition of foreign languages. Core phonological deficit in dyslexia is believed to be transferred from L1 to L2. This line of explanation provides for the difficulties experienced by many poor foreign language learners. Sparks (1995) enumerates several reasons why phonological processing may have an adverse effect on foreign language learning. He mentions the fact that a student may have difficulties perceiving and producing novel phonological strings as well as comprehending spoken language. What is more, poor native language reading skills will generalise to poor reading in a foreign language, which in turn negatively influences listening comprehension, oral expression, reading comprehension, syntax, general knowledge and verbal memory. Chapter 3 is devoted to a more in-depth analysis of native language-based foreign language learning difficulties.

Notes

1. Various methodological designs can be applied in the study of developmental reading disorders – longitudinal versus cross-sectional, group versus case studies. As for the choice of control groups, reading ability/reading-age-matched groups (younger normally developing children matched for reading ability) or chronological age groups (typically developing children of the same age, usually matched for other variables such as gender, IQ, school) can be selected for comparison with clinical cases.
2. The average IQ for the population is 100, with a standard deviation of 15 points. In the UK, obtaining IQ scores between 50 and 70 means having moderate learning difficulties, people with IQ scores below 50 are believed to have severe learning difficulties (Hulme & Snowling, 2009).
3. See Chapter 4 for a discussion on the dynamic change of symptoms in dyslexia.
4. See Chapter 4: 'Identification of dyslexia', for a discussion of the usefulness of reading/IQ discrepancy for diagnosis.
5. See Chapter 4: 'Emotional-motivational disorders in dyslexia', on emotional-motivational problems in dyslexia.
6. See Chapter 5 for a discussion of intervention techniques (HSS and HAS) proposed by Bakker.

Chapter 2
Causes of Dyslexia

Introduction

Dyslexia involves an interdisciplinary study and consensus of neuroscience, cognitive science and learning theory, quite naturally inviting their application in education. It seems to be a very intriguing and controversial phenomenon, widely investigated from many diverse standpoints. Over the past few decades, a considerable amount of research has been devoted to identifying its probable causes, with several important insights from science pathways whose frameworks were not extensively used before to substantiate the nature of dyslexia. Admittedly, the outstanding progress in such scientific fields as neuroscience, brain imaging and genetics has confirmed several intuitively plausible hypotheses lacking earlier empirical verification and has revealed multiple, previously unknown facts indicating the complex, polietiological nature of dyslexia (Bogdanowicz & Adryjanek, 2004). Dyslexia may be caused by a number of factors operating independently or interacting with other factors to produce the outcome; moreover, various causes can be applicable to different children, and, last but not least, there may be several causes of dyslexic problems in place with relation to a particular child. Hulme and Snowling (2009: 30) convincingly argue that in light of current knowledge, causality and causes should be treated in terms of probability rather than certainty – 'Causes are things that increase the likelihood of an outcome'.

All in all, there seems to be general agreement that dyslexia has neurobiological origins with reference to genetic construction as well as structural and functional features of the central nervous system (Knight & Hynd, 2008). These distal causes bring about certain malfunctions on the cognitive level, which, in turn, serve as more proximal causes of reading failure.

Notwithstanding certain characteristics of difficulties encountered by children with dyslexia and manifest causes of their reading disability, which are generally agreed upon (Velutino *et al.*, 2004), several conceptions concerning the underlying causes of dyslexia are currently at large, indeed generating sizeable chaos in terms of available, at times inconsistent and often contradicting evidence and its critical evaluation. Given the complex nature of dyslexia, any decent attempt to understand its multiple facets would necessarily involve a description and explanation with regard to three levels: biological, cognitive and behavioural, with a range of environmental influences operating at each of them

(Frith, 1999, 2008; Morton & Frith, 1995). Explanation at the biological level pinpoints the underlying brain mechanism, for example, disorganisation in the cerebral cortex in the language areas, abnormal magnocellular pathways or abnormal cerebellum. The cognitive level provides a description as regards the theoretical constructs from cognitive psychology such as reduced working memory, poor phonological processing, incomplete automatisation or slow central processing. Finally, the behavioural level refers to symptoms such as poor reading and spelling, difficulty with rhymes, poor motion sensitivity, poor rapid auditory processing and difficulty maintaining balance. No one level of explanation is assigned a more important role than the other levels; all of them are extremely useful in enhancing our understanding of the disorder.

As for the hypothetical causal links between the levels, the indicated direction is from biological through cognitive[1] to behavioural level. In other words, a genetic difference causes a brain abnormality, which in turn is responsible for a cognitive deficit, which in turn brings about certain observed patterns of behaviour. As stressed by Hulme and Snowling (2009), none of the levels can be reduced or replaced with another level. In addition, they extend the understanding of the direction of the hypothetical causal links proposed in the abovementioned causal model by postulating the causal direction 'backwards' – from behaviour, through cognition to biology. It is claimed that alterations at the behavioural level can induce changes at the cognitive level, which in turn depend on the changes in the underlying brain mechanisms. It is possible because experience is likely to modify connections between nerve cells, which can result in long-lasting structural and functional changes. Even more surprisingly, the genetic level is also likely to be influenced by changes at the cognitive and behavioural levels – there is evidence that the way genes are expressed can be altered by experience. Genes carry information that serves to direct development, but influences from the environment in which the development takes place interact with genetic inputs. The course of development, including the development of the brain, is characterised by change and interaction and is said to result from the interplay of genetic and environmental inputs. Hulme and Snowling (2009: 11) stress that: 'learning (an influence from the environment) operates to modify structures in the brain that developed under genetic control and in turn may influence subsequent learning'. Dyslexia seems to be under the considerable influence of genetic risk factors whose activity is connected with altering the development of certain language systems of the left hemisphere of the brain. However, the impact of the environment, in which children learn to read, on dyslexia cannot be underestimated.

Contemporary theories of dyslexia may be applied at any of the levels: brain based, cognitive or behavioural, however, a complete explanation of the dyslexia phenomenon would require forming a complex model aptly representing the relations and the causal links between these separate levels of investigation. In addition, Hulme and Snowling (2009) propose that researching atypical reading development in children should necessarily involve comparing them to patterns of typical reading development in children. Thus, a theory of developmental dyslexia would have to delineate how and why children with dyslexia demonstrate impairment in the processes that are normally involved in typical reading development. Deep and thorough understanding of normal reading development constitutes a necessary prerequisite for successful uncovering of the complex nature of this developmental reading disorder.

The following part of the chapter is devoted to neurobiological substrates (genetic and brain mechanisms) and cognitive correlates of dyslexia. It focuses on familiarising the reader with the major facts and hypothesis brought to light by extensive investigations of the causes of dyslexia.

Genetic Mechanisms in Dyslexia

Genetic theory is one of the oldest attempts to explain the causes of dyslexia. It presupposes the connection between the occurrence of the disorder and inherited anatomical and functional features of the central nervous system, determining the existence of difficulties in reading and spelling. A tendency for the specific reading disorder to run in families was first reported at the turn of the last century (Bogdanowicz, 1989; Spionek, 1985); since then, converging evidence has accumulated in support of substantial heritability in dyslexia (Marino *et al.*, 2007). The genetic basis of dyslexia is verified in population genetic studies, which investigate patterns of inheritance across individuals, and in molecular genetic studies, which attempt to pinpoint particular genes or gene markers that can be linked to dyslexia.

Convincing evidence for the hereditary hypothesis – genetic component to dyslexia – comes from family and twin studies (DeFries *et al.*, 1987; Jaklewicz, 1982; Olson *et al.*, 1989; Pennington, 1989; Pennington *et al.*, 1986; Pennington & Smith, 1988; Ramus, 2006; Stein, 2001). It has been speculated that about 20–30% of the cases of dyslexia are genetically conditioned (Bodganowicz, 1999; DeFries *et al.*, 1987; Pennington *et al.*, 1986); however, some authors claim it might be even 50–60% (Lundberg & Hoien, 2001; Stein, 2001; Stein *et al.*, 2001). Putting the differences in the estimates aside, what follows is that a child of a dyslexic parent can indeed be at considerable risk to develop reading problems. In family studies, children at genetic risk for dyslexia are followed from pre-school age, with their development and progress being documented (e.g. Snowling *et al.*, 2003). Snowling *et al.* (2007) confirm increased risk of dyslexia among adolescent children of dyslexic parents, who were examined when they were 3 years and 9 months, then at the age of 6 and then 8. Their literacy difficulties prevail rather than resolve, they are long-lasting, with no apparent catch-up between 8 and 13 years of age. Still, the genetic risk for dyslexia is not perceived as deterministic in character and the correlation of genes and environment is highlighted instead.

In all likelihood, insufficient phoneme segmentation skills and phonological/orthographic awareness deficits qualify for explanation with regard to genetic influences (Schneider, 1999). According to Snowling (2001a), a low-grade facility to establish relations between orthography and phonology may be an inherited feature of dyslexia. As argued further, the severity of the specific reading disorder encountered by children at risk for dyslexia appears to be directly proportional to the severity of the reading impairment of their parents. Lundberg and Hoien (2001) also point out that children genetically disposed to encounter dyslexic difficulties demonstrate a delay or a deficit primarily in their phonological development; almost invariably lacking the clear-cut mental representations of the sounds of words. Olson *et al.* (1989) have put forward much the same ideas, namely, that word recognition and phonological decoding skills are strongly influenced genetically; additionally, they have indicated lower hereditability for the orthographic coding skills. Stein (2001) claims that even though initially only the phonological ability was assigned a hereditary characteristic, it appears that also the orthographic ability can be transmissible.[2]

Admittedly though, it is unlikely that dyslexia is caused by a single gene, but rather through the combination and interaction of multiple genes (Nicolson, 2001; Ramus, 2006). Molecular genetics studies aim at identifying certain genes (DNA sequences) or gene markers that can be assigned the responsibility for the development of the disorder. It is most likely that it is the combination of the influence of many genes of small effect and the environmental input that the risk of inheriting dyslexia depends on (Hulme & Snowling, 2009). Indeed, there is no indication of the existence of specific genes associated with dyslexia (Vellutino *et al.*, 2004). Even though no single gene for dyslexia has been identified, the approximate positions of the number of gene loci have been mapped (Fisher & Smith, 2001). Chromosomal regions implicated by a number of studies as being likely to contain genes predisposing for dyslexia involve the regions on chromosomes 1, 2, 3, 6, 15 and 18 (Fisher & Francks, 2006; Fisher & Smith, 2001; Stein *et al.*, 2001). Four candidate dyslexia susceptibility genes that are involved in developmental processes including neuronal migration have been identified (Galaburda *et al.*, 2006; Ramus, 2006).

Notwithstanding the utmost difficulty and complexity of the task, establishing transparent connections between genes and behaviour as well as genetic mutations and behavioural disorders seems crucial. In their research, Galaburda et al. (2006) indicate a speculative route between genetic effect, developmental brain changes and perceptual and cognitive impairments characterising dyslexia. Similarly, according to Fisher and Smith (2001), the isolation of gene variants that might possibly be responsible for dyslexia remains a major challenge for research, having great potential benefits for early diagnosis of individuals at risk for dyslexia.

In sum, dyslexia tends to run in families, thus a child of a dyslexic parent naturally falls into the category of children at risk for dyslexia, who are prone to develop dyslexic difficulties. The awareness of a family history of a struggle with literacy acquisition may well serve as an indicator of a necessity of early assessment, followed by appropriate intervention with regard to pre-literacy skills, hopefully reducing or, preferably, preventing the experience of scholastic failure.

Brain Mechanisms in Dyslexia

Moving on from the heritability aspect in dyslexia research to the analysis of brain structure and function, let us concentrate on brain abnormalities in individuals with dyslexia. Since a major difficulty that children with dyslexia experience is poor phonological processing, one would expect certain impairments in the structure and/or function of the brain areas that are assigned the task of language processing. Indeed, individuals with dyslexia are frequently reported to demonstrate distinct characteristics of brain anatomy, brain activity and function from non-dyslexic individuals. Moreover, the abovementioned differences are tentatively assigned responsibility for the occurrence of specific learning difficulties. Minimal brain damage (MBD) or alterations in brain structure (which invite malfunction) to these areas of the brain that are typically allocated the role of mediating the processes of reading and spelling may constitute the underlying cause of dyslexia. Structural anomalies would routinely occur due to damaging activity of various pathogenic factors on the central nervous system in prenatal and perinatal life. However, as rightly highlighted by Hulme and Snowling (2009), despite converging evidence with regard to anomalous functioning of the left hemisphere language areas in dyslexia, it would be premature to evaluate the causal status of these findings. Possibly, reduced reading experience in people with dyslexia becomes in itself an environmental factor potentially capable of exerting certain influences on the structure and function of brain circuits involved in reading. Viewed from such a perspective, differences in patterns of brain activation observed in individuals with dyslexia during the performance of phonological and reading tasks can be treated as a consequence rather than a cause of reading problems.

As far as the measurement of brain function, operationalised as brain responses to cognitive tasks, is concerned, functional neuroimaging is typically utilised in the current studies. Sophisticated techniques[3] allow measuring and mapping of changes and patterns in brain activation, induced by the performance on particular cognitive tasks in terms of place and/or time.[4] Importantly, the outcome of studies using varying methods seem to provide rather consistent findings as to ascertaining particular areas of the brain that show habitually increased activation during tasks involving phonological processing and reading. There exist differences in activation patterns of neural circuits during these tasks in dyslexic brains as compared to non-dyslexic brains. Generally, dyslexics tend to under-activate vital structures of the neural network; the connections between these structures are also fewer than in non-dyslexic brains.

Marino *et al.* (2007) point to an interesting aspect of dyslexia, namely, neurofunctional organisation pattern, being representative of different writing systems. Again, evidence seems inconclusive; data collected in some neuroimaging studies support the existence of unitary mechanisms with regard to alphabetic scripts, irrespective of the orthographic depth. Conversely, other researchers favour the idea that logographic and alphabetic writing systems lead to diversified patterns of neurofunctional organisation.

According to Pugh *et al.* (2005), generally, fundamental principles of speech and reading organisation in the brain seem to chiefly parallel across languages. Despite broad consistency and uniformity in neurobiological foundations, the existence of certain language-specific features is not denied. Particular left hemisphere cortical regions, such as the occipitotemporal, temporoparietal and inferior frontal networks, are repeatedly indicated by the outcome of neuroimaging studies to participate in reading across alphabetic languages, with specific differences between languages, concerning the degree rather than the kind.[5] The same tendency holds true for reading disability, as demonstrated by the results of neuroimaging studies on reading tasks performed by poor readers. Mainly common neurobiological features, such as functional abnormality in the left hemisphere posterior cortex, are displayed across languages (English, Finnish, German, French, Italian) with regard to reading impairment.

However, Hadzibeganovic *et al.* (in press) believe that patterns of activation and neural circuits participating in reading and in reading disorders potentially vary across languages, according to the way written language maps on spoken language (orthographic depth). This view is also supported by cognitive heterogeneity of dyslexia, evident in its varying subtypes across cultures, which cannot possibly be tracked down to the neural impairment of the same type. Hence the existence of a common type of brain abnormality in dyslexia across cultures and languages is perceived as oversimplification. In addition, Siok *et al.* (2008) provide interesting data from Chinese, a non-alphabetic language. They report varying brain anomalies in Chinese dyslexic readers who, unlike alphabetic-language dyslexics, do not demonstrate functional or structural[6] differences from regular readers in the more posterior brain systems. Thus, a structural and functional basis for dyslexia in alphabetic and non-alphabetic languages varies.

Importantly, findings of a number of imaging studies analysing brain activation patterns in English monolingual children with dyslexia before and after intervention, in the form of remedial reading treatment or phonologically driven, indicate the apparent increase in the activation of areas typically employed by good readers. This suggests that instruction plays a vital role in creating the brain activation patterns allowing successful skilled reading in dyslexics (e.g. Blachman *et al.*, 2004; Richards *et al.*, 2000; Shaywitz *et al.*, 2004). For instance, Aylward *et al.* (2003) demonstrate that 28 hours of comprehensive reading instruction results in both behavioural gains in the form of improved reading scores and a change in dyslexic brain function. Namely, increased brain activation during language tasks parallel characteristic patterns of neural processing in non-disabled readers. Similarly, Simos *et al.* (2002) report that dyslexia-specific brain activation maps become normal following successful eight-week intensive remedial training, which results in dyslexics increasing their word reading gains up to average range. The increased activation, resembling patterns usually demonstrated by high-achieving readers, is observed in dyslexic left temporoparietal areas, which equals significant improvement in word reading accuracy.

One would wonder whether children learning English as a second/ additional language (ESL/EAL) demonstrate comparable neurobiological characteristics to monolingual English-speaking children with regard to reading acquisition and disability? In fact, Pugh *et al.* (2005) conclude their literature review with the claim that pronounced differences in the way brain functions between ESL/EAL[7] learners and monolingual children learning to read in English are rather unlikely to emerge, the differences though may be anticipated in the rate of acquisition. What is more, they stress the potential of functional neuroimaging techniques in verifying and evaluating the effects of varying approaches to teaching reading to ESL/EAL learners.

Post-mortem studies as well as non-invasive anatomical magnetic resonance imaging (aMFI) are the most commonly utilised techniques in research on brain structure. A small number of post-mortem analyses of dyslexic brains, amounting to a total of 10 cases (Vellutino *et al.*, 2004), notwithstanding, their instructive force is considerable in that they indicate a complex, and by no means reduced to a single brain area, neuroanatomical basis of dyslexia. On the other hand, methods based on the aMFI make possible the precise evaluation of brain structures and in that way exert substantial influence on the processes of searching for and establishing neural correlates of dyslexia.

Moving on to a more detailed discussion of the brain regions characterised by some structural anomalies in dyslexics as compared to non-dyslexics, let us begin with the planum temporale.[8] Areas in the upper posterior part of the left temporal lobe, in particular the planum temporale, are claimed to be critically involved in phonological processing. Naturally, attempts to explain impairments in phonological processing concentrated on abnormal or non-existent brain laterality in these areas as well as on the structural anomaly of the planum temporale (Hugdahl *et al.*, 2003). Several researchers investigated reduced or reversed leftward asymmetry of the planum temporale, however, the results they obtained varied.

Post-mortem analyses of dyslexic brains have demonstrated substantial evidence for the lack of typical structural asymmetry as regards the planum temporale[9] (Galaburda *et al.*, 1978; Galaburda, 1985, 1993). In addition, several magnetic resonance (MR) imaging studies of the brain structure in individuals with dyslexia have indicated reduced or reversed asymmetry of the language areas in the temporal lobe. Still, this view seems to be challenged by more recent studies of the planum temporale. The abovementioned discrepancies in the results regarding the hemispheric asymmetry of temporal regions in dyslexia might have been brought about by the methodological differences between the studies. For example, Heiervang *et al.* (2000) hypothesised that reduced asymmetry of the planum temporale and/or smaller left planum temporale in children with dyslexia would be connected to reduced right ear advantage (REA)[10] on the dichotic listening task.[11] The study addressed an apparently crucial issue whether deviant structure of the brain areas, which are engaged in speech sound perception and processing, equals functional deficit. However, both normal structural asymmetry, assessed by the size of the planum temporale, and functional asymmetry, indicated by the dichotic listening ear advantage, was demonstrated in dyslexic subjects participating in the study. No significant differences were spotted in planum temporale asymmetry between individuals with dyslexia and controls; both groups demonstrated a mean leftward asymmetry of the area in question. Moreover, dyslexics and controls showed normal REA on the dichotic listening task. However, a small (10%) reduction of the planum temporale size was signified in individuals with dyslexia, while it was apparently absent in controls. Additionally, planum temporale asymmetry and reading in dyslexic group were not correlated, while a positive correlation between these two variables was shown in the control group, thus it would seem that leftward asymmetry as regards the planum temporale may be connected with normal reading but not with impaired reading. Finally, deviant shape of the planar area was demonstrated in dyslexics. Thus, altogether the study has shown that subtle developmental abnormalities may indeed be associated with dyslexia. Another study conducted by the same group of researchers (Hugdahl et al., 2003) provided support for their previous findings.[12]

Leonard et al. (2006) perceive the view that children with dyslexia are characterised by symmetrical planum temporale as a long-lasting misconception. They further report that findings in their sample run counter to the idea of the existence of an association between planum temporale asymmetry and several reading and language variables that were previously indicated in other studies.

A different set of findings refers to anomalies of cell migration (ectopias and dysplasias[13]) reported to exist in the perisylvian cortex of dyslexic brains, principally in the left hemisphere (Ramus, 2004). Ectopias and dysplasias are claimed to result from focal lesions to the maturing brain, which take place during the migration of neurons to the cortex at about the fifth month of fetal life (Borkowska, 1997; Stein, 2001).

Yet another anatomical difference concerns the corpus callosum.[14] It has been indicated that the corpus callosum and, in particular, its back part, called the splenium, which connects the parts realising language functions, are considerably larger in dyslexics (Bloom & Hynd, 2005; Galaburda, 1993; Preis et al., 2000). Plessen et al. (2002) have observed a shorter corpus callosum shape in the posterior midbody region in dyslexic brains as compared to control subjects. As indicated by Bloom and Hynd (2005), most studies report certain abnormalities in the size of the corpus callosum, which are probably directly connected to reduced cortical asymmetry. However, the evidence regarding the size of the corpus callosum in developmental dyslexia is conflicting: both smaller and larger corpus callosi have been found in individuals with dyslexia. Thus, taking into account the anatomical data, it might be hypothesised (Bednarek, 1999; Stein, 2001) that dyslexia is connected with the failure to establish hemispheric specialisation. However, it is difficult to define the activity of the brain organised in that particular way and to qualify the influence it has on the process of reading (Bednarek, 1999).

The most direct evidence that many dyslexics may have impaired development of the visual magnocellular system[15] comes from post-mortem examination of dyslexic brains. This finding has been further confirmed by electrophysiological studies and functional imaging studies (fMRI). It has been found that the magnocellular layers of the lateral geniculate nucleus (LGN) of the thalamus were disordered and the neurons were about 30% smaller in the area as compared to non-dyslexic brains. These abnormalities are known to arise during early development of the brain, as is the case with ectopias, during the phase of rapid neuronal growth and migration in the fourth or fifth month of fetal life (Galaburda & Livingstone, 1993; Ramus, 2004; Stein, 2001).

Fawcett and Nicolson (2001, 2004) believe that problems suffered by people with dyslexia may come down to cerebellar[16] deficit.[17] Indeed, certain structural abnormalities have been reported in the cerebella of dyslexic brains. The abnormality is characterised by greater cell size (Fawcett & Nicolson, 2004). In addition, relatively more large neurons and fewer small neurons were found in the cerebella of dyslexic brains, which might suggest problems in the input to the cerebellum (Fawcett & Nicolson, 2001). Also, a morphological post-mortem anatomical analysis has singled out a significantly larger mean cellular area in the medial posterior and in the anterior lobe of the cerebellar cortex in dyslexic brains (Finch *et al.*, 2002). Moreover, the cerebellar hemispheres in dyslexic brains have been found to be symmetrical, while non-dyslexic controls were reported to possess a larger right hemispheric cerebellar cortical surface (Rae *et al.*, 2002).

As far as brain activation is concerned, it was monitored in individuals with dyslexia and control adults during the performance of a pre-learned sequence and during learning a novel sequence of finger presses, known to result in substantial activation in the cerebellum with non-dyslexic adults (Nicolson *et al.*, 1999). As predicted by the cerebellar deficit hypothesis, the dyslexic group activated their cerebella less during motor learning as far as pre-learned (automatic) and novel sequences were concerned. Moreover, greater activation in their frontal lobes was shown in learning a novel sequence, suggesting they were bypassing the cerebellum to some extent and relying on conscious strategies (Fawcett & Nicolson, 2001).

Additionally, a normally greater density of white matter in the left hemisphere tends to be decreased in people with dyslexia (Klingberg *et al.*, 2000). Studies also report reduced grey matter in the orbital portion of the left inferior frontal gyrus and superior temporal gyrus, but also outside language regions (Brown *et al.*, 2001). Silani *et al.* (2005) provide support for the claim that changed activation noted within the reading system is associated with altered density of grey and white matter of certain brain regions, such as left middle and inferior temporal gyri and the left arcuate fasciculus. They further voice an opinion that their evidence is in accord with the view that dyslexia is associated with local grey matter dysfunction and altered connectivity among phonological/ reading areas.

Also, Temple (2002) supports the claim of the neurobiological aetiology of dyslexia, pointing out that individuals with dyslexia, regardless of age, language and methodology adopted in the study, demonstrate disruptions in temporoparietal brain responses as regards phonological demands and in left frontal brain responses to rapid auditory processing tasks. In addition, individuals with dyslexia show unusual organisation of white matter connecting the temporoparietal cortex to other cortical areas, and the degree of this faulty organisation correlated with reading ability, indicating the important role it plays in reading. However, apparently, more attention should be devoted to the issue of causality and determination of the relationship between the abovementioned disruptions in brain structure and function and the aetiology of developmental dyslexia.

The findings of the post-mortem examination and brain imaging analyses of dyslexic brains indicate the complexity of the underlying neuroanatomical basis of dyslexia that cannot be reduced to a single area of the brain (Galaburda *et al.*, 2006). Leonard *et al.* (2006) highlight the fact that recent studies have revealed a puzzling range of anatomical differences between dyslexics and controls. The neuroanatomical substrates of dyslexia that are pointed out include: reduction in the temporal lobe, frontal lobe, candate, thalamus and cerebellum, insula, anterior superior neocortex and occipital cortex, additionally, subtle changes in callosal morphology, the inferior frontal gyrus and cerebellum have been observed. Similarly, Ramus (2004) enumerates several differences between dyslexic and control brains that have been documented by recent studies, for example, in the left perisylvian cortex, the underlying white matter, the thalamus, the corpus callosum and the cerebellum. However, it is stressed again that the functional significance of the abovementioned brain differences requires decent explication.

The outcome of the neuroanatomical research, even though at times contradictory and hence inconclusive, mostly due to methodological differences, seems to suggest that indeed there exist an anatomical-physiological basis for dyslexia.

Phonological Coding Deficit Hypothesis

Phonological abilities

Phonological processing (implicit phonology) refers to children using speech, without reflecting on the structure of spoken words. Naming and short-term verbal memory (STM) tasks as well as repeating words or non-words are frequently used in studies on phonological processing. Children with dyslexia repeatedly find these simple tasks troublesome (Hulme & Snowling, 2009). *Phonological awareness* (explicit phonology) is the ability to perform explicit judgements with regard to the structure of spoken words and it refers to all kinds of operations on speech sounds, engaging memory, analysis and synthesis of phonological elements. It is basically defined as an ability to identify, distinguish between, detect and manipulate the sound structure of words, stretching from young children's sensitivity to that structure (separate from word meaning) to the skilful handling of manipulation tasks, with regard to constituent phonemes in the speech stream. It is knowledge that spoken words are made of tiny segments – sounds; it is an ability to break apart and put together these sounds. This facility, in turn, forms a prerequisite for later successful mapping of the sounds on the appropriate symbols – letters. *Phonemic awareness* is a type of *phonological awareness*. While the latter deals with various sizes of phonological elements (words, syllables, onset, rimes, phonemes), the former is reduced in scope and related to identification and manipulation of individual phonemes (Krasowicz-Kupis, 2008).

The knowledge of and sensitivity to constituent sound parts of words aids understanding of the written language system and acquisition of the *alphabetic principle* – the idea that written words symbolise spoken words in the following way: single sounds are represented by single letters or groups of letters. *Phonological awareness* is frequently confused with *phonics*, which constitutes a method of reading instruction, aimed at familiarising children with relationships between letter sounds and corresponding printed letters or clusters of letters (Philips et al., 2008).

To ensure terminological clarity, we shall define *phoneme* as the smallest functional unit of a given language, the smallest unit of sound indicating a difference in meaning. It constitutes a class of speech sounds that native speakers identify as the same sound, while members of such a class are called *allophones*. Allophones of a given phoneme – the actual sounds produced by speakers – are phonetically slightly different. For example, even though /p/ in 'pin' and /p/ in 'spin' are phonetically different sounds, aspirated and unaspirated, respectively, native speakers of English ignore (or are relatively insensitive to) the difference because it does not cause any change in the meaning of words. However, /p/ in 'pin' and /b/ in 'bin' are perceived as members of different classes (phonemes) because they are distinctive. As such, a phoneme is an abstract unit and it is unpronounceable. It can be described as an image or a model of a speech sound in our mind. During the course of phonological development, we learn to identify phonemes and ignore allophonic variation because only phoneme change can result in the change of meaning. Phonemes allow us to distinguish between and identify individual sounds that constitute utterances we hear, which, in turn, makes segmentation of these utterances possible.

Turning now to a more thorough discussion of implicit and explicit phonological knowledge, let us begin with a twofold division of phonological competence into *epilinguistic* and *metalinguistic*. The first one is a matter of earlier development and accommodates implicit linguistic knowledge, which is applied in an unconscious, intuitive and automatic way by pre-literate children. The second follows from epilinguistic skills and is connected with a conscious, reflective and intentionally applied explicit knowledge (Gombert, 1992; Goswami, 2000; Krasowicz-Kupis, 2004; Saiegh-Haddad, 2007; Sochacka, 2004). Epilinguistic activities would involve intuitive judgements on similarities between words, for example, comparing words and recognising whether they share syllables, onsets and rimes. Such tasks as identifying and producing phonological segments require conscious knowledge and operation, usually acquired during formal training.

In the course of development of phonological awareness, young children progress from larger to smaller sound units. The awareness of syllables, onsets and rimes develops before the awareness of phonemes. This observation has been confirmed across alphabetic languages when the same phonological awareness tasks are used (Goswami, 2000; Goswami & Bryant, 1990; Miller-Guron & Lundberg, 2000). Consequently, children first find out that sentences are composed of separate words; these words, in turn, can be divided into syllables, onsets and rimes (*intra-sub-syllabic* elements) and, finally, they are made up of sequences of sounds. Children also learn that all these elements can be separated, blended together and otherwise manipulated.

As already mentioned, children begin with handling tasks involving sentences, phrases and words, for instance, compounds (e.g. 'hotdog', 'rainbow'). Then, the ability to identify and manipulate particular phonological units in words naturally refers to bigger chunks, such as syllables within words first, which are more salient and more directly perceivable, and then to individual phonemes. Syllables (or typical, short, single-syllable words in English) can be divided into particular intra-syllabic elements. The model that highlights the most important elements of an inner hierarchical structure of a syllable is as follows – (C)*V(C)*. C stands for a consonant, V stands for a vowel, * shows a possible repetitiveness, and, finally, () indicates a facultative element. A vowel constitutes a peak of a syllable, which can be preceded by a single consonant, consonant blend (e.g. 'fr', 'gl') or digraph (e.g. 'sh', 'ch'), called an *onset*. A vowel can also be followed by a consonant or a consonant blend, named *coda*. A combination of a vowel and a final consonant, consonant blend or digraph forms a *rime*, which constitutes a common part of rhyming words (e.g. 'fan', 'van', 'pan' or 'br*and*', 'gr*and*', 'st*and*') (Kessler & Treiman, 2003; Philips *et al.*, 2008; Sochacka, 2004). Thus, onsets and rimes form bigger intra-syllabic chunks of a syllable or a one-syllable single lexical unit. Each can be further divided into individual phonemes.

Philips *et al.* (2008) stress that the model described above does not hold that a child has to master a given level or stage before moving to the consecutive one, rather the stages overlap. Thus, while still working towards a decent grasp and proficiency at less complicated levels, a child begins to focus on acquiring more complex components. In addition, diversified complexity applies also to the types of tasks that vary in difficulty level. Tasks of identification, synthesis and analysis are typically used in both assessment and teaching of phonological awareness. Tasks aimed at production pose more constraint than recognition exercises. Blending activities tend to be less challenging than analysis tasks. Visual (e.g. tokens, boxes, markers, pictures, gestures) or auditory (e.g. clapping, tapping) cues used to represent a given phonological chunk (word, syllable, onset, rime or phoneme) can considerably back up children's efforts towards completing a given task, because they make oral activities more concrete.

Crucially, there exists a reciprocal supportive relation between phonological awareness and letter-sounds and letter-names awareness development. Instruction in letter-sounds and names should be explicit and systematic in character and included in phonemic awareness teaching (Philips *et al.*, 2008). Goswami and Bryant (1990) stress that acquiring reading skills can efficiently follow the same path, namely, from bigger chunks to smaller ones. The ability to recognise onsets and rimes allows children to categorise words according to sound similarities. Then, sounds are mapped onto letters and letter clusters, and, finally, children are able to read unfamiliar words through analogy, by recognising the chunks they already know. For example, rhyming words often have identical orthographic sequences of letters (Krasowicz-Kupis & Bryant, 2004; Petrus & Bogdanowicz, 2004; Sochacka, 2004). Thus, the more proficient children are in identifying syllables, intra-syllabic elements, phonemes and phoneme-grapheme relations, the faster and more effective is the acquisition of reading ability. On the other hand, children encountering reading difficulties tend to be less sensitive in perceiving rhymes and grapheme/phoneme correspondences (Bogdanowicz & Krasowicz-Kupis, 2005a; Bradley & Bryant, 1983). Direct instruction in grapheme-phoneme relations enhances the conversion of implicit phonological knowledge into explicit. Instruction in orthographic patterns matched with their corresponding sounds proved pivotal in the development of phonological awareness (Wise *et al.*, 2007).

Phonological difficulties in dyslexia

With regard to the investigation on cognitive level, by far the best developed theory of dyslexia states that phonological problems occurring prior to the emergence of reading constitute a cause of later reading impairment. Two strong assumptions made by this theory are as follows: in children later diagnosed to suffer from dyslexia, phonological deficit pre-dates reading instruction, secondly, the severity of the reading impairment (consequence) can be predicted by the severity of the phonological processing (cause). Importantly, phonological deficit is claimed to persist through time, before and after reading has begun. If early phonological deficit is remediated before reading emerges, typical reading development can be expected (Hulme & Snowling, 2009).

The verification of the *core phonological deficit hypothesis* has generated multiple studies, including cross-sectional studies, in which dyslexics' performance is compared to the achievements of chronological age and reading age-matched controls, longitudinal studies conducted in search for best predictors of reading faculty, and, finally, experimental studies whose aim is to verify the effectiveness of early phonological training in enhancing reading skills (Krasowicz-Kupis, 2008). These studies produced an impressive amount of strong and converging evidence in support of the assumption that weak phonological coding constitutes the cause of dyslexia. In addition, the link between phonological processing deficits and atypical brain activation patterns as well as anatomical differences has been demonstrated repeatedly.[18] The description of phonological deficit usually comprises three main elements: phonemic awareness; slow lexical retrieval – best demonstrated in rapid serial naming/rapid automatised naming (RAN) tasks; and poor short-term memory (STM) – evident in non-word repetition and digit span tasks (Ramus, 2004).

Phonological processing difficulties encountered by children with dyslexia are well-documented (Hoien & Lundberg, 2000; Hulme *et al.*, 2005; Lundberg, 2002; Ramus *et al.*, 2003; Snowling, 2001a, 2001b; Szenkovits & Ramus, 2005; Vellutino *et al.*, 2004). Indeed, they seem to be especially evident in attempts to tackle both phonological awareness tasks and tasks requiring memory for phonological sequences. Impaired phonological system in dyslexics is seriously challenged by the activities aimed at identification and manipulation of phonological elements of differing sizes within words. A range of typical symptoms such as problems of verbal short-term memory, non-word repetition difficulties, poor phonological learning of new verbal information, word retrieval and rapid naming problems routinely emerge in dyslexics (Borkowska, 1997; Reid, 1998; Snowling, 2001a). To extend the list, Lundberg and Hoien (2001) enumerate more characteristic indicators of deficiency in phonological processing that may underlie reading impairments: difficulty in segmenting words into phonemes, keeping linguistic material (strings of sounds) in short-term memory, repeating back long non-words, reading and spelling even short non-words, and also slow naming of colours, numbers, letters and objects in pictures, a slower rate of speech sometimes with indistinct pronunciation, not to mention problems in phoneme manipulation. As a consequence, the hypothesis has been put forward that despite relatively appropriate semantic processing, phonology is not as efficiently coded in a dyslexic brain as compared to normally developing children.

According to the phonological coding deficit hypothesis, children with dyslexia encounter specific disruptions in the representation, storage and/or retrieval of speech sounds, which impedes the acquisition of the grapheme-phoneme correspondences, which in turn constitutes the foundation for reading disorders, especially with regard to alphabetic systems (Krasowicz-Kupis, 2008; Ramus et al., 2003). Indeed, a general conclusion, to which there is a growing consensus, is that below standard phonological coding, reflected in incomplete or inaccurate creation of phonological representations of words in one's mental lexicon, proves responsible for the failure in acquiring phonological awareness and alphabetic coding skills alike, which in turn is a key to the reading difficulties experienced by learners with dyslexia (Vellutino et al., 2004). Hence, the most notorious characteristics in dyslexia seem to pertain to poor quality of phonological representations of speech sounds, which, more often than not, turn out to be inaccurately specified, roughly coded, lacking distinctness and/or segmental specificity. As a consequence, phonological processing difficulties and problems in applying the alphabetic principle (segmental hypothesis) emerge. This typically ends up in more or less pronounced reading and spelling impairment (Goswami, 2000; Hatcher & Snowling, 2008; Hulme & Snowling, 2009; Snowling, 2001a; Snowling & Caravolas, 2007). Research findings also appear to confirm the fact that children at risk for dyslexia tend to demonstrate failure in creating mental phonological representations long before they begin their reading instruction. A test of pseudo-word repetition serves well in diagnosing such difficulties because it is an excellent indicator of the ability to form phonological representations (Krasowicz-Kupis, 2008).

With the assumption of the predominating phonological coding deficit hypothesis in mind, presuming only one cause of dyslexic difficulties, it appears to be truly difficult to explain how different subtypes of dyslexia may occur. Especially as regards the cases of individuals with dyslexia whose reading failure is not due to phonological processing impairment. Snowling (2000) proposes that diversified dyslexia manifestations do not necessarily refer so much to differing underlying deficits, but rather to the varying severity of impairment within phonological processing itself. Hence, surface dyslexia, indeed indicating a developmental delay rather than a deficit, may possibly occur due to a much subtler phonological coding deficit than phonological dyslexia. Surface dyslexia is characterised by dominant sublexical strategy in reading,[19] entailing orthographic coding deficit (rather adequate non-word reading, problems with exception word reading), whereas in phonological dyslexia, it is the lexical strategy, which involves recognising whole words, that dominates (relatively normal exception word reading, severe non-word reading problems) (Hulme & Snowling, 2009). This over-reliance on lexical strategy in reading suggests more pronounced phonological coding problems, present due to less-specified phonological representations. It can be expected that the two subtypes differ with respect to neuropsychological basis and represent varying susceptibility to intervention, with the surface type probably promising greater and much more easily achieved pedagogical gains than is the case with the phonological type (Krasowicz-Kupis, 2008). However, several studies provided weak support for the above classification and, in fact, it is suggested that a better way may be to resign from the proposed labels of phonological and surface dyslexia because they describe the patterns of reading impairment that tend to be unstable over time. Instead, it is proposed to treat them rather in terms of continuous variations in the skills that underpin development of reading (Hulme & Snowling, 2009; Snowling & Caravolas, 2007).

Goswami (2000) argues that the phonological representations hypothesis promises a plausible explanation of the role of phonological development in reading and dyslexia, and proposes its potential validity across languages. It is argued that segmental specificity of phonological representations is subject to changes induced by reading and spelling acquisition. Following this line of argument, it is expected, with good reason, that the way distinctness and segmental specificity would be affected by different orthographies depends very much on the transparency of a given orthography.[20] For children learning to read and spell in non-transparent orthographies, the process of restructuring phonological representations towards the phoneme-level is much more time consuming and more painful because of the lack of consistent feedback from reading and spelling at the phonemic level, even with regard to dense phonological neighbourhoods (words with numerous similar-sounding neighbours). For instance, words of low degree of sound-to-spelling consistency, such as 'birch', 'lurch', 'perch', 'search' (several spelling choices for a given sound), are likely to remain less specified phonologically. Accordingly, for children with dyslexia this process requires substantially greater investment of effort and time, frequently without a well-earned profit. On the contrary, while learning to read and write in transparent orthographies, children with dyslexia come across relatively consistent grapheme-phoneme relations and reading practice allows them to specify phoneme-level representations despite their pronounced deficits in phonological processing.

Particular phonological elements of different sizes, which are mentally represented, change over time and can be re-represented several times during the process of development of phonological skills in a given child. This phenomenon has been termed *restructuring*. Intensity of restructuring depends on several factors, for example, vocabulary size, phonological neighbourhood, linguistic features, as well as word frequency and familiarity. Larger vocabularies invite greater restructuring, the same holds true for early-acquired, high-frequency and familiar words as well as for denser phonological neighbourhoods.

Generally, early phonological representations of words are rather holistic and fairly global, then, with age, the change is characterised by an increase in representing segments of sounds in words corresponding to syllables, onsets and rimes and, finally, phonemes, and specifying distinctive features of these sounds (e.g. voicing). Phonemic representation is rather rare in the pre-literacy period, but it is believed to increase with literacy acquisition due to feedback of graphemic information (Wise et al., 2007). However, it needs stressing that inaccessibility of phonemes to pre-literate children is by no means universal. Children from several linguistic backgrounds may demonstrate varying degrees of phonemic awareness prior to formal literacy training; whether and to what extent small grain sizes are available to them depends very much on the nature of the language and its orthography. One might expect that the rapidity of change in restructuring towards achieving the level of individual phonemes would be affected by the level of orthographic transparency of the language in which a child is learning to read and spell. The anticipated effect assumes faster acquisition of the phoneme-level representation in languages with relatively transparent rather than opaque orthographies, since there is a consistent letter representation of a given sound for reading (Caravolas, 2006; Goswami, 2000; Goswami & Ziegler, 2006; Ziegler & Goswami, 2006).

Slow and inadequate phonological coding and poorly developed phonological representations constitute a characteristic feature of children and adults with dyslexia. Additionally, according to Lundberg and Hoien (2001), phonological deficit also tends to be apparent in compensated dyslexics – individuals who manage to achieve an almost normal reading faculty despite experiencing severe dyslexic problems. Snowling (2001a) highlights two possible sources of compensation in dyslexics with phonological processing impairments: visual memory and perceptual speed. Nevertheless, all the phonological tasks appear to be significantly more difficult for compensated dyslexics as compared to non-dyslexics. As pointed out by Shaywitz (1997), despite the undeniable improvement compensated dyslexics achieve in decoding and recognising words, thus automatically gaining access to the higher levels of language processing, their results on tests on reading speed and accuracy prove that decoding still requires considerable effort; words are not recognised automatically and fluently. Poor and slow phonological processing not only makes it increasingly hard, if not impossible, to quickly and effortlessly recognise words, but it is also capable of considerably hampering access to higher levels of language processing (syntactic and semantic), which, even though usually intact, can be reduced in their potential accessibility unless decoding on the phonological level is successful.

Summing up, a pervasive phonological impairment present in preschool years and persisting after the onset of reading instruction constitutes a characteristic feature of dyslexia, which at the cognitive level can be perceived as a delay or difficulty in forming segmental phonological representations. Non-segmental and poorly specified phonological representations present in children beginning formal reading instruction can considerably influence their reading development and aggravate reading difficulties. There exist individual differences in dyslexia with reference to severity and pattern of phonological difficulties. Still, Hulme and Snowling (2009) propose that, despite strong evidence collected in support of the view that the phonological deficit constitutes one cause of failure in the proper development of reading skill in dyslexia, it remains an open question whether other factors may play a causal role here. Indeed, it seems possible and likely. The operation of additional causes can be twofold: they may impact phonological skills and hence become the ultimate cause of phonological impairment or they operate separately from the phonological deficit (reading does not become impaired via the phonological deficit).

It goes without saying that the phonological deficit hypothesis has become the most powerful theoretical framework for dyslexia, but, as it stands, it did not escape criticism. Some scholars believe that the symptoms and causes of reading and spelling difficulties are specific to every child with dyslexia and, apparently, not all of them can be explained by phonological deficit (Nicolson & Fawcett, 1995; Nicolson, 2001). One of the main weaknesses of the phonological coding hypothesis is its inability to explain motor and sensory deficits evident in children with dyslexia. As much as the advocates of the phonological deficit theory appear to accept their co-occurrence with dyslexia, they reject them as insignificant and not critical manifestations of the specific reading difficulty (Krasowicz-Kupis, 2008). No wonder that, as already mentioned, numerous alternative theories have been developed. These theories mostly hold that high-standard phonological processing is indeed crucial for successful development of reading skills and that phonological deficit may deeply compromise reading acquisition. Nevertheless, these problems can be traced back to a more general learning disorder or sensorimotor impairment, which underlies phonological decoding deficit. Additionally, the high-quality controlled research notwithstanding, there seems to remain some scepticism among scholars with reference to such fundamental issues underlying research designs as operationalising and defining the concept of 'phonology' (Uppstad & Tønnessen, 2007).

Indeed, much as the consensus with respect to the link between literacy problems and phonological awareness is common, it is apparently lacking with regard to assigning phonological awareness either a primary/core role or perceiving it secondary to low-level sensory processing deficits (Bishop, 2006; White et al., 2006). Low-level sensory processing impairment theories deal with more basic causes of reading disability, involving the visual system, auditory system and the cerebellum. They usually refer to the faulty processing of rapid, transient stimuli most probably originating from neurobiological underpinning in the form of cerebellar or/and magnocellular malfunction, and possibly underlying the phonological deficit. Finally, apart from attempting to account for the phonological deficit in terms of the secondary impairment, they also propose a range of other deficits.

Goswami (2006) perceives those theories as complementary; probably underlying the phonological deficit and undertaking an attempt to decipher why otherwise cognitively well-functioning children struggle with phonological processing. As an example, the domain of processing auditory clues to the rhythm of speech is given; it is claimed that 'dyslexics just don't get the beat' (Goswami, 2006: 259). The temporal processing theory of dyslexia (or temporal order perception theory) (Tallal, 1980) sees the non-linguistic, auditory deficit, characterised by problems in temporal processing of rapidly changing auditory stimuli, responsible for dyslexic reading difficulties. In a similar vein, the magnocellular theory (Stein, 2001) proposes that the phonological deficit be traced back to the auditory deficit. In addition, Nicolson and Fawcett (2006: 261) point to the fact that the 'cerebellar deficit is the only single explanation of problems in balance, phonology and speed, and also one explanation of "pure" phonology/speed problems'.

By contrast, White et al. (2006) and Ramus et al. (2006) admit that the connection between phonological dyslexia and disordered sensorimotor processing is unquestionable, probably also indicating a common biological characteristic; in addition, they acknowledge the existence of a subgroup of children with dyslexia whose reading problems cannot be plausibly explained in terms of phonological deficit and this is where the sensorimotor deficit comes into play as a viable alternative. Nonetheless, they heavily criticise the proposition that phonological deficit could be causally related to and convincingly explained by low-level processing. Accordingly, if it were the case, then all dyslexics with phonological processing problems should be expected to demonstrate auditory deficit. However, in their study, only a small subgroup with clear phonological deficit also showed auditory deficit. Moreover, phonological deficit not accompanied by any sensorimotor deficits, including visual, auditory and motor, was observed in some children with dyslexia. White *et al.* (2006) and Ramus *et al.* (2006) interpret the results obtained in their multiple case study as strongly supportive of a primary role of phonological deficit, which is expected to be biologically based, at the same time discrediting and unequivocally rejecting the sensorimotor theories as generally incapable of explaining dyslexia. Interestingly, as already mentioned, they admit though that phonological deficit itself cannot explain all cases of dyslexia. Thus, the remaining subgroup of dyslexics, a non-phonological type, is believed to suffer from a visual impairment, more precisely visual stress, causing their reading difficulties. Altogether, summarising White *et al.*'s (2006: 253) position, 'specifically linguistic phonological deficit' is clearly favoured and argued to be 'directly and exclusively' responsible for dyslexic reading failure, furthermore, it is not believed to follow from auditory or motor deficits. Last but not least, in rare cases, visual disorder possibly accounts for dyslexic reading problems.

Still, the character of this visual disorder is not totally clear in light of evidence produced by other studies. Shovman and Ahissar (2006) point out that, in fact, individuals with dyslexia often complain about vision-related symptoms such as 'jumping letters', 'dancing lines' or blurred text; in addition, some of their reading errors tend to be explained in terms of visual processing impairment. However, in their examination of the visual aspect of reading in dyslexia, they did not confirm this kind of deficit to have any debilitating effect on the dyslexic single word reading ability. The subjects were tested on a specially designed task that was intended to be as similar as possible to single word reading with respect to visual aspects, at the same time lacking all the others – phonological, morphological or semantic. Shovman and Ahissar (2006) admit that children with dyslexia more frequently reported visual difficulties in reading compared with controls. The proposed explanation of this phenomenon involves the idea that, rather than in the context of single word decoding, which was simulated in the study, individuals with dyslexia encounter greater visual stress during normal reading conditions, namely, when approaching texts. The visual stress they experience seems to follow from the additional burden of the need for accurate saccades and tracking along the lines of the text, which altogether requires more visual attention necessary to compensate for poor phonological representations. Thus, the visual stress itself appears to stem from rather than to cause dyslexic reading difficulties.

In line with a multifactorial and multifaceted view of dyslexia, visual attention span deficit, possibly contributing to dyslexic difficulties irrespective of phonological impairment, was investigated by Bosse *et al.* (2007). Reduced visual attention span is characterised by poor multi-element processing, stemming from disorder in allocating attention across letter or symbol strings, which in turn limits the number of elements that can be simultaneously processed from a short visual display during reading. The outcome of the study indicates that poor visual attention span can explain some dyslexic reading difficulties independently of their phonological abilities. In fact, Bosse *et al.* (2007) qualified dyslexics into three subtypes, including those with identified single phonological processing or visual attention span deficits and a subgroup with a double deficit.

It seems that the debate on theories of dyslexia is very unlikely to end soon as new evidence, fresh insights and reinterpretations of the previous findings are regularly added to the field. Such a state of affairs naturally gives rise to numerous questions, especially as practitioners tend to find themselves at a loss while trying to interpret and understand research findings and translate them into plausible implications for intervention and teaching.

Double-deficit Hypothesis

Beyond doubt, some scholars do not seem to share the view of the exclusive and primary nature of poor phonological coding as a cause of dyslexia. The *double-deficit hypothesis* (DDH) proposes the existence of two independent underlying sources of dyslexic difficulties, namely, the phonological core deficit and naming speed impairment (Wolf & Bowers, 1999). Cirino *et al.* (2005) extend the applicability of DDH beyond children, supporting the fact that both phonological processing and visual naming speed seem likely to predict reading deficits in adults.

Let us move on to a more detailed revision of the nature of the second core deficit in dyslexia – the naming speed impairment. Deficits in the rate of processing are best elucidated by the serial naming speed, which is usually measured by RAN. Individuals' responses during their performance on tasks of naming speed are analysed with respect to the time needed for providing verbal labels for randomly presented high-frequency visual stimuli, such as numbers, letters, colours or objects (Vukovic & Siegel, 2006; Wolf & O'Brien, 2001). Slow naming speed may translate into low-level ability to recognise words quickly, which typically invites reading difficulties. In other words, children who exhibit difficulties in developing adequate rapid processing rates can be expected, with good reason, to experience some turbulence in reading development. Cirino *et al.* (2005) stress that poor visual naming speed may be responsible for slower word decoding, without being affected by accuracy, and as a consequence, reading comprehension may considerably diminish. Thus, RAN tasks seem to prove of service in formulating predictions and identifying children at risk for reading failure. However, Vukovic and Siegel (2006), due to the lack of a clearly operationalised and consistently used definition of rapid naming, call for the need to delineate particular features of RAN tasks that make the processes of naming speed crucial to reading development. Having reviewed the literature on reading difficulties in children, they arrived at the conclusion that naming speed deficit lacks specificity. In addition, they raise considerable doubts as to the existence of a sufficient amount of supporting evidence for DDH, especially as relates to the claimed independence of naming speed skills of phonological processing ability in explaining reading difficulties. By contrast, Wolf and O'Brien (2001) propose that the processes underlying naming speed indeed constitute a second core deficit in dyslexia, generally independent of phonological processing and manifesting itself in children and adults alike, a fact verified by numerous research outcomes.

Admittedly, the presupposed independence of the rapid naming impairment of the phonological deficit allows identification of three major subtypes of reading-impaired individuals, who can be categorised according to the presence or absence of these underlying processes. More precisely, the phonological deficit subtype concerns poor readers suffering solely from the disorder of phonological processing, at the same time demonstrating normal naming speed. By contrast, the naming speed deficit subtype refers to reading-impaired individuals with average phonological and word attack skills, but exhibiting below standard naming speed and later comprehension disorders. Finally, the most notoriously and severely disordered poor readers, characterised by low-grade gains with regard to both phonological processing and rapid naming, constitute the double-deficit subtype (Wolf & Bowers, 1999). Katzir *et al.* (2008) provided support for the valid framework of the DDH by investigating distinct subtyping of reading-disabled individuals. In their sample, as many as 46% of poor readers were categorised under the double-deficit subtype, approximately 25% were ill-at-ease when performing phonological processing tasks but proved average in terms of naming speed, in 18% of cases the reverse was observed, and finally, the remaining 11% could not be classified into any of the subtypes under the DDH framework. Similar findings were reported in other studies as well (Lovett *et al.*, 2000). As stressed by Wolf and O'Brien (2001), the continually growing bulk of data on the abovementioned subtypes of reading-impaired individuals indicate certain applied implications of the

DDH, namely, the need for adequate treatment and reading intervention, especially as regards two subtypes with poor rate of processing and low-standard fluency in reading. However, Vukovic and Siegel (2006) point to the improper design of intervention studies as constituting an apparent gap in research devoted to verification of the DDH.

Naming speed deficits are also existent in languages with more transparent orthographies, posing readers with fewer phonological demands than English. Taking German as an example, it has become evident that the naming speed deficits differentiated groups of readers in that language and predicted a reading ability better than a phoneme deletion task, which is considered the most well-known phonological measure. Apart from German, serial naming speed also proved a powerful predictor in Dutch, Finnish and Spanish. Wolf and O'Brien (2001) highlight the fact that in languages with more regular orthographies, phonological skills play a reduced role, while it is the carrying out of the naming speed tasks that becomes a stronger predictor of the reading performance.

However, language processing disorders do not hold a total potential for the explanation of reading disorders. Frequently, these problems seem not to be provoked by or fully dependent on poor language skills, quite the contrary, they may be invited by other deficits, thus proper attention is given to them in the forthcoming sections.

Magnocellular Deficit Hypothesis

As already signalled, a huge bulk of evidence has been provided supporting the thesis that the majority of people with dyslexia have impaired phonological processing (Bradley & Bryant, 1983; Hatcher & Snowling, 2008; Hulme & Snowling, 2009; Shaywitz, 1997; Snowling, 1981, 2001a), which correlates with their reading difficulties and, to a great extent, can explain them. According to Vellutino et al. (2004), visual system deficit theories in dyslexia, despite poor empirical support, were fairly influential and occupied an important position in research from the turn of the 20th century, through the 1970s and 1980s. Then linguistic deficit hypotheses started to gain increasing prominence. In those days, the proposed causes of reading difficulties included, for example, faulty visualisation, visual sequences and visual memory. Some interest in disordered visual processing as a cause of reading difficulties remained, but the scope has changed into analysing visual tracking problems, visual transient system deficit, abnormalities of perception of visual motion, the last two associated with functional distortions in the visual magnocellular subsystem.

In the search for possible causes of dyslexic difficulties, the studies on psychophysiology of the visual system arrested the attention of researchers, especially as pertains to the role of functional differences between the two structurally independent subsystems of the visual system – magnocellular and parvocellular.[21] Indeed, the fact has been accepted that some dyslexics show a certain degree of visual deficit (Stein et al., 2000b; Bednarek, 2003).

Stein (2001), Stein et al. (2000b) and Talcott et al. (2000a) demonstrated that the contrast sensitivity in individuals with dyslexia is impaired as compared to non-dyslexics, especially as low spatial frequencies, low luminance and high temporal frequencies (short stimulus duration) are concerned. Detection of such stimuli depends on the sensitivity of magnocells (M-cells) that comprise the retino-cortical M-pathway and this transient pathway is said to be the locus of the subtle visual impairments in dyslexia. On the other hand, people with dyslexia perform better at high spatial frequencies realised by the parvocellular system, which indicates that they are not as poor at all visual tasks. What is more, dyslexics exhibit low contrast and flicker sensitivity that are well-accepted measures of the visual transient/magnocellular system function. That is why it has been suggested (Stein, 2001; Stein & Talcott, 1999; Talcott et al., 2000a, 2000b) that individuals with dyslexia may have a specific impairment of the visual magnocellular/transient pathway, however the impairment is said to be mild and non-existing in all dyslexics. Those individuals with dyslexia who show visual symptoms are likely to have significant magnocellular deficit. The impaired transient sensitivity has been claimed (Stein et al., 2000b) to result in unsteady binocular control, which may bring about the impression, frequently reported by people with dyslexia, of letters moving around and over each other.

Stein (2001), Stein et al. (2000a, 2001) and Talcott et al. (2000a, 2000b) further state that reduced sensitivity of the magnocellular system is indicated by reduced sensitivity to visual motion.[22] Visual motion sensitivity has been measured with the use of a random dot kinematogram (RDK) test prepared for adults and children. Sensitivity to coherent motion is significantly reduced in the dyslexic group in comparison to controls. It appears to be independent of the changes in the temporal and spatial parameters of the RDK as well as its density. It can be related to poor integration of the changes in time that are characteristic of dynamic visual stimuli. Moreover, the reduction in motion sensitivity in an individual has been shown to correlate with his/her reading impairment. These findings have been confirmed by electrophysiological studies, fMRI and post-mortem examination of dyslexic brains (Galaburda & Livingstone, 1993).[23]

As argued by Stein (2001) and Talcott et al. (2000b), more evidence is being accumulated to show a causal connection between the function of the magnocellular system and reading. The direction of visual attention and eye movements as well as visual search are claimed to be dependent on the magnocellular system functioning. It is maintained that dyslexics show reduced motion sensitivity as well as unsteady binocular fixation, causing poor visual localisation, particularly on the left side (left neglect). Binocular and visual perceptual instability in dyslexics can cause an impression that the letters they are trying to read move around. Individuals with dyslexia also tend to complain (Bednarek, 2003; Stein, 2001; Stein et al., 2001) that small letters they are trying to read seem to change places, to merge with each other, to move in and out of the page, to blur, to get larger or smaller. It can happen because binocular instability causes the lines of sight of the two eyes to cross over each other. Therefore, it is not surprising that dyslexics cannot remember the proper order of these letters in words and that is why they fail to form reliable memories of these words' orthography. It is claimed that the smaller the letter size, the greater the number of visual errors committed by children with binocular instability (Cornelissen et al., 1991). Consequently, magnocellular sensitivity, being essential for motion sensitivity and stable binocular fixation, can thus predict the visual orthographic component of the reading skill of good and poor readers. For example, the spelling of irregular words and homophones[24] cannot be attained by sounding the letters out; their orthography must be remembered visually. Stein (2001) and Talcott et al. (2000b) demonstrated that the ability to spell irregular words and performance on the pseudo-homophone test correlate with visual motion sensitivity. Moreover, motion sensitivity accounts for the orthographic skills of an individual independently of his/her phonological skill.

There is another trend in research on the role of the visual system, dealing with the specificity of eye movements in people with dyslexia (Bednarek, 1999). According to Pavlidis (1986), eye movements highly correlate with the ability to read. It is maintained (Bednarek, 1999; Bogdanowicz, 1999, 2002a; Borkowska, 1997, 1998; Maruszewski, 1996; Pavlidis, 1986) that the movement of eyes during reading is not continuous; it consists of moments of fixation and saccades allowing perception of the next fragment of text. Successful reading is said to depend on achieving stable visual perception during each fixation on the word to be read and rapid shifts of visual attention to the next (Stein et al., 2001). Good readers move their eyes more regularly along the lines of the text than people with dyslexia. Abnormal saccade control has been demonstrated in people with dyslexia (Biscaldi et al., 1998). The pattern of eye movement in dyslexics during reading is disordered; the movements are more irregular, less harmonious and smooth. Significantly, more movements during reading have been noticed, especially as pertains to the occurrence of successive regressions (moving back and fixating on the already processed fragment of the text). Moreover, there are more fixations and they are longer (Borkowska, 1997; Pavlidis, 1986).

As much as the severity of reading difficulties may correlate with impairment in the pattern of eye movements, there is no agreement as to the causal status of the disordered pattern of eye movements with regard to dyslexia. It seems that reading difficulties induce an abnormal pattern of eye movements because poor readers seek ways of compensating, thus longer fixations may be traced back to decoding problems and numerous regressions can be brought about by the necessity to go through a given fragment of the text again in order to integrate and understand it. It might be suspected then, with good reason, that the incorrect pattern of eye movement in dyslexia may be caused by the difficulties in understanding the text, particularly in the cases of unknown words and grammatically complex sentences (Everatt, 2008).

On the other hand, some studies show a tendency in individuals with dyslexia to demonstrate the same pattern of eye movement in tasks that do not require reading and understanding of the text. For example, in watching numbers, pictures or fixating eyes on lights that are moving sequentially along the line from left to right and from right to left. Furthermore, children with dyslexia, when compared to other reading-impaired individuals, also perform more eye movements on reading tasks, especially regressions. These findings may indicate that they show a consistent eye movement pattern irrespective of the task. Thus, this pattern seems to be independent of reading. It is probably brought about by the central neurological mechanism, connected with small developmental changes in the cerebral cortex (Bednarek, 1999; Bogdanowicz, 1999; Borkowska, 1997; Ott, 1997). Apparently, these findings have not been successfully replicated in other studies; some children with dyslexia demonstrate typical patterns of eye movements, characteristic for non-dyslexic individuals, in tasks that do not involve reading (Everatt, 2008). Stein et al. (2001) consider the visual magnocellular system responsible for controlling eye movements during reading, thus it might be concluded that the disordered pattern of eye movement in individuals with dyslexia may be caused by inadequate functioning of the magnocellular system. Biscaldi et al. (1998) speculated that the neural substrate for the disordered saccade performance in dyslexics might be the parietal cortex.

The magnocellular theory is not reduced to the visual system. Even though the visual magnocellular pathway has been widely studied, there also exist magnocellular pathways in other sensory and motor systems, in which magnocells are specialised for temporal processing. For example, Stoodley et al. (2000) tested skin sensitivity to mechanical vibration in dyslexics and found mild deficits; moreover, reduced tactile sensation in dyslexics has been indicated as well (Grant et al., 1999). Even though these magnocellular deficits do not affect reading directly, the projections from all the magnocellular systems are received by the cerebellum, which is also known to be important for the acquisition of reading (Stein, 2001).

As far as the auditory magnocellular system in dyslexia is concerned, similar to its visual counterpart, deficits in detecting rapidly presented and changing stimuli are observable (Bednarek, 1999; Talcott et al., 2000b). As maintained by Stein, Talcott and others (Stein, 2001; Talcott et al., 1999, 2000b), the ability to differentiate between the letter sounds is dependent on the capacity to perceive changes in sound frequency and amplitude that characterise them. Spoken language occurs at low frequency. Thus, sensitivity to low frequency (FM) and amplitude modulation (AM) (ability to spot slower modulations in speech) is necessary for speech perception and thus for the development of phonological skills. It has been demonstrated that FM (2 Hz) and AM are significantly lower in individuals with dyslexia than in non-dyslexics, which can possibly explain dyslexic difficulties with phonological processing. Auditory FM and AM sensitivity in dyslexics has been compared to their ability to read nonsense words (considered to be the purest test of phonological skills) and high correlation has been found. Dyslexics are claimed to require considerably larger changes in frequency and amplitude to distinguish between them, however they are good at differentiating much higher rates of FM (240 Hz), which are not used for phoneme detection. Again, as in the case of the visual system, people with dyslexia are not poor at all auditory tasks, but they tend to show specific difficulties with modulations that are important for distinguishing letter sounds.

Measures of auditory temporal sensitivity correlate with measures of phonological skill, which might mean that people who are good at detecting modulations (changes in pitch) of low-frequency sounds are better at phonological processing (distinguishing and manipulating the speech sounds) and reading. Whereas measures of visual temporal sensitivity correlate with measures of orthographic skill, thus it might be the case that people who are good at spotting changes in the motion of dots across the computer screen are better spellers (Bower, 2000). The auditory frequency modulation (FM) sensitivity at 2 Hz but not at 240 Hz strongly predicts phonological ability but not orthographic skill, while visual motion sensitivity predicts orthographic skill but not phonological ability (Talcott et al., 2000b). It is further argued that even though these correlations do not prove a causal relationship, low-level visual and auditory function seem likely to be important in learning to read.

Despite solid research, some scholars (Fawcett & Nicolson, 2004) claim that the relationship between the magnocellular deficit and reading is not transparent, and others (Vellutino et al., 2004) consider the evidence provided by the advocates of the magnocellular hypothesis as inconclusive, equivocal and controversial.

Cerebellar Deficit Hypothesis

The advocates of a different concept to explain dyslexic difficulties have advanced an alternative model to the phonological core deficit hypothesis (Fawcett & Nicolson, 2001, 2004; Fawcett, 2008). While not denying the widely investigated and strongly confirmed connection between dyslexic reading difficulties and faulty phonological processing, they propose that problems suffered by children with dyslexia may be attributed to the more generally perceived automatisation deficit, capable of causing reading impairments and poor phonological processing alike. The *dyslexic automatisation deficit hypothesis* operates on the cognitive level and can be traced back to the biological level, namely, to an underlying cerebellar malfunction.[25]

Typical signs of cerebellar malfunction such as problems with muscle tone and disturbance in posture, gait or limb movements can be observed in children with dyslexia. It has been shown (Fawcett et al., 1996; Fawcett & Nicolson, 1999) that dyslexics perform worse than non-dyslexics on a wide variety of motor tests, including balance and other functions that the cerebellum is responsible for, thus clear behavioural evidence of the existence of cerebellar abnormalities in children with dyslexia has been provided. However, in a more recent study (Stoodley, 2006), which compared adults with dyslexia and controls on rapid pointing and balancing measures, no significant between-group differences were indicated with regard to balancing tasks; only when speed and accuracy of pointing were combined, a slight advantage of controls over dyslexics was recorded. The authors concluded that the tentative explanation can be twofold – either the tasks were too easy for adults with dyslexia participating in the study, or it is possible that with time, balancing deficits diminish and they are no longer apparent in adults with dyslexia. If the latter is true, then it would mean that balancing deficits evident in children with dyslexia are indeed a sign of a developmental delay rather than a true deficit. There is a need for more research to verify these propositions.

Traditionally, the cerebellum has been seen as a motor area involved in learning and automatisation of motor skills. Recently it has also been claimed that the cerebellum is important for language-related cognitive tasks, so called language dexterity. Thus, it is involved in the automatisation of any skill, whether motor or cognitive, including reading. Learning a skill fluently, making it automatic, means that one can perform it without thinking. These facts have led to the formulation of the automatisation deficit hypothesis (Nicolson & Fawcett, 1990, 2001), which states that children with dyslexia find it abnormally difficult to make any skill automatic (to become expert in any skill), despite extensive practice, regardless of whether the skill is cognitive or motor. Even if children with dyslexia succeed in achieving reasonably good literacy skills, their reading remains slower, more effortful and less automatic than normal readers of the same age. The quality of the automatised performance is lower, dyslexics are less skilled and their performance on any task is comparable with that of much younger children (Fawcett & Nicolson, 2004). What is more, the difficulties are greater when the time needed to master the skill increases.[26] Even though the behaviour of children with dyslexia appears normal, they experience lapses of concentration and get tired more quickly than other children while performing a given activity. Hence the suggestion that dyslexics are able to perform at normal levels by consciously compensating (concentrating, controlling) during the performance of the skill that might normally be automatic. A difference in learning rate has also been observed between dyslexics and controls, if a skill takes a typical child 100 hours to master, it would take a dyslexic child 1000 hours to acquire the same level of performance of the skill. The dyslexic automatisation hypothesis provides for reading problems and also for deficit in phonological and motor skills and rapid processing (Fawcett & Nicolson, 2001). It also offers an explanation why everything needs to be made explicit in teaching a child with dyslexia, while non-dyslexic children can pick up the skill without effort (Fawcett & Nicolson, 2004).

An ontogenetic causal chain proposed by Fawcett and Nicolson (2001, 2004) highlights the connection between cerebellar abnormalities, phonological problems and eventual difficulties in writing, reading and spelling. It indicates how deficits in the brain structure can lead, via disorders in cognitive processes such as automatisation and phonology, to reading disorder. It provides an account of patterns of difficulties encountered by dyslexics and shows how they arise developmentally. Children with dyslexia show poor quality handwriting, which can be explained in the view of the cerebellar deficit hypothesis as a motor skill that requires precise timing and coordination of muscles. It is further argued that cerebellar deficit in infants would first manifest by mild motor difficulty in sitting, walking, muscle control and articulation (the most complex motor skill), resulting in later start as far as babbling and talking are concerned. Moreover, even after the development of speech and walking, these skills remain less fluent than in infants without any cerebellar impairment. Consequently, articulation and speech that is less fluent than normal may lead to less complete processing of auditory, phonemic structure of spoken words, bringing about the loss of onset, rime and the phonemic structure of language. Spelling difficulties arise from over-effortful reading, poor phonological awareness and difficulties in automatising skills. According to the proponents of the hypothesis in question, in order to minimise reading and spelling difficulties, the involved subskills should be automatised through specialised teaching, with the use of carefully designed, monitored and long-term training programmes.

Altogether, cerebellar deficit would be responsible for the phonological processing deficit that together with the learning and automatisation deficit lead to reading and spelling difficulties. However, as seems to be the case with any other, more or less popular, assumption concerning the possible underlying causes of dyslexia, the cerebellar deficit hypothesis also invited considerable criticism from scholars dealing with dyslexia. For instance, Savage's (2007) findings discredit Fawcett *et al.*'s (2001) claim that the cerebellar deficit is specific to dyslexia and hence capable of distinguishing between groups of children with dyslexia and readers without IQ discrepancy, more precisely, children with moderate intellectual disability. In light of these findings, the value of IQ measures in dyslexia assessment, argued in favour of by Fawcett *et al.* (2001), apparently loses its potential, since the cerebellar deficit appears not to be reserved solely for this group.

The scale and scope of research devoted to discovering the underlying cause of dyslexia is beyond doubt impressive. Complicated and variable neurobiological patterns have been revealed. Apparently, the diversity of behavioural indications of dyslexia does add to the complexity of the nature of the neurological and cognitive basis of the disorder. It seems obvious that a massive amount of research findings, quite frequently controversial or inconclusive, involving anatomical, physiological and behavioural investigations, requires integrating with evidence of genetic and cultural influences as well. Altogether, it seems that a comprehensive causal explanation of dyslexia, incorporating a huge bulk of scientific facts, still remains a matter for the future.

Notes

1. The term *cognitive* refers here to the level between the brain and behaviour; the level of 'mind' or 'mental processes' (Hulme & Snowling, 2009).
2. It is implied (Stein, 2001; Stein *et al.*, 2001) that at least three genes may be important, one for orthography alone, one for phonological skills alone and one controlling linked orthographic and phonological abilities. Moreover, there seems to be noticeable agreement that the gene responsible for phonological and orthographic control is located on the short arm of chromosome 6 (Stein *et al.*, 2001).
3. For instance, electrophysiological methods, positron emission tomography (PET), functional magnetic resonance imaging (fMRI), magnetic source imaging (MSI) and magnetic resonance spectroscopy (MRS).

4. More precisely, what can be successfully captured during cognitive processing are, for instance, the metabolic changes reflected by glucose utilisation or blood flow shifts from one part of the brain to another, as measured by PET or fMRI (Richards, 2001).
5. For example, Hadzibeganovic *et al.* (in press) indicate the brain regions of abnormal function and atypical structure in dyslexics identified in recent neuroimaging studies with regard to alphabetic languages. Among the enumerated regions, there are the left temporoparietal areas, claimed to be involved in letter-to-sound decoding during reading, the left middle-superior temporal cortex, taking part in speech sound analysis, and, finally, the left inferior temporo-occipital gyrus, participating in quick word recognition.
6. For instance, volumetric grey matter.
7. ESL learners – learn English as a second language; EAL (EFL) learners – learn English as an additional (foreign) language.
8. The planum temporale is a region located in the superior temporal gyrus, between Heschl's sulcus anteriorly and the end of the Sylvian fissure posteriorly (Hugdahl *et al.*, 2003).
9. The planum temporale is normally bigger in the left hemisphere in non-dyslexics, while in people with dyslexia it is of similar size in both cerebral hemispheres.
10. The dichotic listening test constitutes a functional measure of phonological processing. It allows the evaluation of the auditory processing of verbal input in the temporal lobe. It entails simultaneous presentation of two different competing auditory stimuli, one to each ear. Typically, a REA indicates left hemisphere dominance for phonological processing. In other words, when reporting what they have heard, individuals with left hemisphere language lateralisation more accurately repeat verbal stimuli presented to the right ear.
11. Other studies have also pointed to the existence of reduced or absent REA in individuals with dyslexia encountering phonological difficulties, e.g. Bloom and Hynd (2005).
12. The left planum temporale was significantly larger than the right one in dyslexics and controls. However, the left planum temporale appeared significantly smaller (9%) in the dyslexic group, whereas the right planum temporale was similar in size in both groups. Again, both groups demonstrated a significant REA, however, right ear scores in the dyslexic group were reduced as compared to controls, while the left ear score resembled the scores gained by the control group. It has been suggested that normal REA in subjects with dyslexia, despite a smaller left planum temporale, means that the planum temporale is not unique for phonological processing.
13. Ectopias are defined as small areas of inadequately placed neurons clustered around the temporoparietal junction; they consist of about 50–100 neurons that missed their target in the cortex during the course of neural migration. Dysplasias – described as focal malformations of the architecture of the cortex, have been shown to be bilaterally located; nevertheless, their number was greater in the left hemisphere in all the examined brains (Ramus, 2004).
14. The tissue connecting the two cerebral hemispheres, allowing communication and flow of information between them; the largest neural pathway connecting the two cerebral hemispheres. It is built of several parts connecting particular areas of the left and right cerebral cortex.

15. See the section 'Magnocellular deficit hypothesis' for more information on the magnocellular deficit hypothesis in dyslexia.
16. The cerebellum is a subcortical brain structure at the back of the brain.
17. See the section 'Cerebellar deficit hypothesis' for more information on the cerebellar deficit hypothesis in dyslexia.
18. Neuroimaging studies of phonological processing indicate differences in the left temporoparietal cortex in adults and children with dyslexia when compared to non-impaired controls (Shaywitz et al., 2003; Temple et al., 2001).
19. See Chapter 1: 'Reading strategies and stages of reading development'
20. See Chapter 1: 'Orthographic depth and grain size: A cross language perspective on reading and dyslexia'.
21. The stimulus analysis in perceptual systems is conducted sequentially (hierarchically), it means that the information sent from the lower levels of the central nervous system is further analysed and integrated on the higher levels. In these systems, there exist considerably independent pathways, specialising in transmitting information concerning different features of a given stimulus (Grabowska, 1997). At all levels of the visual system, two subsystems of cells, which fulfil different roles in analysing visual stimuli, can be separated. According to their anatomical structure, these subsystems are called magnocellular and parvocellular (Bednarek, 1999; Bogdanowicz, 1999). Thus, the retino-cortical visual stream consists of magno (larger) and parvo (smaller) cells, which transmit signals (electrical impulses) from the retina in the eye to the brain (Grabowska, 1997; Stein, 2001; Stein et al., 2001; Talcott et al., 2000a). The parvocellular system is responsible for the analysis of details, recognition of small shapes, perception of colours, and clear, sharp vision, while the magnocellular system deals with peripheral vision (reacting over a larger area), perception of rapidly presented, rapidly changing and moving stimuli, it is sensitive to contrast and luminance (Bednarek, 1999; Grabowska, 1997) and low spatial frequencies (Grabowska, 1997). Magnocells project to the primary visual area in the occipital cortex (Stein, 2001).
22. Experiments on monkeys have demonstrated that detecting coherent motion in a display of dots moving around randomly (random dot kinematogram) proves to be a sensitive test for probing the whole magnocellular system.
23. See the section: 'Brain mechanisms in dyslexia' on brain abnormalities in dyslexia.
24. Words that sound the same but have different spelling.
25. See the section: 'Brain mechanisms in dyslexia' on brain abnormalities in dyslexia.
26. Impairment is said to increase as the square root of the necessary learning time.

Chapter 3
Dyslexia and Foreign Language Learning

Native Language-based Foreign Language Learning Difficulties

Obviously, familiarity with foreign languages is a must in the multilingual society we live in today. Thus, a foreign language requirement has to be fulfilled at schools and universities, posing a substantial burden on a number of students, who repeatedly demonstrate varying degrees of difficulty in learning a foreign language, quite frequently at the same time doing well at other courses. Many explanations have been proposed and debated in order to explain this phenomenon. Suggestions included lack of foreign language aptitude, poor attitude, low motivation, high levels of anxiety, failure to use appropriate learning strategies, mismatch of teacher-student learning styles, much less personality variables. Seemingly, some correlational linkages between affective variables and successful foreign language learning appeared to be strong. However, no single variable or set of variables have been proved to account for successful or unsuccessful foreign language learning. Foreign language researchers have not managed to explicitly specify any clear pattern of the relationship between foreign language achievement and cognitive, attitudinal and personality variables (Brown, 2000; Ellis, 1994; Lundberg, 2002; Sparks, 1995, 2006).

In the 1960s, Carroll attributed individual differences in foreign language learning to the overall language ability of the learner and to variables related to instruction. Pimsleur observed that foreign language underachievers tend to demonstrate poor sound discrimination skills and hardness in sound-symbol learning, responsible for the foreign language learning differences that could not be explained by low motivation or intelligence. Dinklage documented cases of students achieving well at other courses, yet failing their foreign language component at Harvard University. Again, the failure could not be traced back to lack of motivation or poor attitude, as their attempts to perform well in foreign language courses and positive stance were evident. Dinklage was the first to suggest that the hindrance experienced by those students resembled dyslexic problems, namely, difficulties in learning to read and spell, occurrence of letter/symbol reversals, sound confusions, poor discrimination of sounds in a foreign language and verbal memory deficit (Ganschow *et al.*, 1998; Schneider, 1999; Sparks, 1995; Sparks *et al.*,

1989, 1991, 1992b, 1995b). In the 1980s, a plausible bond between foreign language learning difficulties and problems with native language learning was put forward. Apparently, foreign language learners with specific learning difficulties share various aspects of language functioning that might negatively influence their ability to learn a foreign language (Sparks *et al.*, 1989). Skehan believes that second or foreign language learning is the equivalent of the first language learning faculty and children who develop faster in their first language also score higher on foreign language aptitude tests (Ganschow & Sparks, 1995; Schneider, 1999; Sparks *et al.*, 1995b). It is claimed that successful foreign language learning draws on intact language skills. Thus, logically, foreign language acquisition can be blocked by any physiological or biological deterrents that handicap the learning of one's native language (Sparks *et al.*, 1995b; Spolsky, 1989).

Ganschow and Sparks (1986) have presented detailed case studies of four college students, who faced foreign language learning problems most probably related to their native language learning impairment. Gajar (1987) compared a group of students with identified specific learning difficulties with a control foreign language-enrolled group for their aptitude for learning a foreign language, measured by the Modern Language Aptitude Test (MLAT; Carroll & Sapon, 1959). Specific learning-disabled students performed significantly more poorly than the control group on all five subtests of the MLAT, namely, auditory comprehension in a listening memory task, sound-symbol association ability, vocabulary knowledge, sensitivity to grammatical structure and visual rote memory for words. This emerging body of evidence suggested that students with foreign language learning difficulties had early histories of language problems, which were either unrecognised or compensated for due to their high IQ and remedial help (Sparks *et al.*, 1989).

In the same vein, Chodkiewicz (1986) highlights the fact that individuals struggling with reading in their native language are prone to face failure in their attempts to become fluent in foreign languages. A close interdependence between the ability to read in one's native and foreign language is suggested. Thus, individuals who are low-grade readers in their native language are very likely to read poorly in the foreign language, while, conversely, good readers apply their competencies equally well in the native as well as foreign language.

Kahn-Horwitz *et al.* (2006) borrow the notion of the so called 'Matthew effects' from native language (L1) reading research (Stanovich, 1986) and aptly use it to characterise weak English as a foreign language (EFL) readers. Possessing stronger reading subskills such as, for example, phonological awareness and knowledge of letter sounds and names at the beginning stages of learning to read in a second/foreign language (L2) typically assures faster and more accurate L2 reading acquisition. This, in turn, by and large secures greater reading experience, almost invariably necessary to produce skilled readers. Being disabled with respect to the abovementioned decoding skills puts children at an obvious disadvantage, since their slow and laborious reading experience results in difficulties with comprehension, decreases motivation and, finally, makes them lag behind good foreign language (FL) readers. Additionally, developing an ability to read in a foreign language is believed to trigger progress of the parallel skill in a native language and vice versa. However, such a transfer can take place after a learner has reached a certain level of proficiency in a foreign language (Chodkiewicz, 1986). It seems that in this way a vicious circle closes, unless learners with dyslexia are provided with appropriate tutoring assistance.

Since the 1980s, Sparks *et al.* have conducted pioneering research in the matter of foreign language learning difficulties of individuals for whom reading and spelling in their native language constituted an obvious challenge. Among these poor FL learners, there are students classified as learning disabled (LD)/dyslexia and low-achieving (at-risk) students without diagnosis towards LD. In 1989, Sparks and Ganschow (Ganschow *et al.*, 1998; Ganschow & Sparks, 2000, 2001; Sparks, 1995; Sparks *et al.*, 1989; Sparks & Ganschow, 1991) proposed the *linguistic coding deficits hypothesis* (LCDH) as a model for explaining language problems encountered by poor foreign language learners. They revived the speculations of Pimsleur, Carroll and others about the salience of the native language skills, language aptitude differences, and, particularly, phonological processing in foreign language learning. It is claimed that poor foreign language learners have in common a disability in linguistic coding. There are three types of linguistic coding deficits: phonological (involves identifying and distinguishing between speech sounds and processing the sound/symbol connections), syntactic (involves understanding and applying grammatical, structural concepts of a language system) and semantic (connected with understanding meanings). Phonological and syntactic tasks are fundamental to language acquisition in its earliest stages, whereas semantic undertakings depend on the conceptual understanding of the messages conveyed through language units (Sparks *et al.*, 1989). The model proposed by Sparks and Ganschow is based on findings in native language research on reading disabilities by Vellutino and Scanlon (Ganschow & Sparks, 1995; Sparks *et al.*, 1989), who claim that poor readers exhibit difficulties with phonological and syntactic aspects of their native language, with phonological coding being especially weak.

To recapitulate, LCDH puts forward an idea that foreign language learning is built on native language skills, that phonological/orthographic, syntactic and semantic competences in the native language form the foundation for foreign language learning (and FL aptitude). Thus, the strength of the native language codes considerably determines the extent to which a learner can become proficient in a foreign language. Weak L1 skills tend to inhibit FL proficiency development. Students with stronger native language skills will demonstrate higher FL proficiency and achievement than students with weaker native language skills. In a similar vein, poor L1 readers are expected to transpose low automaticity and efficiency to L2 reading.

It is also speculated that both native and foreign language learning depend on basic language learning mechanisms, moreover problems with one language skill are likely to have a negative effect on both the native and foreign language systems. Furthermore, it is assumed that the majority of poor foreign language learners experience most difficulty with the phonological/orthographic rule system of L2. LCDH predominantly focuses on linguistic variables because foreign language learning is the learning of language (Ganschow *et al.*, 1998; Ganschow & Sparks, 1995; Sparks, 1995; Sparks *et al.*, 1989; Sparks & Ganschow, 1991).

The comparison between good and poor language learners shows that poor students show significant degrees of variation rather than deficits in language performance. As already mentioned, it especially pertains to the tasks that place specific demands on phonological processing, within which the ability to isolate and manipulate consciously the sounds of the language – phonemic awareness[1] – tends to be particularly deficient. Measures of phonological awareness appear to be significant predictors of the disparities between children with and without impaired reading (Sparks, 1995). According to Sparks (Sparks, 1995; Sparks *et al.*, 1989), students with obstructions in the phonological component of their native language are likely to confront an immediate hurdle in foreign language learning.

The native language difficulties of at-risk learners may be overt or subtle; in the latter case, they may only be apparent in one language code – phonological/orthographic, syntactic or semantic. Four prototypes of poor foreign language learners, characterised by diverse linguistic profiles, have been described. Weak phonology, average or strong syntax and strong semantics constitute one prototype; the second prototype is characterised by strong phonology, average or strong syntax and weak semantics; the third has weak phonology, syntax and semantics; and the last prototype entails average to strong phonology, syntax and semantics, but low motivation and/or high anxiety. The most commonly occurring combination is the first prototype (with weak phonology) (Ganschow & Sparks, 1995; Sparks, 1995).

As already indicated, Spark and Ganschow (Sparks *et al.*, 1995b) suggest that foreign language learning problems of students at secondary and post-secondary level may be due to earlier problems with phonological/

orthographic processing of their native language. It is further hypothesised that even though these students may be able to compensate for their phonological/orthographic processing problems and achieve average or above-average grades in most school subjects, when it comes to learning a new sound-symbol system of a foreign language, the difficulties with phonological/orthographic processing re-emerge.

Bearing in mind that these difficulties may hamper the process of FL learning to a lesser or greater extent, one might, quite naturally, consider an extreme case and ask whether they are capable of making a decent command of a foreign language a totally unattainable goal. In other words, should we conceptualise the notion of an absolute inability to learn a foreign language as a plausible explanation of FL learning difficulties in the cases of LD students, and only those students?

Foreign Language Learning Disability versus Continuum Notion of Language Learning Differences

The aim of this section is to provide arguments, supported by evidence from research findings, for the negative answer to the question, whether a disability for FL learning (FLLD) can be perceived and treated as a distinct type of disability. On the contrary, the position that language learning ability, with reference to LD as well as non-LD (low-achieving) students, exists on a continuum, with the foreign language learning difficulties ranging from mild to severe, is advocated. It seems reasonable to expect that in the majority of cases, learners with dyslexia (LD) could be placed on this continuum more towards its severe end.

Sparks et al. (1989) initially termed their hypothesis, the linguistic coding deficit hypothesis, and concentrated on describing barriers that students with specific learning disabilities (SLD) encounter in foreign language learning. SLD students are claimed to face subtle or overt deficits in the oral and written aspects of their native language and to exhibit a discrepancy between their measured intellectual ability (IQ) and specific areas of academic achievement (e.g. reading, spelling, mathematics). Then, Sparks et al. expanded their interest onto a large group of students without SLD, who, nevertheless, experience substantial trouble in foreign language learning. The term, at-risk foreign language learners, has been introduced to refer to students with identified learning disabilities, most of whom experience obstructions in foreign language learning, and students who are not ascertained as LD but still struggle with substantial pitfalls in foreign language learning in the formal classroom environment (Ganschow & Sparks, 1995). Since in the USA the study of foreign languages does not usually start until high school, in their studies, Sparks and colleagues have concentrated on these older students.

The name, *linguistic coding deficit hypothesis*, was changed to the *linguistic coding differences hypothesis* (LCDH) in 1994 (Ganschow et al., 1998), firstly, in order to highlight the individual differences in basic language propensities; secondly, to focus attention on the fact that language learning ability exists on a continuum, with foreign language learning difficulties ranging from mild to severe; and thirdly, to place emphasis on the fact that there is no such phenomenon as a *foreign language learning disability* (FLLD). According to Schneider (1999), the differences between poor LD and non-LD foreign language learners pertain to the degree of complication and appear primarily in spelling and performance on foreign language aptitude tests. On the proposed continuum, the students with diagnosed LD constitute the most severely affected cases.

Sparks (2006) proposes convincing arguments against the existence of a distinct entity, such as a disability for FL learning (FLLD), as a notion separate from terms more neutral in character, for example, learners with FL learning difficulties, or at-risk, poor, low-achieving FL learners. The term *foreign language learning disability* (FLLD) seems to have gained some acceptance over the past couple of years, in both learning disabilities and foreign learning field, and even when it is not used explicitly, a relation between LD and FL difficulties is apparently implied (e.g. Shaw, 1999; Reed & Stansfield, 2004; Smith, 2002). In their earlier work on FL learning problems, Sparks and colleagues (e.g. Ganschow & Sparks, 1986, 1987; Ganschow et al., 1991) also theorised about a plausible explanation of the abovementioned difficulties in terms of an assumed existence of the link between a classification of LD and FL learning problems. However, having conducted a number of studies in order to verify the hypothesised connection, they revised their stance on this matter and acknowledged that research findings had not confirmed their speculations, and that the earlier use of the term FLLD was unjustified and incorrect (Sparks, 2006; Sparks et al., 2002, 2003).

It turned out that secondary and post-secondary students, both classified as having LD, and poor FL learners without LD diagnosis, signed on for FL courses, rarely significantly differed with respect to cognitive, native language and FL aptitude measures (e.g. Sparks et al., 1996, 1998b). LD students did not always experience problems with FL learning, in fact, many of them easily got credits in their FL courses, completing them with little or no obvious difficulty (Sparks & Javorsky, 1999; Sparks et al., 2002, 2003), while many students who could not formally be classified as having LD experienced difficulty and failure in their attempts to complete FL requirements. Additionally, it has been shown that LD students do not substantially differ from non-LD low-achieving students when it comes to the severity of the FL problems they experience or their language learning profiles (Sparks *et al.*, 2002, 2003, 2006).

Ferrari and Palladino (2007) find the results described above concerning relative similarity between LD and non-LD high-risk FL students somewhat misleading. On the one hand, low-achieving students identified as at-risk for FL learning problems lack formal (and former) diagnosis of LD, on the other hand, they closely resemble LD students with regard to phonological and syntactic difficulties. Potentially, the answer may lie in the analysis of FL learning profiles demonstrated by high-risk students, with the most frequently and consistently emerging poor phonological and syntactic abilities but rather average semantic faculty. In addition, age could be a factor as well. Since most of the studies by Sparks *et al.* concentrate on young adults, high school or college students, arguably, it seems a challenging task to actually reconstruct individual's development and native learning difficulties, which might have been compensated to some extent by the time they advanced in their academic career to the level of high school or college. Thus, tracking down their FL learning difficulties to poor phonological and syntactic abilities in their native language poses a considerable problem.

The abovementioned research outcomes indeed seem to run counter to the commonly accepted proposition that students with LD struggle with markedly more severe native and foreign language learning problems than non-LD learners. The controversy may have also been caused by the lack of a congruous, unambiguously operationalised and empirically well-grounded definition of LD (Sparks *et al.*, 1995a, 1998a, 2002, 2003, 2006, 2008a) that would allow the diagnosis of a large number of children who do not function well in regular classroom settings and do not exhibit other malfunctions such as mental retardation, visual or hearing impairments, or physical handicaps as LD. The lack of scientifically sound criteria for the identification of LD has been very problematic and has led to the formation of heterogeneous research samples of LD students (Sparks *et al.*, 1995a, 1995c, 1998b). For example, in their study, Sparks *et al.* (2003) report that at least 50% of LD students did not meet either the legal or research criteria for LD classification. The fact was attributed to problematic definition and classification system of LD that, quite logically, produces problematic students' classifications as LD.

Although poor foreign language learners exhibit statistically significant native language and foreign language dissimilarities when compared to good foreign language learners, their performance, as already indicated, may still be in the average to low-average range (Sparks, 1995). The analysis of the grades of LD foreign language students showed that a number of them had successfully passed at least one foreign language course in college. The majority of petition students also admit having passed FL courses in high school, often with average and above-average grades. Thus, one might wonder why these students had been able to fulfil the FL requirement in high school and then, surprisingly, were granted FL course substitutions or waivers in college. According to Sparks *et al.* (2003, 2008b), there exist several unfounded assumptions adopted by students, diagnosticians, university officials and disability service providers. The prevailing belief among LD students and diagnosticians is that these students are bound to confront excessive difficulty with FL learning and are most likely to fail FL courses. Moreover, diagnosticians may falsely assume that students of average and above-average intelligence, who struggle with and achieve low grades in FL courses, must be LD, notwithstanding high scores obtained on tests verifying their native language ability. Even more importantly, there is a possibility that educational officials and disabled service providers adopt a view that only students classified as LD are prone to experience extreme problems in FL learning and fail FL courses, and therefore should be provided with educational accommodations in the form of special instruction, course substitution or waiver. Educators may further assume that non-LD low-achieving students with L2 learning problems do not encounter subtle or overt L1 difficulties and, unlike in the cases of LD poor L2 learners, they do not need and would not benefit from direct, explicit instruction and other educational adjustments. However, the aforementioned assumptions have been negatively verified by the research results and, in all likelihood, they seem to be false.

Sparks (Sparks, 2006; Sparks *et al.*, 2008b) claims that research findings unequivocally denote LD classification as an irrelevant factor in determining the ease of FL acquisition. Still, despite quite incontrovertible research conclusions, typically the practice in many high schools, universities and colleges is that in order to be eligible for FL course substitution or waiver, students need to be diagnosed as LD. At the same time non-LD FL underachievers, with legitimate special needs in the area of FL learning, are generally not granted the abovementioned accommodations because they lack formal identification and evaluation of their learning problems. Furthermore, LD students are too frequently automatically assumed to be likely to exhibit difficulties in FL learning, and low-achievers struggling with FL learning are routinely expected to be LD (Sparks *et al.*, 2002, 2003; Sparks, 2006). Since, at present, there is no empirically supported sound ground to offer FL course substitutions or waivers to LD students at the same time denying them to non-LD students with FL learning problems – it would seem fair to either offer the educational adjustments, following some school-selected criteria, to all students struggling with FL provisions or not to make any students eligible for such options (Sparks *et al.*, 2003; Sparks, 2006).

It needs stressing here that FL learning difficulties experienced by low-achieving non-LD students as well as these diagnosed to have LD can be, in all probability, attributed to the same factor, namely, weaker L1 skills, which, almost invariably, are linked to lower L2 aptitude, achievement and proficiency. LD and non-LD poor FL learners, whose results on measures of L1 skills and FL aptitude are on the whole significantly poorer than those of high achievers, have been repeatedly observed to demonstrate similar skills on measures of L1 and L2 literacy. In addition, they commonly exhibit comparable L2 aptitudes, cognitive abilities (IQ) as well as levels of motivation for L2 learning (Sparks, 2001, 2006; Sparks *et al.*, 2008a, 2008b).

What follows from the above is that, firstly, most probably there is no such phenomenon as FL learning disability and language learning ability exists on a continuum, with foreign language learning difficulties ranging from mild to severe. Secondly, intelligent students struggling with FL courses should not be perceived as having any kind of special disability. Thirdly, non-disabled low-achieving learners may have, just like their LD counterparts, subtle or overt language learning problems. Finally, students classified as LD can, to some extent, become proficient in a foreign language. Beyond doubt, native language problems will manifest themselves in students' attempts to learn a foreign language, nevertheless, they do not necessarily have to impede successful foreign language acquisition (Mabbott, 1995). Thus, obviously enough, poor FL learners should rather not be withdrawn from foreign language courses but encouraged to enrol and provided with tutoring assistance (Ganschow *et al.*, 1998; Sparks *et al.*, 1998b, 2008a; Sparks, 2006).[2]

What follows is a comprehensive, however, by no means exhaustive, review of research findings in support of the LCDH, promoting the claim that native language skills form the basis for FL aptitude and learning, so, logically, students with weaker native language skills are expected to routinely demonstrate markedly lower FL aptitude, achievement and proficiency than students with stronger native language skills. In addition, linguistic factors have repeatedly proved responsible for FL learning success or failure, while affective variables seem to be secondary with respect to this matter. Poor attitude, unfavourable self-perception, as well as motivational-emotional disorders are likely to occur as a result rather than the cause of the difficulties in question.

Review of Research in Support of Linguistic Coding Differences Hypothesis

Sparks and Ganschow initiated their research on the aetiology of foreign language learning difficulties concentrating on cognitive, affective and linguistic factors. They accumulated a sound empirical support for their hypothesis that foreign language potential is in essence directly linked to the native language capacity. In their studies, a rich battery of tests involving phonological, syntactic and semantic measures of language and a foreign language aptitude test were administered to good and poor foreign language learners, who consistently turned out to have substantial native language learning deficits (Sparks, 1995).

It needs highlighting that, as far as the cognitive domain is concerned, no significant unlikeness in the level of intelligence (IQ) has been found between the students with and without foreign language learning difficulties. As relates to the affective domain, poor attitude and lack of motivation invariably turned out to be the result of hardness with language rather than its cause. In the face of it, the linguistic factors are believed to constitute the primary causal determinants in successful or unsuccessful foreign language learning. Thus, let us stress again, poor foreign language learners almost inevitably suffer from either subtle or overt native language impairments, which are blame-worthy for the foreign language acquisition problems these students encounter (Ganschow et al., 1998; Sparks et al., 1998a).

Anxiety and perception studies

As pertains to the affective variables, it is speculated that students' low level of motivation and high level of anxiety regarding foreign language learning exist due to certain deficits in their native language skills (Sparks, 1995; Sparks & Ganschow, 1991; Sparks et al., 1989). In one of the studies providing support for the above hypothesis, the students were grouped by the level of foreign language anxiety. Native language skill and foreign language aptitude differences were documented across high-, average- and low-anxiety groups (Ganschow et al., 1994). In another study (Sparks et al., 1997b) with similar grouping criteria, significant differences were spotted in oral and written foreign language proficiency among high-, average- and low-anxiety groups. In general, it can be concluded that students with lower levels of anxiety about foreign language learning, stronger native language skills and greater foreign language aptitude score significantly higher on measures of foreign language proficiency than students with higher levels of anxiety about foreign language learning, lower native language skills and lower foreign language aptitude.

In order to study affective states, several investigations with reference to students' self-perceptions about their foreign language learning have been conducted (Javorsky et al., 1992; Sparks et al., 1993). Other studies concerned teachers' perceptions about their students' foreign language learning aptness and affective characteristics (Sparks & Ganschow, 1995). Moreover, parents' perceptions about their children's native and foreign language learning faculties (Sparks & Ganschow, 1996) have also been investigated.

In one of the self-perception studies (Javorsky et al., 1992), both LD and non-LD foreign language college students were equally motivated to learn a foreign language. However, the LD foreign language learners perceived themselves as less capable of mastering the content of foreign language courses in both the oral and written requirements. Additionally, they admitted feeling more anxious when taking tests and studying for foreign language lessons. In another study of this kind (Sparks et al., 1993), high school first-year foreign language course students characterised as high-risk, low-risk or diagnosed as LD were compared with respect to their academic skills and attitudes towards foreign language learning. Low-risk students reported significantly higher foreign language grades and demonstrated markedly more positive attitudes about their language learning potential than high-risk and LD students. Furthermore, high-risk and LD students perceived themselves as deprived of the academic capacities to acquire satisfactory competence in a foreign language. Nevertheless, all students participating in the study admitted they possessed readiness and a desire to learn a foreign language. As maintained by Sparks et al. (1993), the fact that high-risk and LD students perceived themselves less positively resulted from their substantially weaker native language propensities and foreign language aptitude as compared to low-risk students.

In the perception study conducted by Sparks and Ganschow (1996), the high school students were allocated into high, average and low groups in compliance with their scores on the native language and foreign language aptitude tests. Students who scored lower on the testing measures were perceived by their teachers as possessing weaker foreign language academic skills and less heartening affective characteristics, pertaining to higher anxiety, lower motivation and less optimistic attitude than students who demonstrated superior native language skills and foreign language aptitude.

In the study on parents' perceptions of their children's language ability, first-year high school foreign language learners were divided into low-risk, average-risk and high-risk groups with regard to the scores of the questionnaire (completed by their parents) on the subject of their native language learning history. The students also underwent the native language faculty and foreign language aptitude testing. All-embracing significant group differences were detected favouring the low- and average-risk groups over the high-risk group on the native language, foreign language aptitude and cognitive measures. What follows from the above studies is that students who are perceived, both by their parents and foreign language teachers, as holding weaker native and foreign language skills indeed exhibit inferior competencies touching on the native and foreign language and they achieve lower grades in foreign language courses than students who are perceived as the ones demonstrating strong native and foreign language abilities.

The results of the aforementioned studies clearly provide support for the claim that foreign language learning difficulties are not induced by the affective variables. Quite the opposite, the affective differences between good and poor foreign language learners seem to be dependent on the intensity of difficulties they struggle with during foreign language acquisition.

Comparison studies between good and poor foreign language learners

Moving on from perception to comparison studies, let us note that Sparks and Ganschow conducted a number of studies in which they compared good and poor foreign language learners. In the studies examining native language skills and foreign language aptitude differences, it was shown that successful college foreign language learners exhibited significantly stronger native language phonological/orthographic skills (but not semantic) and greater foreign language aptitude (as measured by the MLAT) than unsuccessful foreign language learners (Ganschow et al., 1991). This distinctness has been demonstrated not only at post-secondary, but also at secondary level (Sparks et al., 1992a), with the use of a similar battery of native language strength (reading, spelling, vocabulary and writing) and foreign language aptitude measures. First-year foreign language learners in high school were grouped into low and high risk in line with their first quarter foreign language grade (A and B – low risk, D and F – high risk) and the recommendation of their foreign language teachers. Low-risk foreign language learners displayed impressively stronger native language phonological/orthographic and syntactic but not semantic capabilities and greater foreign language aptitude than high-risk foreign language learners.

In another study (Sparks et al., 1992b), LD first-year foreign language learners were compared to low- and high-risk foreign language learners on the same measures. Again, low-risk foreign language learners manifested stronger native language phonological/orthographic and syntactic but not semantic skills and greater foreign language aptitude than LD and high-risk foreign language learners. The salient outcome of the study is that no significant contrasts were identified on most native language and foreign language aptitude tests between the LD and high-risk foreign language learners. High-risk foreign language learners outperformed LD foreign language learners only on the spelling measure. Hence, the hypothesis that high-risk non-LD foreign language learners and LD foreign language learners present similar native and foreign language aptitude complexity.

Finally, foreign language grades of poor and good foreign language learners were compared, relevant to their native language abilities and foreign language aptitude. As expected, students who obtain higher foreign language grades reveal impressively stronger native language skills and foreign language aptitude than students who earn lower grades (Ganschow et al., 1998).

Prediction studies

Sparks and Ganschow tested the efficacy of the LCDH by examining the best predictors of foreign language grades in the first year of study. Sparks et al. (1995b) conducted two experiments involving ninth and tenth grade students. They found that the best predictor of foreign language grades in both experiments appeared to be the native language variable – the eighth English grade. This grade is related to one's oral (listening and speaking) and written (reading and writing) linguistic abilities, both of which are crucial for foreign language learning. Another predictor was the result on the MLAT – long form, consisting of four independent variables, namely, the phonetic coding, grammatical sensitivity, inductive language learning ability and rote memory. Native language spelling turned out to be a predictor variable in one of the experiments, thus confirming the importance of the native phonological/orthographic ability for foreign language learning. Furthermore, separate analyses of various foreign languages (Spanish and French) were conducted. The findings indicate that similar testing measures best predict the achievement in Spanish and French.

Sparks et al. (1997c) examined the best predictors of overall (oral and written) proficiency in a foreign language after two years of study in two experiments. Foreign language word decoding, which is a direct measure of the phonological-orthographic (sound and sound-symbol) component of a foreign language, and end of first-year foreign language grade (as an indicator of achievement in a foreign language course) were claimed to predict comprehensive foreign language proficiency in both experiments. Additionally, the native language vocabulary contributed to the general foreign language proficiency in experiment 1.

In another study conducted by Sparks et al. (2006), students were followed from first through tenth grade and tested on L1 reading and spelling, L1 receptive vocabulary and listening comprehension, as well as general IQ at specific time intervals over this period. The scores on the abovementioned measures were used as predictor variables in order to analyse their effects on oral and written FL proficiency and FL aptitude. All students participating in this study completed a two-year high school FL course in Spanish, French or German. The study findings strongly support the existence of the connection between L1 (reading, spelling) and subsequent L2 skills (reading, spelling, listening, speaking) and FL aptitude, as well as the importance of lower-level phonological abilities for oral and written FL proficiency. A vital implication that follows from the outcome of the study is that intelligence cannot be treated as a good predictor of students' future FL proficiency. Thus, to determine placement levels and to predict FL proficiency, native and foreign language educators are advised to use measures of students' L1 achievement rather than IQ scores. Explicit teaching of FL phonological and phonological/orthographic skills to secondary school FL students is strongly recommended by the authors. Touching on the native language elementary graders, direct instruction in L1 sound and sound/symbol systems would better prepare those students for L2 study.

Proficiency studies

Proficiency studies aim to determine the relationship between native and foreign language skills. The results of research conducted by Sparks *et al.* (1998a) disclosed the existence of fair overall differences in native language capability, foreign language aptitude and the end-of-year foreign language grade. High school students taking part in the study were grouped according to the level of their oral and written competencies in a foreign language (Spanish, French and German) into high foreign language proficiency group, average foreign language proficiency group and low foreign language proficiency group. It turned out that students who obtain higher scores on oral and written foreign language proficiency tests have stronger native language skills in phonology/orthography and semantics than students who gain lower scores. The outcome of the study also suggests that generally average and low foreign language proficiency students did not differ noticeably on the phonology/orthography measures, thus only defined differences in phonological/orthographic skills differentiated low and high foreign language proficiency students. Moreover, students with low foreign language competence would score significantly lower than students with high foreign language faculty on the foreign language aptitude measure. Finally, the abovementioned findings imply that the students exhibiting different levels (high, average, low) of foreign language proficiency show disparities in their foreign language course grades, especially at the end of the first year, on the side of the high foreign language ability group. It has been argued that even though the students' grades in foreign language courses do not compose a measure of actual foreign language proficiency, the results of the studies suggest that, at least to some extent, higher grades may reflect superior oral and written foreign language skills. Following the results of these studies, it is quite apparent that the performance on the standard measures of native language skill is straightforwardly related to the level of foreign language proficiency. Students with higher levels of native language abilities tend to achieve greater oral and written foreign language proficiency. In a similar vein, groups of students who manifest critical variance in the overall foreign language proficiency almost certainly display decent divergence in the native language skills. Hence the conclusion that learners faced with either subtle or overt difficulties in reading, writing, listening and speaking in their native language are likely to experience similar pitfalls in foreign language learning.

To sum up, the research evidence cited above suggests that native and foreign language aptitude differences between good and poor foreign language learners inevitably exist. Poor foreign language learners consistently score lower on the native and foreign language aptitude measures than good foreign language learners. Moreover, most of the poor foreign language learners have trouble primarily with the phonological code – the ability to break down, put together and relate the sounds of the language to the appropriate letters or letter combinations, while semantic difficulties (language comprehension problems) do not appear to trigger most foreign language learning difficulties (Sparks et al., 1992b).

Studies on English as a foreign language

Sparks' claims concerning the learning profiles of native English-speaking young adults, learning various foreign languages, attracted the attention and interest of many researchers. The results of numerous recent studies, with reference to various L1 languages, with English as a foreign language, seem to be in line with Sparks' findings; however, in some experiments, the LCDH assumptions were not quite positively verified.

For example, Chen (2001) supported the validity of the LDCH by concluding that difficulties which Chinese college learners of English in Taiwan experience in FL learning can be attributed to their underlying problems with the Chinese language. Ho and Fong (2005) examined Chinese dyslexic learners of English in Hong Kong who had difficulties learning English as a second language and found that, regardless of the distinctive characteristics of the two scripts, Chinese non-dyslexic children outperformed children with dyslexia on FL measures. Chinese dyslexic children with a phonological deficit in their native language proved at high risk of encountering difficulties learning English. The fact that children participating in the study demonstrated weak phonological awareness in both Chinese (L1) and English (L2) supports the notion of cross-linguistic transfer and the proposition that L1 skills form a foundation for the development of L2 skills. However, importantly, weak phonological awareness demonstrated by the participants of the study in Chinese did not translate into reading problems in that language, unlike in English, where their poor phonological skills were most often, though not without exceptions, linked to reading failure. In conclusion, despite being concomitant at a high rate, reading difficulties in Chinese (L1) and English (L2) occur due to both common and specific causes.

Helland and Kaasa (2005) focused on Norwegian 12-year-old students with dyslexia, who learned English as a second language. Generally, the dyslexic group, when compared to non-dyslexic controls, demonstrated significantly poorer results on a specially designed English proficiency test, including the measures of morphology, syntax, semantics and orthography. However, group differences among learners with dyslexia, relating to success on all linguistic skills measures except for L2 spelling, have been noted. The assumption that dyslexics, who show L1 skill impairments of differing severity, confront more hurdles in learning foreign languages than non-dyslexic students also holds true in the Polish secondary school environment (Jurek, 2004a, 2004b, 2004c; Nijakowska, 2004).

However, by way of contrast, Miller-Guron and Lundberg (2000) seem to challenge the assumption that L1 dyslexic reading problems are bound to translate into L2 reading failure. They report a truly surprising and extraordinary preference for reading in a foreign language (English), exhibited by adult Swedish dyslexics. The authors termed the phenomenon the *dyslexic preference for English reading* (DPER) and hypothesised that its occurrence may be caused by several socio-cultural and emotional factors, such as enhanced L2 input through television and music media, early exposure to L2 literature, along with factors specific to English orthography. The relatively shallow Swedish orthography puts high demands on readers with regard to phoneme by phoneme decoding. That is why Swedish readers with dyslexia, who possess weak phonological skills at the level of phonemes, may paradoxically develop a preference for reading the deeper English orthography, most probably because they are continuously inefficient in applying the graphemephoneme (small grain size phonological unit) strategy when approaching Swedish texts. Reading English texts, on the other hand, requires word recognition strategies concerning larger orthographic segments such as rimes or whole words.[3] The proposed explanation seems to be in accord with the phonological grain size theory (Ziegler & Goswami, 2006). Still, Swedish, as a highly inflected and derivational language, places greater morphosyntactic demands on its readers than English, which is the fact that may additionally contribute to the explanation of DPER. DPER proponents (Lundberg, 2002; Miller-Guron & Lundberg, 2000) also seek supportive arguments for their claims among the results of neurobiological investigations, speculating that neurological dissociation of languages in bilinguals may help to explain DPER. As much as the assumption that the neurological substrate of L2 in the brain may function more effectively than L1 tissue is indeed a tempting speculation, it seems a matter of future research to be confirmed.

Van der Leij and Morfidi (2006) suggest that even though the universal phonological core deficit is responsible for transferring reading difficulties from L1 to L2, variable orthographic competence may possibly exist independently of phonological decoding and be capable of explaining differences between reading-disabled individuals in L2 with a deep orthography and L1 with a shallow one. Following this line of argument, they speculate that the subgroup of Swedish dyslexics with preference for English reading from Miller-Guron and Lundberg's (2000) study might have demonstrated advantageous orthographic competence, which was mainly applied to L2 inconsistent orthography, while there was limited opportunity to use it in the quite shallow orthography of L1. It is further implied that poor readers exhibit differing cognitive profiles and may vary in their sensitivity to irregularities of the non-transparent English orthography.

Sparks *et al.* predominantly focused on young adults consistently exhibiting minor to more severe phonological and syntactic coding impairment in L1. However, the apparent constraint of such research is that direct analysis of developmental and academic advancement as well as early histories of L1 acquisition hurdle, which the FL learning problems might be traced back to, is rather impossible. It can only be reconstructed, usually from a self-report assessment. Hence the need to extend the existing findings to younger children and varying languages. In this vein, Ferrari and Palladino (2007) investigated seventh- and eighth-grade Italian students qualified either into a group of high or low achievers with regard to learning EFL. Native language reading comprehension was consistently deficient in low-achieving FL students, whereas their reading speed and accuracy, even though slightly poorer (though usually not reaching statistical significance) when compared to high-achieving FL counterparts, proved average according to Italian norms. The findings are not quite in accord with the LCDH assumptions, according to which poor FL learners are expected to demonstrate impairment in particular in phonological-orthographic skills with regard to L1. All in all, the pattern of learning difficulties in Italian children was not parallel with that of native English-speaking young adult students at risk of FL learning difficulties described earlier.

By contrast, analogous findings to those of Sparks *et al.* concerning best predictors of FL proficiency have been reported by other researchers with regard to younger students as well. For example, Kahn-Horwitz *et al.* (2005, 2006) analysed individual differences among beginning readers of EFL and concluded that L1 skills in Hebrew strongly predicted their L2 skills. Similar to Sparks *et al.* (2006), Kahn-Horwitz *et al.* (2006) opt for early detection of L1 difficulties in word recognition, phonological awareness and vocabulary knowledge in students beginning their FL acquisition in order to identify at-risk FL learners. It is expected and suggested that such identification followed by appropriate intervention and instruction would very likely prevent those students from falling behind good FL readers. Dufva and Voeten (1999) studied Finnish children and found that L1 literacy and phonological processing in first grade predicted their performance in foreign language (English) in the third grade. Similarly, a significant relationship between L1 phonological/orthographic skills (especially an ability to decode words) of Spanish first-graders and their later decoding and reading skills in EFL has been indicated by Lindsay *et al.* (2003).

Oren and Breznitz (2005) investigated the differences in accuracy and reading rate of words in L1 and L2 in adult dyslexic and regular readers. They maintain that as much as dyslexic deficits in L1 (Hebrew) and L2 (English) seem to share some universal underlying features, their behavioural manifestations may well be dependent on specific orthographic characteristics, inherent to each and every language. Thus proposed is the idea of the possibly complementary relation between the following assumptions: individual differences in foreign language learning can be predicted and caused by native language deficits and particular features of different orthographies may cause varying problems in learning and reading these languages. Hence, frequently, certain impairments, not necessarily evident in L1, may emerge with the commencement of second or foreign language learning. In Oren and Breznitz's study (2005) in both languages dyslexic attainments on measures of speed of information processing, phonological short-term and working memory, and phonological processing proved considerably poorer in comparison to regular readers. In Hebrew and English alike, the dyslexic reading rate was substantially slower than in regular bilingual readers. With regard to accuracy measures, regular readers outperformed individuals with dyslexia in English but not in Hebrew, the effect most likely traceable to the non-transparent, irregular character of English orthography. All in all, dyslexics performed consistently better in the shallow orthography of a pointed Hebrew than in the deep English orthographic system, where their difficulties were considerably more severe and apparent. What follows from the outcome of this study is a presupposed importance of the orthography-specific mechanisms in determining success in the acquisition of the reading skill.

It seems that, generally, native language competence serves as a basis for foreign language faculty and children who develop faster in their native language tend to manifest higher foreign language aptitude. Then, logically enough, hampered ability to learn a foreign language in students with dyslexia can be attributed to the lack of solid foundation in their native language. Implications for the assessment of foreign language learning difficulties explicitly indicate both native language ability and foreign language aptitude measures as a must.

Notes

1. See Chapter 2: 'Phonological coding deficit hypothesis', for a discussion on phonological processing.
2. A review of the research on the effectiveness of the MSL instruction in FL teaching can be found in Chapter 5: 'Multisensory Structured Learning Approach and Foreign Language Study'.
3. See Chapter 1: 'Orthographic Depth and Grain Size: A Cross-language Perspective on Reading and Dyslexia' for a discussion on orthographic depth and grain size.

Chapter 4
Symptoms and Identification of Dyslexia

Lifelong Nature of Dyslexia

Dyslexia is a lifetime and chronic condition; children once diagnosed as dyslexic do not outgrow dyslexia, but remain dyslexic through their youth into adulthood (Downey *et al.*, 2000; Gregg *et al.*, 2005; Oren & Breznitz, 2005). However, substantial inter- and intra-individual variance makes the overall picture of dyslexia quite complicated (Krasowicz-Kupis, 2008). The way dyslexia leaves its imprint on behaviour varies across individuals. In addition, throughout life, behavioural symptoms of dyslexia manifest in a given person are subject to a dynamic change, under the influence of education, effectiveness of therapeutic activities and efficiency of compensatory strategies. Thus, some features of dyslexia alter with age – characteristic symptoms tend to be evident but can diminish or disappear at given points in development because certain deficits get compensated, while other disorders prevail into adulthood (Bogdanowicz, 1997c, 1999; Mickiewicz, 1997; Snowling, 2001a).

The most fundamental and primary behavioural symptom of dyslexia seems to be a pronounced and persistent difficulty in the acquisition of skilful word decoding (reading) and encoding (spelling), forcing the child to lag behind his/her peers with regard to literacy development. Decoding and encoding are interrelated, they can be collectively perceived as print processing or a mechanical aspect of reading and spelling ability (Szczerbiński, 2007). The difficulties often remain intractable, despite special educational efforts at alleviating them. The key dyslexic difficulty related to decoding words is reflected in slower rate and poor accuracy of reading. Dyslexic word decoding problems are best evidenced during single word and pseudo-word reading tasks. Difficulties in non-word processing are highly indicative of late or deficient phonological development (poor phonological representations). Reading difficulties are frequently accompanied by low-grade orthographic spelling. Phonological processing disorders, by definition, constitute a characteristic trait of dyslexia, while linguistic functioning with reference to syntactic, semantic or pragmatic levels may well be within average. All other symptoms associated with dyslexia, which are discussed in the following sections, have been reported to exist in some individuals with dyslexia, so they can, but by no means have to, go along with basic reading impairment. These symptoms may form multiple diversified sets and constellations, specific to each child (Krasowicz-Kupis, 2008).

Risk for dyslexia

Multiple warning signs and areas of poor performance, to a considerable extent indicative of later low-grade reading skill, can be quite accurately identified in children before or at the very beginning of their school education, when any adeptness regarding reading and spelling skills is naturally not yet evident (Bogdanowicz, 2002a; Johnson et al., 2001; Ott, 1997). Areas of weakness identified in post-infantile and preschool stages, including, for instance, late development of speech, poor epiphonological skills or late development of motor ability, constitute the warning signs or indicators of the *risk for dyslexia*, denoting high probability of later learning difficulties (Bogdanowicz, 2002a; Ott, 1997). With the commencement of school education and formal literacy instruction, isolated difficulties in learning to read and spell, frequently emerge in children with these early signs.

A group at risk for dyslexia is composed of children with hereditary transmission – coming from families with a history of dyslexia (Snowling et al., 2007), children showing speech delay, ambidextrousness or left-handedness and partial/fragmentary disorders of psychomotor development. Children from a pathological pregnancy and delivery and those prematurely born qualify to the at-risk group, as do pupils who might not have explicitly demonstrated any worrying signs of developmental delay or deficit at a very young age, but with the onset of formal instruction, they clearly begin to face intensified problems in literacy acquisition. They experience learning difficulties despite normal intelligence, good sight and hearing as well as favourable educational and didactic conditions (Bogdanowicz, 2002a). The malfunctions observed in at-risk children are mild, not resulting from the more global developmental delay or reduced cognitive capability.

Detailed inventories of symptoms, which parents and teachers of young pre-school and school children should be aware of and especially sensitive to, have been compiled by several authors (Bogdanowicz, 1999, 2002a, 2003a; Bogdanowicz & Adryjanek, 2004; Ott, 1997; Tomaszewska, 2001). As already indicated, the main prevailing symptom of dyslexia is reading difficulty, in particular single word decoding, tracked down directly to the core linguistic deficit at the level of phonological processing. All the other symptoms related to dyslexia, grouped into collections specific to each child, can but, let us stress again, do not necessarily accompany the basic reading problem. Moreover, their intensity varies as well. One can imagine that the more characteristic

Symptoms and Identification of Dyslexia 87

signs (listed below) one notices in a particular child, the greater the likelihood of the risk for the disorder.

Spheres of child development and activity demanding careful attention of caretakers include language functions and speech, sequencing (including both visual and auditory sequential memory), fine and gross motor skills, visual functions and visual-motor co-ordination, orientation in body schemata, space and time, and, last but not least, reading and spelling competence. Unusual, low-grade performance of young children within these areas cannot be missed or ignored, since failure to recognise problematic spheres and risks may result in far-reaching consequences.

Individual differences among regular readers as well as children with dyslexia can be, to a great extent, explained by the degree of efficiency with respect to phonological processing. Children at risk for dyslexia tend to demonstrate late or incomplete phonological development, evidenced in low scores on non-word processing tasks. It seems that these children experience marked impairment in their ability to form phonological representations before they make a start with reading instruction and they are disadvantaged in comparison to normally developing children, since their representations are much less specified and stable[1] (Snowling, 2000). This, in turn, has a debilitating effect on the ability to map orthography on phonology.

Language impairment can be manifest in several ways, for example, late development of speech, word-naming problems, word mispronunciations, jumbling words, difficulties with rhyme and alliteration, and also poor use of syntax (inappropriate word order and ungrammatical forms). Other problematic aspects include poor memorisation of nursery rhymes, short poems and songs, below-standard aptitude to repeat messages and follow a series of instructions, and a tendency to use circumlocutions. Difficulty in remembering names and common sequences (e.g. the alphabet, days of the week, months of the year) and retrieving them from memory is also unexceptional. Sound discrimination and manipulation, including blending, sequencing, adding and deleting tasks usually poses tangible difficulty as well.

The symptomatic behaviour with regard to poor automatisation[2] of gross motor skills (arms and legs) involves lack of a crawling stage, awkwardness in keeping balance, laboriousness in hopping, catching, throwing or kicking a ball, frequent bumping into people and objects, knocking things over or dropping them, struggling to learn to ride a bicycle, to swim or to dance. In view of the above, playground games may constitute a problem, which can be additionally intensified by the use of commands such as left/right, up/down, backwards/forwards, in front of/behind. Poor co-ordination when climbing ropes, standing on one leg or walking along a bench are further signs. Late development of fine motor skills (fingers and hands) leads to low dexterity in using cutlery, scissors, rubber, tracing, dressing up, tying up shoe laces, buttoning a shirt, manipulating small objects (building blocks) and, last but not least, drawing and writing (due to an awkward pencil grip).

Disorders of visual function and visual-motor co-ordination concern low-grade grapho-motor activity, difficulty arranging building blocks or puzzles according to a given pattern and drawing. What is more, poor ability to remember letter shapes, to distinguish between similar shapes (geometric figures or letters, e.g. m-n, l-t) or letters of similar shape but different position in space (p-d-g-b), low graphic level of drawings and written work as well as mirror writing are frequently observed. Children at risk for dyslexia may experience problems in orientation in body schemata and space, at times can be confused when discriminating right from left, moreover, they can exhibit low-level orientation in time (yesterday, tomorrow, later, earlier) and poor concentration.

Persistent below-standard abilities to decode words, encountered at the beginning of school education, qualify as symptoms of the risk for dyslexia. Slow and laborious reading can be so time consuming that even if accuracy approximates normal, comprehension is invariably hampered. A tendency towards skipping certain fragments, repeating lines and losing a place in the text can be habitually observed. In addition, instead of being properly read (decoded), words are often guessed, drawing on the first letter, syllable or on overall appearance of a word, or substituted with a semantic counterpart ('was' for 'lived', 'car' for 'bus'). Decoding seems to arrest most attention, which, unsurprisingly, often leads to problems with comprehension.

As for spelling ability, some young learners at risk for dyslexia typically commit multiple mistakes in rewriting and dictation; they continually find it oddly difficult, in comparison to other children, to remember and properly distinguish between the language sounds and their corresponding graphic symbols – letters. At times, they also use mirror images of letters and often write down words awkwardly, for instance in reverse direction – from right to left.

Generally, the following types of errors are principally committed by children with dyslexia in reading and spelling: omission, insertion, displacement, condensation, rotation, reversal, substitution and guessing (Critchley, 1964; Kaja, 2001b; Levinson, 1980; Ott, 1997). Thus, letters, parts of words, syllables and whole words are often omitted or inappropriately inserted. Peculiarly, skipped elements can resurface in distant parts of the same sentence and letters or syllables of successive words can be condensed and read as new words. In addition, reading is often characterised by noticeably awkward intonation. Handwriting can be barely legible and full of corrections, while rate of writing tends to be unnaturally slow.

Quite naturally, screening for early dyslexia signs has great potential with regard to indicating children at risk, who can then undergo special training aimed at reducing the areas of difficulty and, in the long run, avoid scholastic failure and the potential danger of emotional damage. Hopefully, such a procedure becomes a widespread and common practice.[3]

Notwithstanding massive evidence for early predispositions to literacy difficulties as well as sound usefulness of screening, Lindsay (2001) maintains that any attempts to develop early educational screening methods frequently prove problematic due to low accuracy, resulting in high rates of false positives (children incorrectly identified as being at risk for dyslexia, who later show no reading impairment) and false negatives (children not identified as being at risk for dyslexia, who later encounter reading difficulties) (Kalka, 2003).

Regardless of the hypothetical difficulties, children at risk for dyslexia stand in need of early detection, most valuable during the pre-school stages, which, indeed, is undeniably dependent on both teachers' and parents' alertness and sensitivity to early signs of late development or difficulty. Obviously, the role of observant and attentive adults, who are knowledgeable about the symptoms and inescapable consequences of dyslexia in later life, especially when they are not properly identified at the right time, cannot be overestimated.

Provided considerable attention and time is devoted to the remedial activities, there is a realistic chance that reading problems can substantially decrease or even disappear. Spelling difficulties tend to be much more persistent and manifest in childhood through adolescence to adulthood, despite an adequate knowledge of the orthographic rules. Thus, even in adulthood, spelling usually remains a painful task, in spite of the attainment of typically fluent reading. If the usually isolated difficulties in learning to read and spell, evident at the beginning of school education, are not correctly diagnosed and subject to adequate pedagogical intervention, almost invariably they can grow into the global learning difficulty. Reading impairments may hamper educational progress in many areas of the school curriculum and beyond it. Individuals with dyslexia, being poor readers, to a great extent can be deprived of unlimited access to a wide range of information, touching on multiple scientific disciplines and spheres of life (Bogdanowicz, 1999; Dockrell & McShane, 1993).

All in all, dyslexia is a life-long condition, whose behavioural signs differ and change as a function of age, from pre-school age (risk for dyslexia) to adulthood. Several phenomena may shape the dynamism of symptom change, for instance, an increase in the range of difficulties with regard to specificity of various school subjects; possible occurrence of the emotional-motivational and personality disorders (consequence of scholastic failure), but also compensation or reduction of the disorders and improvement in reading and spelling skills due to intensive remedial activities and learning. Importantly, withdrawal from special educational activities and training, lack of sufficient self-control while reading and spelling, intensive stress, tiredness or inability to concentrate can bring about the re-occurrence or intensification of specific learning difficulties (Bogdanowicz & Adryjanek, 2004).

Signs of dyslexia in older individuals

Let us now concentrate on older individuals with dyslexia. It appears that certain symptoms described above with regard to younger children are no longer discernible in older learners, but some other difficulties endure. What is more, new areas of difficulty, for example, problems in foreign language learning (FLL) or in undertaking sports with success may emerge. Other problematic domains include geography (reading maps; directions), arithmetic, geometry, chemistry, music (musical notation), biology (complex terminology) or history (dates, names, chronology), to mention just a few.

Frequently, intensified reading difficulties largely diminish and what usually remains unchanged is a slow rate of reading and a negative attitude towards the activity of reading as such. Still, intensity, types and prevalence of reading errors would certainly depend on the orthographic depth of a given language and adopted reading strategies.[4] For instance, vowel misreadings frequently occur in English. It can be attributable to complicated letter-to-sound mappings, with yet much more complex relations for vowels than for consonants. Whereas in Italian or Spanish, vowel misreadings are rather rare because of the roughly equally consistent grapheme-phoneme relations for vowels and consonants. In fact, young Spanish-speaking children tend to commit most reading errors with regard to three context-dependent consonants – (c, g, r – which have two distinct pronunciations, depending on the other letters in a word) – and not in visually similar consonants (d, b, g, p, q) (Goikoetxea, 2006). Davies *et al.* (2007) observe that Spanish dyslexic and regular readers differ significantly with respect to quantity but not the type of errors they make. Children with dyslexia are less efficient readers and produce significantly more errors than controls. The errors in decoding print mainly take the form of additions, deletions or substitutions, reflecting possibly both impaired phonological and orthographic (grapheme-to-phoneme) processing.

The number of specific spelling mistakes, such as additions, deletions or substitutions of parts of words, or reversals, may slightly decrease with age and education, however, recurrent orthographic mistakes (difficulty choosing the appropriate spelling choice for a given sound, which is especially conspicuous in deep orthographies) notoriously prevail. Telling similar sounds apart and writing dictations remains a demanding task both in terms of singling out and recognising individual sounds in the right sequence as well as applying the phoneme-grapheme conversion rules.

The following are examples of dyslexic spellings with skipped, added or changed letters, syllables or parts of words: 'trick' for 'tick', 'walk' for 'walking', 'sudly' for 'suddenly', 'rember' for 'remember', 'amt' for 'amount', 'merember' for 'remember', 'tow' for 'two', 'pakr' for 'park', 'sitesr' for 'sister'. Peculiar dyslexic difficulty also lies in the lowered ability to divide sentences into words – or to keep word boundaries, for instance 'a nother' for 'another', 'firstones' for 'first ones', 'halfanhour' for 'half an hour'. Similarly, dividing words into syllables and constituent phonemes and difficulty in differentiating between similar sounds, which leads to choosing an incorrect graphic representation for the targeted word, proves problematic. Time and time again, phonetic spelling (e.g. 'yoos' for 'use', 'wokt' for 'walked', 'mendid' for 'mended') but also bizarre and inconsistent spelling, unusual sequencing of letters or multiple attempts at spelling a target word (e.g. 'schule', 'skchool', 'school') may occur in one piece of dyslexic writing. Spelling of individual words can be so deformed that their decoding proves virtually impossible.

Occasionally, some older students with dyslexia can continually show below-standard ability to distinguish between letters of similar shape and to rewrite texts correctly, which is characteristic for younger children. Low-grade ability to discriminate and remember letter shapes applies, in particular, to letters similar in shape (a-o, m-n, l-t, hence 'cat' for 'cot', 'moon' for 'noon') as well as letters similar in shape but differing in their position in space – (p-g-b-d; m-w, n-u, hence 'bady' for 'baby', 'dot' for 'got', 'brown' for 'drown', 'pig' for 'dig', 'pug' for 'bud'). Inverting words dynamically ('no' for 'on', 'was' for 'saw', 'dog' for 'god', 'gip' for 'pig'), neglecting diacritical marks and misusing lowercase and uppercase letters ('daDDy' for 'daddy') happens at times (see Appendix 3 and Appendix 4).

The traditional division of reading and spelling errors into visual and auditory, being directly traced back to disorders of visual and auditory perception, respectively, though not completely free from faults, is frequently presented in the literature and, at least in the Polish context, heavily relied on by diagnosticians and practitioners (Czajkowska & Herda, 1998; Górniewicz, 1998; Jędrzejowska & Jurek, 2003; Mickiewicz, 1997; Opolska, 1997; Saduś, 2000, 2003; Skibińska, 2001; Zakrzewska, 1999). Beyond doubt, the plausibility of dividing dyslexic errors into auditory and visual seems questionable because an unequivocal qualification of the nature of an error into visual or auditory seems highly problematic (e.g. confusing the letters 'b' and 'p') (Mickiewicz, 1997). Despite the apparent unreliability of such divisions, they serve as foundations for typologies of dyslexia based on symptoms (reading-spelling pattern and types of errors). For example, such a typology of dyslexia, frequently referred to in the literature (Bakker et al., 1995; Bednarek, 1999; Borkowska, 1998; Dockrell & McShane, 1993; Johnson, 1978; Krasowicz, 1997; Krasowicz-Kupis, 2008; Ott, 1997; Reid, 1998; Stamboltzis & Pumfrey, 2000), was proposed by Boder (1973). Three subtypes of dyslexia suggested by Boder are as follows: *dysphonetic* (auditory), *dyseidetic* (visual) and *mixed*.[5] Bogdanowicz (1997a/2000, 1999) suggests the following subtypes – *visual, auditory, integrative* and *mixed*, again based on differing underlying pathomechanisms, responsible for certain types of errors.[6]

The reliability of classifications based on symptoms may be reduced by uncertainties regarding the credibility of qualifying errors as visual or auditory (Borkowska, 1998). Notwithstanding the considerable popularity of such classifications among practitioners, in light of the present knowledge about the causes of dyslexia, they seem to have rather historical value (Krasowicz-Kupis, 2008). For example, research verifying the causal mechanisms of visual and auditory spelling mistakes in Polish did not indicate that they are caused by distinct mechanisms, hence the reliability of the abovementioned typology remains unconfirmed (Pietras, 2007, 2008).

Pietras (2007) proposes that spelling errors be qualified into three categories. *Language errors* constitute the first category, which a given spelling attempt is phonologically inaccurate – the phonological structure of a word is distorted, thus the corresponding orthographic mapping is inaccurate for the targeted word. The second category – *memory errors* – are phonologically accurate spelling attempts but orthographically inaccurate, they are decodable and retain the phonological structure of a word, however the choice of sound-to-letter mappings is inappropriate (e.g. 'rein' for 'rain', 'eeg' for 'egg'). Finally, errors involving skipping the tiny elements, such as diacritical marks, or confusing letters similar in shape are called *visual*. Krasowicz-Kupis (2008) suggests that, generally, it seems to be the quantitative factor that is more important in evaluation of dyslexic errors, hence taking the total number of errors as an indicator of dyslexic spelling difficulty. While with regard to qualitative analysis, a broad division into phonologically accurate or inaccurate spellings is advised.

Low-standard level of precision of hand and finger movement (fine motor skills), causing unintelligible handwriting, is again and again reported in individuals with dyslexia. Due to an awkward pen grip, writing tends to be slow and subject to numerous corrections. Additionally, co-movements of other parts of the body (legs, tongue) can be observed during writing. Letters tend to be poorly formed and not appropriately connected; they may well drift off the intended angle, direction and spatial position (see Appendix 5 and Appendix 6). Finally, details such as periods, commas and capitals are very often omitted, spaces between letters and words can be irregular, and, as already mentioned, lines are continually skipped.

Language deficit in dyslexia, by definition connected with poor phonological processing, in some cases may also extend to lowered morphological, syntactic and/or syntactic abilities, which accompany disordered phonological functions. Students with dyslexia have been reported to produce ungrammatical utterances, especially with regard to applying phrases that describe spatial relations (Borkowska, 1997, 1998; Krasowicz, 1997; Krasowicz-Kupis, 2003, 2006; Oszwa, 2000; Schneider, 1999). Comprehending and retrieving abstract and complex sentences, especially those composed of multiple clauses, such as relative or subordinate clauses, frequently poses irrefutable difficulty on children with dyslexia. The most pronounced problems in understanding syntactic structures can concern questions, relations between direct and indirect objects as well as the passive voice (Rosenthal, 1970; Schneider, 1999; Slobin, 1971; Wiig & Semel, 1984). Learners with dyslexia may demonstrate poor familiarity with syntactic rules, pertaining to the transformational complexity and length of the sentences; as a consequence, they may produce less structurally advanced sentences – mostly short, positive, declarative and in the active voice. Often, numerous syntactic mistakes occur, including grammatically incorrect structures and inappropriate use of parts of speech. These deficits have been observed in dyslexic children and adolescents alike (Wiig & Semel, 1976).

Similarly, research conducted by Krasowicz (1997) among Polish children regarding the interdependence between the level of language acquisition and reading ability in children, has shown that the syntactic structure of the utterances produced by children with dyslexia is characterised by the following factors: reduced content of the utterance, use of significantly shorter sentences, more instances of simple than complex sentences, and, finally, greater number of incomplete sentences when compared with the utterances produced by non-dyslexic children. Oszwa (2000) discusses indications of agrammatisms as pertains to the use of prepositions by Polish children with dyslexia. The number of prepositions used by children with dyslexia while describing a picture is significantly smaller as compared to non-dyslexics. Additionally, derivation of nouns and adjectives as well as the use of complex prepositions tend to be difficult for these children.

According to Vogel (1983), the use of inflectional, grammatical morphemes is sometimes considerably reduced in children with dyslexia as compared to good readers. Correct use of the third person singular present tense marker '-s', the progressive aspect marker '-ing', tense markers, regular and irregular plural markers, the comparative marker '-er', the superlative marker '-est', the adverb marker '-ly' as well as suffixes can constitute a source of perceivable confusion for children with dyslexia who learn English (Wiig *et al.*, 1973; Wiig & Semel, 1984).

Furthermore, children with dyslexia can also show a subtle deficit on the semantic level of language processing. According to Krasowicz (1997), this is mainly reflected in disordered organisation of the narrative utterances, their poor structure and content. Syntactic deficit concerns difficulties in identifying the setting of a story (characters, time and place), the main plot and the resolution. The utterances formed by learners with dyslexia contain a considerable number of omissions and deformations of the basic information in the story. The most often neglected elements concern the identification of characters and the sphere of spatial-temporal relations. The observed disorders may be caused by deficits in cognitive functions, relating to the linguistic processing and organisation of information. Similarly, Wiig and Semel (1984) mention dyslexic semantic difficulty in discriminating between the spatial ('in', 'on', 'by', 'at', 'to') and temporal ('yesterday', 'today', 'tomorrow') references, adjective and adverbial time markers ('last', 'first', 'before', 'after'), directional changes ('up', 'down') and indefinite ('someone', 'anyone', 'something'), demonstrative ('that', 'those') and reflexive ('a girl washed himself') pronouns. Moreover, it is argued (Wiig & Semel, 1976) that some individuals with dyslexia may experience plausible difficulties in differentiating between the various meanings of a word, which depends on the changes of context. Sometimes, they also demonstrate sizeable difficulty in understanding synonyms, semantic transformations, connected with recognising the alterations in meaning, and semantic implications – defined as an ability to comprehend information that is indirectly presented.

As Borkowska and Tarkowski (1990) claim, linguistic competence, defined as a capacity to use language, as well as communicative competence, signified as an ability to use language efficiently in social interactions, are beyond doubt limited in children with dyslexia. Borkowska (1998) further argues that there exists a relationship between the level of acquisition of semantic rules as well as communicativeness of discourse and the occurrence of specific difficulties in reading and spelling. Learners with dyslexia may show deficits in the acquisition of semantic rules, which leads to construal of poorly organised narrative discourse (e.g. in the situation of describing a picture and telling a story), which is characterised by significantly simpler, shorter or incomplete episodic structure. Moreover, in reported research, children with dyslexia construct their narrative discourse from the reduced number of pieces of information, thus making it appreciably less communicative. Additionally, children with dyslexia often encounter difficulties in accommodating discourse to the social situation that they find themselves in and these difficulties tend to increase with age (Borkowska, 1998).

Some older students with dyslexia are reported to display poor gross motor skills and deficient balance, hence an impression of overall clumsiness, which, unfortunately, does not help them in undertaking sports activities. For that reason, these students may find PE classes least enjoyable. In addition, they can be characterised by poor orientation in space and body schemata, especially with reference to denoting the right side versus left. Proper time management seems to pose a noticeable burden on these students, as they struggle trying to organise their time efficiently as well as to remember dates and events, particularly in chronological order. In addition, phonological sequential memory can be deficient, which translates into extreme difficulty in recalling sequences of terms and names, such as months of the year, or calling to mind and following a series of complex multistep instructions. What is more, doing simple mental mathematical calculations and using multiplication tables may seem obscure. Furthermore, students happen to pronounce distorted words and spoonerisms, they are often lost for words and forgetful, and apparently require more time for retrieving information from memory. As for the poor manual precision or low-grade fine motor skills, drawings can be of a particularly poor quality, written work messy or even unintelligible, with badly formed letters and spellings crossed out. However, handwriting may be surprisingly neat but, at the same time, writing speed substantially decreases. Generally, an ability to organise and compose a piece of writing is much below standard in terms of accuracy, content and time efficiency, unlike frequent advanced oral capability (Bogdanowicz & Adryjanek, 2004).

It needs stressing that individual students with dyslexia demonstrate certainly not all but only diversified sets or clusters of the above-mentioned difficulties. There apparently exists an impressive variance as to the areas and severity of difficulties, levels of creativeness or sporting faculties across individuals with dyslexia, let alone various talents and strengths they have at their disposal.

Most of the symptoms described above may persevere in secondary school students with dyslexia. In addition, problems more specific to particular school subjects, for instance foreign languages, can intensify. Generally, the difficulties encountered by learners with dyslexia at higher educational stages undeniably become more global in character.

Among adults with dyslexia, two types of readers are usually observed and reported in research findings – those who, despite considerable problems experienced during literacy acquisition, manage to achieve high-grade reading proficiency, allowing access to higher education facilities. The second group is composed of individuals whose compensation mechanisms did not prevent failure in developing sufficient reading skills, hence their enormous struggle in adapting to common formal schooling requirements. Still, even those adults who are capable of compensating for their dyslexic difficulties and demonstrate comparatively high reading performance are characterised by a relatively stable cognitive profile, with prevailing phonological processing difficulties. They may demonstrate inadequate phonological representations and find it abnormally difficult to form new ones as well (Snowling & Nation, 1997). These difficulties are most evident in approaching tasks, which call for heavy reliance on phonological skills, such as unfamiliar word reading or pseudo-word decoding, in addition, spelling seems quite painful (Oren & Breznitz, 2005). All in all, dyslexic symptoms in adulthood can be summarised as the impairment of varying degrees in the accuracy of decoding and speed of word recognition (fluency) (Breznitz, 2003). Inasmuch as the former can possibly improve in adulthood, especially with regard to text, the latter may remain slower in comparison to regular adult readers. It appears that the skill of inferring meaning from contextual cues enables some adult dyslexic readers to achieve high-standard reading comprehension. Nonetheless, rather poor accuracy still seems quite prominent in single word and pseudo-word decoding. Converging research findings indeed confirm that dyslexic students' accuracy gains increase as they progress in school, however they continually show low-grade reading and spelling fluency. In fact, reading fluency level can best discriminate between college students with and without dyslexia (Gregg *et al.*, 2005).

Some individuals with dyslexia also self-report being disorganised and forgetful throughout life, which can probably be traced back to poor concentration abilities. As children, they may often fail to recall their homework, while as adults they admit letting slip telephone numbers, messages, names, appointments and dates; getting an impression that they most certainly are in the wrong place at the wrong time. Sometimes adults with dyslexia fail in distinguishing left from right and finding their way in an unknown place, not to mention getting on a wrong bus because of erroneous perception of the position of figures (e.g. 69 for 96). In addition, they report misarticulating multisyllabic words, mispronouncing names and surnames, committing spelling mistakes and avoiding reading. Driving a car, especially in an unfamiliar area, filling in forms, learning the sequences of movements in an aerobics or dance class, quickly retrieving information from memory – all constitute examples of activities that can be confusing for adults with dyslexia, who are otherwise perceived as intelligent, talented and creative people

(Bogdanowicz, 2003a; Bogdanowicz & Adryjanek, 2004; Bogdanowicz & Krasowicz-Kupis, 2005a).

Emotional-motivational Disorders in Dyslexia

The advocates of the *psychogenic aetiological theory* of dyslexia (psycho-dyslexia) claim that specific reading difficulties in children are caused by disorders in the emotional sphere. In view of the above statement, dyslexia should be treated as a symptom of emotional disorders (Krasowicz, 1997). However, it needs stressing that in light of recent findings pertaining to the causes of dyslexia, this theory underwent heavy criticism and was discredited, as no convincing evidence was provided to support it (Zakrzewska, 1999). Naturally, an inappropriate course of the emotional-motivational processes may exert negative influence on the ability to read and spell, however, in these cases the resulting difficulties are not of a dyslexic character (Bogdanowicz, 2003a).

In fact, the emotional-motivational and social perturbations that can be experienced by individuals with dyslexia are beyond doubt secondary to their scholastic failure in acquiring literacy skills. Their onset is not evident at the beginning of children's educational career but later, when reading problems become increasingly pronounced and, sometimes, close to impossible to overcome. Thus, disorders of emotional and social functioning and personality disorders can indeed coexist with dyslexia, but as a consequence rather than a cause of difficulties in reading and spelling (Bogdanowicz, 1989, 1999, 2002a; Czajkowska & Herda, 1998; Krasowicz-Kupis, 2008; Zakrzewska, 1999). Individuals with dyslexia are reported to frequently suffer from emotional-motivational problems of various intensity with regard to low self-perception, low self-esteem, lack of confidence, feelings of shame, fear, embarrassment and frustration, caused by experiencing constant failure in the acquisition of reading and spelling skills. Common negative attitudes of peers and, sometimes, parents, lack of their acceptance and support can markedly enhance the abovementioned negative feelings (Bogdanowicz, 1985a; Elliott & Place, 2000; Gindrich, 2002; Ledwoch, 1999). Possible frustration experienced by children with dyslexia, brought about by their lowered ability to successfully acquire literacy skills, can frequently be aggravated by feeling unable to meet the expectations of their relatives, teachers and peers (Ryan, 1992).

Importantly, dyslexics constitute a group at considerable risk for emotional disorders, still they do not constitute a homogeneous group as regards their emotional functioning (Porter & Rourke, 1985). Some children with dyslexia do not categorically manifest any evident symptoms of emotional disorders, which would noticeably distinguish them from their peers at school and they function well in the educational environment (Krasowicz-Kupis, 2008). By contrast, in some children with dyslexia the relationship between reading and spelling difficulties and emotional disorders appears to be more apparent and undeniable than in others. Research outcomes indicate the occurrence of difficulties in getting to sleep, nightmares, aversion to school, constant worrying, increased self-criticism, shyness, timidity, all too often leading to difficulty in establishing contacts with peers, isolation at school, grossly disordered interpersonal encounters and even symptoms of child depression. What is more, several somatic disorders such as losing consciousness, frequent headaches and dizziness, the feeling of constant tiredness and exhaustion, not to mention stomach aches and pains in the chest, may at times be evidenced (Porter & Rourke, 1985).

Failure in learning to read and spell and in meeting the expectations of others, unsurprisingly, can invite misbehaviour of diverse harshness, from daydreaming, not focusing and getting distracted by virtually everything to employing avoidance tactics (sharpening pencils, looking for books, going to the toilet) and disruptive (class clown) or withdrawal tendencies. In rare cases, low resistance to frustration can culminate in attacks of anger and rage, hostility or aggressive manner towards other people and, unfortunately, sometimes even turn to juvenile delinquency. Ryan (1992) claims that the obvious target of this anger would be school, teachers and parents.

Anxiety appears to be frequently reported as an emotional symptom in children with dyslexia, who become fearful due to continual dissatisfaction, disappointment and confusion at school. Anxiety forces people to avoid whatever frightens them. As a consequence, new situations and experiences may become extremely anxiety provoking, hence steering clear of undertaking challenges. All too often there seems to exist a marked tendency among teachers and parents to interpret such avoidance behaviour as laziness. Carroll and Iles (2006) extend the research on dyslexic vulnerability to anxiety as an emotional consequence of scholastic failure to higher education students, who, being highly capable, most probably manage to adapt successful coping strategies in order to compensate for the learning difficulties they experience. Hence the shift of focus from detrimental feelings of inadequacy and academic incompetence in the context of literacy acquisition in children, towards the current worries of the university undergraduates. Observed are the elevated *trait anxiety* (defined as a rather stable personality feature) levels in students with dyslexia, much higher in comparison to what is shown by age-matched reading unimpaired students. Sadly, the dyslexic emotional perturbation is not limited to academic tasks, but it generalises to involve social functioning as well. In addition, tasks and situations demanding literacy accuracy, e.g. reading skills, repeatedly evoke the feelings of stress and worry, translatable into *state anxiety* (defined as a subjective feeling of emotional tension evoked by a particular situation perceived as self-threatening).

With regard to foreign language study, Piechurska-Kuciel (2008) investigates the effect of dyslexia on *language anxiety* at different stages of language processing in high school students. Individuals with symptoms of dyslexia typically and repeatedly demonstrate significantly higher levels of language anxiety at all stages of language processing (input, processing and output) than regular foreign language learners. Dyslexic language anxiety at input and processing stages seems to parallel the general tendency observed among unimpaired students to decrease substantially after the first year of learning and then to remain stable till the end of the three-year study period at secondary school. However, when it comes to output anxiety, unlike their peers, learners with dyslexia evidence permanently high levels throughout the time of high school foreign language study, which potentially detracts from the standard of their foreign language production.

Interestingly, Ledwoch (1999) claims that particular developmental deficits of cognitive processes have a diverse influence on the emotional conduct of children with dyslexia. Thus, on the one hand, children who repeatedly demonstrate a hurdle in the auditory-linguistic processing are often observed to experience more perplexity in establishing interpersonal contacts, manifested by apprehensiveness, lack of confidence and low self-esteem. Nevertheless, they seem to function quite adequately in social situations requiring good visual-spatial abilities and inter-modal integration. On the other hand, children with non-verbal learning disabilities seem to be markedly more prone to experiencing emotional disorders due to perceptual and cognitive deficits, which are crucial for social functioning. The difficulties pertain to visual-spatial information processing, responsible for interpreting such non-verbal indicators as, for example, face expression, gesticulation or body movements. In addition, as stressed by Ryan (1992), some individuals with dyslexia may show a tendency to encounter problems in interpreting social clues; moreover, their reluctance to initiate and maintain relationships with other people (drawing on the habit of avoidance of potentially difficult and failure instigating situations) can give an impression of them being awkward, which may lead to ill social functioning.

The following is a seemingly obvious concluding remark – it is of paramount importance that educators and parents possess an adequate understanding of the nature of dyslexia and are sensitive to problems experienced by individuals with dyslexia. Then, hopefully, fewer children will be prone to developing emotional and personality disorders due to scholastic failure.

Identification of Dyslexia

A detailed description of all aspects of assessment, including a broad battery of diagnostic tests, is beyond the scope of the present section, rather our aim here is to draw the attention of the reader to the general objectives and main issues related to identification.

It appears that intensive research on dyslexia invites multiple attempts, which often depend on general discrepancy and exclusion criteria, to define the condition. The discrepancy criterion concerns significant incongruity between the unexpectedly poor scholastic achievement of a child in a certain area of study and his/her age and/or level of intelligence. The exclusionary criterion indicates critical differences existing between dyslexic and other reading disordered individuals whose reading and spelling problems, unlike in dyslexics, may stem from mental retardation, sensory and emotional impairment, or the influence of an environment disadvantaged with respect to financial, economical, cultural or pedagogical aspects (Kasowicz-Kupis, 2008).

The discrepancy criterion basically allows to distinguish between general and specific learning disorders. It touches upon the significant gap between the actual reading ability and the level of this ability that could be expected of age and/or IQ. The exclusionary criterion indicates that reading difficulties stemming from lowered intellectual capacity, severe sensory, health or emotional impairment and the influence of a disadvantaged background should not be qualified as dyslexia (e.g. Vellutino, 1979). Finally, a clinical criterion is anchored in identification of key symptoms. However, the reliability of this criterion seems to be considerably reduced by the prevailing lack of consensus as to the collection of the most telling symptoms of dyslexia. Much as it is agreed that persisting reading and spelling difficulty constitute the key signs in dyslexia, however a precise description and definition of this difficulty remains a matter of discussion (Kasowicz-Kupis, 2008). It seems to be the case that clinicians conducting diagnosis towards dyslexia are confronted with the lack of definitional consensus of the disorder (Helland, 2007; Snowling, 2001b).[7]

Dyslexia is routinely diagnosed no sooner than a child starts learning to read and spell. In Poland, for instance, it is usually at the end of the second grade of primary school (Bogdanowicz, 1997c, 1999). Similarly, Wagner et al. (2005) report that in the USA, children with learning disabilities are typically identified and provided with remedial services not until the second or third grade, due to the formal requirement of the significant discrepancy between expected (based on IQ) and observed levels of achievement.

While there is common agreement that early diagnosis of learning disorders is pivotal to the further educational career of at-risk children, especially in light of research findings indicating that with age, reading difficulties become progressively intractable, it appears that too frequently this postulate cannot be easily put into practice. Various universally applicable but also country- and language-specific factors seem to contribute to such a state of affairs, including lack of agreement as to the underlying causes, definition and assessment criteria among researchers, unsatisfactory degree of awareness among some of the stakeholders or lack of resources in terms of appropriate standardised diagnostic measures, formal regulations, let alone money. This already complex situation is apparently aggravated in the bilingual or multilingual context.

Assessment of dyslexia in speakers of varying languages proves intricate, especially in light of the fact that the same phonological deficit can be capable of bringing about different manifestations of reading problems across languages, depending on their orthographic depth. Wagner *et al.* (2005) speculate that as much as a mild phonological impairment in Spanish-speaking children tends not to deter them from acquiring accurate word reading ability, though slightly hampering fluency, in Spanish due to its transparent orthography, it would do more harm if they were English L1 speakers. Hypothetically, if the same children had an English native-language family background and were to fulfil the reading requirement in English, the same phonological impairment would be very likely to invite considerable problems in accurate and fluent reading, possibly even further exacerbated by inappropriate instruction, neglecting explicit reference to the alphabetic principle. Such a view can be substantiated by the findings of research on reading acquisition in alphabetic languages (Ziegler & Goswami, 2005, 2006) indicating that, first, reading difficulties in all alphabetic languages studied to date can be tracked down to phonological processing disorders, second, the way letter-to-sound mapping is executed in different languages influences the reading strategies adopted by readers in these languages.[8]

Naturally, identifying the cases of dyslexia among the multitude of poor readers is a difficult task. In the Polish context at least, diagnosis towards dyslexia is interdisciplinary in character and requires a reliable, discerning and multidimensional opinion of various specialists, mainly a teacher therapist and an educational psychologist. However, time and time again, depending on the individual needs and set of symptoms, the consultation and co-operation of other experts, including a speech therapist, a laryngologist, an ophthalmologist, a psychiatrist, a paediatrician or a neurologist may be necessary (Bogdanowicz, 1999, 2002b; Czajkowska & Herda, 1998; Jędrzejowska & Jurek, 2003; Mickiewicz, 1997; Tomaszewska, 2001). A medical examination, if it takes place, is usually selective and aimed at excluding the conceivable defects (e.g. of vision and hearing) and illnesses, potentially bearing responsibility for the occurrence of difficulties in reading and spelling (Jaklewicz, 1997).

Generally, the aim of the assessment procedures is to provide well-grounded information concerning: firstly, the classification of the disorder, secondly, an unequivocal identification of the deficient functions that directly condition the processes of reading and spelling, thirdly, a tentative indication of the possible underlying causes which dyslexic difficulties can be traced back to (Bogdanowicz, 2003b; Reid, 1998). Last but not least, a diagnostic policy should involve the anticipation and prognosis of further development as well as inspire the design of an individual educational plan, tailored to the needs of a given child (Bogdanowicz, 2002a; Górniewicz, 1998; Jędrzejowska & Jurek, 2003). Likewise, Reid (1998) rightly claims that assessment should be linked to teaching at all times. Thus, recommendations as to the design of the therapeutic programme make up an indispensable part of an official post-assessment opinion. In fact, Vellutino et al. (1998) advocate that intervention should constitute a vital part of the longitudinal diagnostic process, thus making it more reliable. Pedagogical assessment should be conducted repeatedly in order to verify the effects of therapeutic intervention (Górniewicz, 1998; Oszwa, 2000). Finally, the appropriate formal (ministerial) regulations pertaining to the individualisation of the teaching process, types of accommodations of scholastic requirements to the needs and abilities of children with dyslexia as well as provision of special help ought to be cited in the assessment report as well (Bogdanowicz, 1999; Tomaszewska, 2001). Reading impaired children, deprived of access to professional therapeutic activities, remain in danger of intensifying the already persistent difficulties in reading and spelling, which in turn often negatively influences their overall scholastic career (lower marks, repeating classes, resignation from further education) and personality development (low self-esteem, group-dependence, emotional disorders) (Bogdanowicz & Wszeborowska-Lipińska, 1992; Jaklewicz, 1997).

Assessment procedures involve both clinical and experimental methods. Clinical methods such as interview, observation, analysis of samples of writing, drawings, medical and educational documentation are useful in collecting information with reference to developmental history, learning difficulties and the ways they have been dealt with, home and school environment, personality features and behaviour patterns. Diagnosing the family and school environment yields an invaluable insight into a multitude of factors influencing the child's development and contemporary situation at school, including a record of up-to-date successes and failures concerning all school subjects. Consultation with the teacher therapist, native and foreign language teachers as well as physical education teacher constitutes a source of particularly useful data (Bogdanowicz, 1997a/2000, 1999, 2002b, 2003b; Bogdanowicz & Krasowicz-Kupis, 2005b; Górniewicz, 1998; Mickiewicz, 1997; Szepietowska, 2002).

The introductory stage of the assessment process described above is followed by the evaluation of reading and spelling ability, pertaining to accuracy, rate, strategy of reading and level of comprehension, all of which constitute the essential part of the diagnostic procedure. It covers: verification of the letter knowledge with regard to their shape, name and sound, single word decoding, pseudo-word reading, reading text aloud, silent reading with comprehension, dictation, writing an essay and sometimes rewriting and writing from memory (Górniewicz, 1998; Jędrzejowska & Jurek, 2003; Krasowicz-Kupis, 2008; Turner, 2003). In fact, defining dyslexia with reference to decoding and encoding difficulties naturally invites certain diagnostic procedures. Since pseudo-word reading and spelling tests constitute the most direct measures of decoding and encoding skills, then, logically, they should become an integral element of the assessment battery (Szczerbiński, 2007).

Another crucial component part of such a battery would be the evaluation of the cognitive functions. The description of the phonological deficit usually comprises three main elements, namely, phonological awareness defined as conscious ability to identify and manipulate speech sounds, slow lexical retrieval, best demonstrated in rapid serial naming tasks, and, finally, poor short-term verbal memory, evident in non-word repetition and digit span tasks (Ramus, 2004; Turner, 2003). Krasowicz-Kupis (2008) enumerates the following areas of cognitive development that require decent evaluation: speech and language functions, mainly with regard to phonological processing but also morphological, syntactic and semantic (pragmatic) processing, language awareness, again mainly with reference to the phonological level (e.g. phonemic analysis and synthesis), rapid automatised naming, phonological memory, and last but not least, intellectual ability (IQ).

Admittedly, some doubts have been cast on the role of intelligence tests in diagnosing dyslexia (Stanovich, 1996), the issue is subject to intense debate, indeed generating substantial controversy. Traditionally, a discrepancy between the reading capacity of children and that expected of their IQ and age is used to distinguish dyslexics from other poor readers (Lindsay, 2001; Reid, 1998; Schneider, 1999). The probable score on the reading test can be estimated in line with the score obtained on the intelligence test. Considerable disparities between the expected and actual reading scores are claimed to indicate the presence of specific difficulties in reading and spelling (Elliot & Place, 2000). However, Miles (1996) believes that the concept of the global IQ may be misleading because some of the items in IQ tests are, in fact, inappropriate for children with dyslexia in that they cannot possibly reveal the real capabilities of these individuals. There is no denying that children with dyslexia repeatedly achieve significantly reduced scores in the following subtests: Information, Arithmetic, Digit Span and Coding – forming a profile called ACID, hence a worry that the evaluation of the general IQ can be imprecise (Bogdanowicz, 2003b; Krasowicz-Kupis, 2008; Lindsay, 2001; Reid, 1998; Wszeborowska-Lipińska, 1996).

Furthermore, Reid (1998) highlights the fact that the unexpected discrepancy between low literacy achievement and high IQ in dyslexics may not necessarily be predicted by IQ but by some other cognitive measure, e.g. listening comprehension. Szczerbiński (2007) adds that as much as intellectual ability highly correlates with reading comprehension, its relation with decoding is poor, in fact, decoding ability can be better predicted by phonological processing ability. Moreover, the causal relationship between IQ and reading faculty appears doubtful in light of evidence from hyperlexia studies, indicating that children with poor comprehension and low general IQ can demonstrate good decoding skills, which means they can be good mechanical readers (Siegal, 1989).

Yet another argument is that dyslexia can theoretically exist in all children, independently of intelligence. What follows from the above is that it is possible to diagnose dyslexia across the levels of intellectual development, provided children's reading achievement is below a typical reading score for their age and intelligence level. However, it is not recommended with respect to mentally retarded children, as it would change nothing in their educational situation. It can be expected though, with good reason, that they may manifest decoding difficulties of dyslexic type and benefit from pedagogical interventions designed for children with dyslexia. All in all, Szczerbiński (2007) concludes that decoding and encoding difficulties are not directly caused by low intelligence because, simply enough, print processing is not dependent on intelligence, hence the secondary role that IQ measurement holds in dyslexia assessment. Nevertheless, despite the intense debate on the usefulness of the discrepancy between the IQ level and the ability to read, it continually tends to be treated as a dyslexia indicator in everyday clinical practice (Bogdanowicz, 2003b; Bogdanowicz & Krasowicz-Kupis, 2005b; Elliot & Place, 2000). Moreover, with reference to research practice, the use of IQ-discrepancy-defined groups proves to be a common approach in studies on dyslexia. This cautious selection of poor readers of average IQ is conducted in hope of excluding more general learning difficulties and in that way creating better chances for depicting cognitive disorders that reading difficulties can be traced back to (Hulme & Snowling, 2009).

Moving on from the role of IQ to other components of the assessment battery in dyslexia diagnosis, let us enumerate the evaluation of perceptual-motor functions (e.g. visual perception and memory) and their integration (e.g. visual-motor or auditory-visual-motor coordination) as well as motor function (gross and fane motor skills) and lateralisation, which are routinely perceived valid in the Polish context for instance (Krasowicz-Kupis, 2008). However, in the face of non-existent unanimous agreement with regard to the underlying causes and pathomechanisms of dyslexia, its diagnosis, unsurprisingly, proves a complex and difficult process. For the same reason, there are differences with reference to the choice of tests and functions to be measured. Szczerbiński (2007) suggests that since it can be concluded from research findings that dyslexia does not follow from visual memory deficit or is not significantly related to the lateralisation formula, it seems reasonable to give up on their verification to concentrate on more telling indicators of the disability. At the same time though, he admits that among all familiar pivotal dyslexia indicators, none is, in fact, totally specific to this disorder (they occur in other contexts as well), thus the assessment towards dyslexia is to a great extent probabilistic in nature. The presence of particular features increases the chances that we are dealing with dyslexia, however some doubts and uncertainty may remain. Importantly, a high degree of severity and persistency of occurrence of these characteristics magnifies the likelihood that the problem we cope with is indeed dyslexia.

In fact, the level of severity and persistency can be verified by the responsiveness to intervention, which most desirably should become a critical element of the assessment procedure. It would translate into preceding final diagnostic decision about the nature of reading and spelling difficulties by intensive and individualised treatment, aimed at enhancing decoding and encoding abilities. Only non-responding individuals, who do not benefit from such a treatment and still struggle with reading, could be diagnosed dyslexic. Thus, ineffectiveness of special remedial teaching (which nevertheless proved useful for other poor readers) serves as an indicator of dyslexia. It needs stressing here that low-responding children are not impossible to teach, they simply require much more intensified and longer treatment (Szczerbiński, 2007; Vellutino et al., 1998).

Helland et al. (2008) verify the relation between school performance, operationalised as responsiveness to remedial activities and support, and a dichotic listening (DL) task with consonant-vowel (CV) syllables realisation in dyslexic 12-year-olds. Typically, children with dyslexia demonstrate reduced REA[9] on the DL task, which is a frequently used measure tapping phonological processing. Given that the phonological processing deficit is the core deficit in dyslexia, then reduced REA and lack of the left hemisphere dominance would be related to dyslexic reading and spelling difficulties. Children with dyslexia who do not respond well to special education show significantly lower REA in comparison to non-dyslexic age-matched children as well as children with dyslexia who positively react to remedial teaching. DL scores highly correlate with scores on language test, and Helland *et al.* (2008) speculate that children achieving average REA on the DL test should be capable of properly distinguishing between similar sounds, unlike those with reduced DL scores. The potential validity and usefulness of the DL task as a tool that can be successfully applied in clinical practice, with regard to differential diagnosis, is indicated. It is further implied that training in differentiating between and sequencing speech sounds can improve dyslexic linguistic skills and exert a normalising effect on the activation pattern in the left planum temporal, as evidenced by fMRI brain imaging.

Finally, in order to get an overall picture of an individual with dyslexia, it is worth devoting some thought to their emotional functioning. It is proposed that emotional state and well-being, self-esteem, self-control as well as attitude and motivation become a part of the assessment of individual needs of children with dyslexia (Carroll & Iles, 2006; Krasowicz-Kupis, 2008; Turner, 2003).

Identification of Dyslexia: Bilingual/Multilingual Perspective

On the one hand, there is a growing literature touching on the identification and remediation of dyslexia in a monolingual population; on the other hand, very little research has been initiated with respect to individuals from bilingual and multilingual backgrounds (Deponio *et al.*, 2000; Everatt *et al.*, 2000a, 2000b; Ganschow *et al.*, 2000; Stamboltzis & Pumfrey, 2000). There is an increasing and widespread sensitivity and concern over the issues of literacy acquisition and assessment of reading disabilities among school children in multicultural and multilingual settings, in particular, those who learn English as a second or subsequent language. Inasmuch as the assessment under such conditions is indeed a great challenge, achieving it early enough may equal enhanced effects in terms of treatment and later reading success. Conversely, delaying diagnosis and intervention leads to under-identification and, in the long run, to disadvantage and cumulative educational failure, not to mention the fact that it proves cost ineffective. As Geva (2000) rightly stresses, in attempting diagnosis towards dyslexia in a multilingual environment, first of all there is a need to differentiate between the phenomena that could be characterised as common, regular problems related to second language (L2) acquisition and true warning signs of reading fiasco. In addition, it is vital to understand whether the abovementioned signs prevail in L1 and L2 alike.

Children from ethnic and linguistic minorities, raised in a bilingual environment (living in a target/L2 speaking country and using their native language (L1) at home), frequently possess considerably weak L2 language skills before the commencement of formal schooling. Many educators apparently share a view that these children necessarily need to acquire a decent spoken command of L2 in order to learn to read it. Such an attitude also extends to promoting a view that waiting for the L2 oral proficiency to fully develop is required to ensure the reliable and valid identification of learning/reading problems. In research on at-risk learners of English as a second language (ESL), Geva (2000) confirms that elementary classroom teachers are rather reluctant and hesitant in qualifying ESL children as potentially at-risk for reading failure due to the prevailing belief that reading disabilities cannot be identified until these children reach a certain threshold of L2 oral proficiency. However, according to Geva (2000) there is no need to wait because, notwithstanding the crucial effect of L2 oral proficiency on reading comprehension, it seems to play a minor role in explaining poor word-based reading skills (word and pseudo-word decoding abilities) in L2, which prevail despite adequate instruction. Hence the need for early assessment of word decoding skills in L2, even if children still lack adequate L2 facility. As a matter of fact, it may be the case that children decode words much more accurately in L2 than in L1, which would depend on how letters map onto sounds (orthographic depth) in a given language. On the one hand, substantial differences may not be spotted between the accuracy and rate of word decoding in L1 and L2 in spite of varying levels of proficiency. Under such circumstances, reading comprehension seems greater in L1 than in L2 due to the facilitating effect of children's command of L1. On the other hand, along with not fully developed L2 oral proficiency, also poor decoding skills are capable of inhibiting reading comprehension.

Another important issue is that poor word recognition abilities can be traced back to low-grade phonological processing, which holds true across languages. Skilful phoneme manipulation enhances the development of good decoding skill, which, in turn, translates into high-level reading from the first grades. By contrast, below-standard phoneme manipulation ability has a debilitating effect on word decoding skill, possibly leading to reading failure. Importantly, several cross-linguistic studies consistently report the linguistic interdependence of phonological processing skills (and related processes, such as naming speed and phonological memory), in other words, these skills in one language are capable of predicting word recognition ability within and across languages, irrespective of existing differences between alphabetic systems of phoneme-to-grapheme conversion. All in all, most important for diagnosing reading disabilities in the multilingual context is the fact that differences in phonological processing abilities are critically related to word recognition skills across languages, which means that phonological processing abilities in one language, no matter whether L1 or L2, can predict individual differences in word decoding in another language. Diagnosing reading difficulties in a cross-linguistic context proves plausible even in view of not yet fully developed L2 proficiency (Geva, 2000).

In sum, Geva (2000) suggests, first of all, that heavy reliance on L2 oral proficiency in the identification of ESL learners who can be at-risk for reading disability is unreasonable, second, that two sets of complementary procedures (useful in L1) can be successfully applied in assessing towards dyslexia in bilingual or ESL individuals. The procedures involve phonological processing abilities and rapid basic reading skills assessment as well as looking for the gap between listening and reading skills. A small gap is expected in average-achieving children, by contrast, the discrepancy between much greater scores on listening comprehension tasks and poor reading comprehension is a vital indicator of a child experiencing print processing difficulties rather than problems with processing and comprehending verbal information. To stress again, postponing diagnostic activities in the case of ESL children who encounter substantial difficulties in developing word recognition faculty can have far-reaching damaging consequences for these children, as they are simultaneously deprived of the chance for intensive instruction in word recognition/attack skills.

Nowadays, the ethnographic reality poses new requirements on educators and clinicians in terms of dyslexia screening procedures and tools as well as individual education plans in order to cater for the needs of children from ethnic and language minorities, e.g. English as an additional language (EAL) learners. The estimates are that ESL children constitute almost 10% of the entire public school enrolment in 2000–2001 in the USA, with the numbers expected to grow to 40% by the year 2030. Still, the vast majority of the non-English-speaking population (about 80%) is mainly Spanish (Wagner *et al.*, 2005), unlike in Canada, where the student population is much more diverse in terms of native languages of ESL children and more numerous (approximately 18% as of 2001) (Geva, 2000; Lovett *et al.*, 2008).

In fact, it seems that early screening procedures designed primarily with monolingual children in mind can benefit bilinguals, as demonstrated in the case of learners of EAL. Everatt *et al.* (2000a) maintain that, in particular, phonological measures seem to be useful in identifying students with literacy problems, regardless of language background. Everatt *et al.* (2000b) found that young English/Sylheti bilingual children demonstrating below-standard spelling and reading skills can be accurately distinguished from the control group by the scores they achieve on several tests, including the measures of phonological processing ability and rapid naming. Apart from these two, the ability to recite high frequency sequences and repeat novel sequences of unknown or non-linguistic information, as well as the ability to recognise previously seen shapes also proved vital. Everatt *et al.* (2000b) stress that phonological measures indeed provide consistent results with reference to bilingual and monolingual learners alike.

Hutchinson *et al.* (2004) support the view that early identification and assessment towards dyslexia of children with EAL translates into more desirable effects in terms of therapy and treatment. They, nevertheless, admit that in the cases of children with EAL such a diagnosis is much more difficult than in monolingual children due to frequently poor L2 proficiency, the lack of L1 assessment and poor teachers' awareness of the effect dyslexia has on bilingual language processing, which altogether often leads to under-identification. In the UK, almost 10% of children attending primary schools speak EAL, including British Asian children investigated by Hutchinson *et al.* (2004). They report the phonological assessment battery (PhAB) of service in identifying individuals with poor phonological skills, responsible for reading accuracy difficulties in both EAL and monolingual children, with the EAL learners ready for PhAB in the second year at school and above, on condition that their language skills allow to understand test instructions. All in all, as indicated by Lovett *et al.* (2008), it seems that, principally, the components of the assessment of reading disorders in ESL children would be similar to those used in the diagnosis of reading deficits in L1.

Wagner *et al.* (2005), as mentioned above, report that approximately every fifth child in US public schools speaks an L1 other than English, in a rough estimate about 80% are Spanish-L1 speakers, however some urban districts document around 100 languages spoken among students. Understandably, such a situation forces educators and policy makers to respond to the educational needs of such learners, also with respect to the appropriate identification procedures. Given the facts cited so far about the necessity to distinguish between problems regularly occurring in the FLL context and signs of forthcoming reading failure as well as the facts about assessment procedures originally designed for monolingual speakers but applicable also in multilingual context, whether such children should undergo the identification process in their L1 or L2 seems to remain an open question. Generally, that would depend on the levels of proficiency in both native language and English. On the one hand, assessment of ESL learners in English may prove troublesome in that they may simply find the task instruction incomprehensible, despite the potential for performing the task itself. On the other hand, while assessment conducted in L1 may offer greater insight into the range of abilities and knowledge, it cannot possibly prognosticate reading acquisition in English to the same extent as the assessment in English can.

Wagner et al. (2005) rightly point to the fact that the identification of learning disabilities in ESL learners needs to comprise the evaluation of the course of literacy instruction, which is useful for the examination of both opportunity (access) to learn and the skills learned, especially when children are given such instruction in their native language prior to training in English. Thus, if children demonstrate good phonological skills developed in their L1 and at the same time experience difficulty in mastering reading ability in English, it may possibly be attributed to the quality and amount of instruction in English rather than to the underlying phonological deficit. If a student who gets literacy training in his L1 does not successfully develop reading ability in L1, it can be suspected, with good reason, that the prevalent phonological deficit constitutes the underlying cause. However, such factors as the varying instructional and cultural background of speakers sharing the L1 but having different origins, as is the case with Spanish speakers who are Puerto Rican, Mexican or Spanish, can play a role as well.

All in all, Wagner et al. (2005) advocate developing a *comparable assessments* procedure, grounded on examining at-risk ESL learners with regard to both native and English language. Ideally, these comparable assessments should touch on the same domains and levels with similar precision. In practice, availability of such compatible, valid and high-standard procedures is extremely rare. Such an enterprise poses considerable demands for multiple reasons, for instance, designing comparable assessments across languages varying in terms of orthography (both the type of the alphabet and orthographic depth) or alphabetic and non-alphabetic languages is indeed a challenge. Nevertheless, Wagner et al. (2005) report successful work on compiling a comparable assessment procedure for Spanish, developed from an existing one in English and comprising the following domains: knowledge of letter names and sounds, phonological awareness, rapid naming, word reading accuracy and efficiency, and reading comprehension.

Faced with mounting problems concerning assessment procedures in EAL students, one might also turn to the model of assessment involving the dynamism of response to instruction (Szczerbiński, 2007; Vellutino et al., 1998; Wagner et al., 2005). The model assumes that the identification of students at-risk for reading failure, who require additional remedial teaching, should be based on their reduced response to instruction. In the context of EAL students, limited reaction to ESL or EFL services is applicable.

Yet another perspective on the assessment of learning difficulty follows from the research on the native language-based FLL difficulties.[10] Here we concentrate on individuals who find the study of L2/foreign language, mainly executed in the formal, classroom environment rather than in the naturalistic setting of the target language-speaking country, a considerably demanding task. Identifying the problems they encounter, which can most possibly be traced back, as mentioned above, to their poor native language skills, is helpful in designing effective remedial teaching methods with regard to foreign language study.

The finding that students encountering either subtle or overt difficulties in reading, spelling, listening and speaking in their native language are likely to experience similar difficulties in FLL is, naturally, of vital importance for the assessment of their potential performance in foreign language courses. Generally, a comprehensive evaluation procedure should best involve several components, such as a review of a developmental history of the student and a scrupulous survey of his/her native as well as FLL accounts (Ganschow et al., 1998). Implications for the assessment of difficulties in FLL drawn from the studies conducted by Sparks et al. (Ganschow & Sparks, 1995; Sparks et al., 1995b, 1997c) explicitly indicate both native language (English) and foreign language aptitude measures as a must. Administration of the standardised measures of the native language skills (reading, phonological/orthographic processing, grammar, writing, vocabulary and oral language) and the foreign language aptitude test (MLAT) sheds light on FLL potential (Ganschow et al., 1998). Native language phonological/orthographic measures consist of tests of phonemic awareness, pseudoword reading and spelling, which is an additional indicator of future foreign language performance. It is known that the score on the long version of the MLAT turned out to be a key predictor of the foreign language performance, hence the proposition to use it as a screening tool for diagnosing students' aptness for FLL. Furthermore, since the subtests of the MLAT measure different aspects of language learning, they could serve as diagnostic tools for detecting the possible problem areas in FLL. Additionally, attention should be paid to whether the language background, together with the current native language difficulty, are adequately documented as well as whether there exists a corroborated record of a failure in or an excessive struggle with the foreign language courses. Finally, it needs stressing again that the data collected during the psycho-educational assessment pave the way for the development of alternative foreign language instruction, with adequate adjustments made with reference to the FLL methods and strategies (Sparks et al., 1989).[11]

A different approach towards evaluating learning difficulties in L2, though sharing some elements with the one presented above, especially with regard to the assessment procedures involving L1, is the one proposed by Helland (2008). Helland gives an account of the principles that served as guidelines in designing a test battery – 'English 2 Dyslexia Test', used for testing English as L2 in Norwegian learners with dyslexia of Grade 6 and 7. Such a L2 test would necessarily integrate the following: differences between L1 and L2, with reference to language typology and features of the orthographic system, customary signs of dyslexia in L1 and typical symptoms of the disorder in L2, also vital elements of a language test and crucial components of a dyslexia test. In fact, Helland (2008) proposes that the above assessment tenets could equally be applied to other languages learned as L2 besides English.

Interestingly, functional neuroimaging techniques can also be potentially utilized during the diagnosis of ESL/EAL learners in order to identify certain markers of reading disability (Pugh *et al.*, 2005).

Admittedly, despite the increasing recognition of dyslexia throughout the world, tests for identification of individuals with dyslexia exist in relatively few languages (Smythe & Everatt, 2000). Not only in deep orthographies, such as English, but also in highly transparent and logographic languages there are reports of individuals faced with problems in learning to read and spell. As maintained by Vellutino *et al.* (2004), impaired fluency and speed in word identification and text processing, which lead to reading comprehension difficulties, are claimed to be the key markers for dyslexia in such languages. Thus, quite naturally, diagnosing dyslexia in different languages cannot be reduced to the assessment of phonological awareness, but requires the examination of a broad scope of cognitive identifiers, for example, the speed of processing or visual recognition skills, depending on the orthographic features of a given language, possibly conducive to diverse occurrence and manifestations of dyslexia across scripts. It is suggested that for students with dyslexia learning English, the processes related to phonological awareness constitute the main obstacle. However, the likelihood of occurrence of other deficits in these learners is not denied, still, the nature of the script seems most problematic. Thus, deficits in visual processing are more liable to be responsible for dyslexia in Chinese dyslexics, while Hungarian dyslexics would probably experience deficits in the speed of processing (Smythe & Everatt, 2000).

Summing up, beyond doubt, timely diagnosis provides opportunities for immediate intervention, designed to prevent a child from encountering intensified, severe dyslexic difficulties. Early diagnosis, conditioning the efficient help, paired with an opportunity to compensate for their developmental delays, should be offered to children at risk for dyslexia. The necessity of preventive treatment, the prophylaxis, drawing on early diagnosis has been highlighted by practitioners (Benton, 1978; Bogdanowicz, 2002a; Elliot & Place, 2000; Górniewicz, 1998; Jędrzejowska & Jurek, 2003; Johnson *et al.*, 2001; Ott, 1997). The earlier the pedagogical intervention, the more efficient it is in terms of time and effort. Moreover, it can possibly hold back high anxiety and low self-esteem from developing (Everatt *et al.*, 2000a). On the other hand, if the dyslexic difficulties are not adequately recognised and dealt with instantly, they are forceful enough to exert considerable influence on the course of the scholastic career of the child. The assessment towards dyslexia is a typically complex task in monolinguals, it gets even more complicated in bilingual and multilingual environment, however, there is no doubt that it is worth every effort.

Notes

1. See Chapter 2: 'Phonological coding deficit hypothesis', on the phonological deficit in dyslexia.
2. See Chapter 2: 'Cerebellar deficit hypothesis', on the cerebellar deficit in dyslexia.
3. Several early screening tests are available, for example the phonological assessment battery (PhAB) (Frederickson et al., 1997), the dyslexia early screening test (DEST) devised by Nicolson and Fawcett (1996) and the scale of the risk for dyslexia (SRD) developed by Bogdanowicz (2002a). DEST can be administered by teachers or school health professionals who could test all pupils on entry to school. It is suitable for children aged from 4.6 to 6.5 years and provides information concerning the areas of strengths and weaknesses of the children. It is in the pencil and paper form and requires 30 minutes per pupil to administer. SRD can be applied to pupils aged 6–7. Its aim is to reveal delays in the psychomotor development and denote the functions that can be disordered. The administration of the SRD should most suitably be accompanied by an early assessment of reading and spelling skills. The advantage of the SRD is its uncomplicated form – the questionnaire can be relatively quickly filled and compiled by teachers or parents.
4. See Chapter 1: 'Reading Strategies and Stages of Reading Development', on reading strategies and Chapter 1: 'Orthographic Depth and Grain Size: A Cross-language Perspective on Reading and Dyslexia', on the orthographic depth.
5. Dysphonetic dyslexics (63%) suffer from deficits in phonological decoding, given rise to by disorders of auditory-linguistic processing. This type is characterised by problems in differentiating and identifying individual speech sounds, poor phonological word analysis, and difficulties in integrating written words with their sounds. In other words, dysphonetic dyslexics face problems applying the grapheme-phoneme rules and, for that reason, they are forced to rely on their sight-vocabulary when recognising words. Thus, dysphonetic writing exploits the visual memory of words. Typical misspellings are phonetically inaccurate (e.g. 'catteg' for 'cottage', 'coetere' for 'character'), while in reading, words are often guessed or replaced (semantic substitution, e.g. 'laugh' for 'funny', 'bus' for 'car'). By contrast, in dyseidetic dyslexia (9%) visual perception and memory as well as visual-spatial processing is deficient. Dyseidetic dyslexics find it particularly difficult to make use of visual whole-word information in reading; additionally, their performance on irregular words is also significantly below standard. Confusion of letter shapes and phonetic writing are characteristic features of this type of dyslexia. Thus, visual-spatial reversals, static and dynamic inversion are usually observed ('dab' for 'bad', 'was' for 'saw'). Typical misspellings, as suggested above, are phonetically accurate and can be easily decoded (e.g. 'laf' for 'laugh', 'berd' for 'bird', 'wok' for 'walk'), while reading is based on phonological analysis and synthesis. However, dyseidetic dyslexics appear to be relatively better than dysphonetic dyslexics

in applying grapheme-phoneme conversion rules. Finally, the third, mixed type (28%) presumes co-occurrence of dysphonetic and dyseidetic difficulties. As can be noticed from the percentages cited above, dysphonetic dyslexics constitute the majority of cases, which is in accord with a commonly accepted claim that phonological processing deficit is a core deficit in dyslexia.
6. Disorders of visual or visual-spatial processing, caused by impairments of visual attention, perception and memory, markedly connected with hand motor disorder as well as visual-motor coordination deficits, generate visual dyslexia. By way of analogy, auditory dyslexia is provoked by disorders of language processing brought about by deficits in auditory attention, perception and memory, together with poor representation of speech sounds. Mixed type entails cumulative characteristics, involving co-occurrence of both visual and auditory deficits. Finally, disorders of integration of perceptual-motor and language functions produce integrative dyslexia. In this case, no disturbances in simple perceptual-motor functions measured in isolation are signified, but the integration and co-ordination of stimuli coming from different receptors on the cortical level is disordered.
7. See Chapter 1: 'Defining dyslexia', on the definition of dyslexia.
8. See Chapter 1: 'Orthographic Depth and Grain Size: A Cross-language Perspective on Reading and Dyslexia', on the cross-language perspective on reading and dyslexia.
9. Right ear advantage (REA) indicates left hemisphere superiority for language, with the activation of the left planum temporale.
10. See Chapter 3 for a discussion of the native language-based FLL difficulties.
11. The findings of multiple studies conducted on successful instructional methods to at-risk foreign language learners are referred to in Chapter 5.

Chapter 5
Treatment and Teaching

Issues in Dyslexia Treatment

The issue of supporting individuals with dyslexia in their attempts to overcome reading and spelling difficulties, experienced both in their native language as well as in a second or additional language, which they frequently struggle to learn, invites three (at least) diverse perspectives into play, namely, that of a researcher, teacher-therapist and language teacher. Serving one overall goal – searching for the best practices in order to enhance the chances of successful literacy acquisition for children with dyslexia – each is predominantly preoccupied with research-based interventions and treatments, special education services (pedagogical therapy) and teaching approaches and techniques, respectively.

Theoretically, it seems that teachers' choices can be well informed by research findings, providing evidence that either supports or fails to support the effectiveness of specific educational approaches and instructional practices. However, an apparent lack of enthusiasm and relative reluctance of teachers with regard to implementing research-validated educational activities can be observed (Philips *et al.*, 2008; Ritchey & Goeke, 2006), thus forming a gap between research and practice. Similarly, Hurry *et al.* (2005) highlight a particular difficulty and, at the same time, salience of transforming the educational research into teacher practice, thus making research-based and verified techniques available to teachers.

This complex process of transformation consists of several levels and steps, including a national policy and curriculum design to finally end at the level of the classroom. Philips *et al.* (2008) suggest that one of the reasons for the mismatch might be that teachers lack awareness as well as specialised thorough knowledge and understanding of the concepts that are to be successfully converted from research and applied in practice. Indeed, one can be truly confused with the massive amount of conflicting research outcomes, competing theories and alternative treatments offered in the study of dyslexia. In light of the above, some reluctance seems justified.

It appears that bridging the research-practice gap would first involve translating and disseminating research findings so that one would not fail to distinguish between the issues that still constitute a matter of intense debate and the facts that have already gained widespread recognition and acceptance in dyslexia research and practice. For instance, the importance and necessity of phonological training for children with dyslexia is widely approved by researchers, practitioners and teachers alike, and supported by constantly accumulating scholarly and pedagogical knowledge. Naturally, there have been several propositions with regard to alternative modes of treatment in dyslexia, to which some attention is devoted in this chapter as well.

In order to minimise the literacy problems of individuals with dyslexia, it is necessary to enhance automatisation of the reading and spelling skills through carefully designed, monitored and long-term reading instruction (Nicolson & Fawcett, 2001). Importantly, direct instruction in phonological awareness and letter-sound correspondences typically brings highly positive effects in terms of enhanced word identification, spelling and reading ability (Vellutino *et al.*, 2004). The influence of phonological training on reading acquisition is deemed especially effective when it is combined with instruction in letter-sound mappings (Bogdanowicz, 2002a; Gustafson *et al.*, 2007; Reid, 1998; Wise *et al.*, 2007).

What additionally follows from the research findings is that neural networks necessary to mediate word recognition can be successfully produced through the interaction of brain and environment (pedagogical intervention, instruction or early literacy support) (Vellutino *et al.*, 2004) – probably the most crucial implication for all those preoccupied with developing literacy faculty. As has been mentioned,[1] findings of several imaging studies investigating brain activation patterns in English monolingual dyslexics before and after phonologically driven reading intervention indicate the increased activation of areas typically employed by regular readers, which means that instruction plays a vital role in creating brain activation patterns, allowing successful reading in children with dyslexia. In other words, dyslexia-specific brain activation maps may become normal following intensive remedial training (e.g. Aylward *et al.*, 2003; Blachman *et al.*, 2004; Richards *et al.*, 2000; Shaywitz *et al.*, 2004; Simos *et al.*, 2002). Similarly, functional neuroimaging techniques can be potentially applied to assessing the effectiveness and success of various reading instructions/interventions in English as a second/foreign language (ESL/EAL) learners (Pugh *et al.*, 2005).

Wagner *et al.* (2005) imply that inasmuch as special education activities typically serve well in putting a stop to further distancing of the observed and expected achievement, they are incapable of normalising performance. At the same time, research-based treatments lead more frequently to improvement and larger gains, though mainly with regard to accuracy rather than fluency or comprehension. Another problem seems to be the apparent lack of universality of a given intervention in terms of effectiveness. Significant differences between treatment and control groups are shown, indicating usefulness and efficiency of a given set of educational actions. Still, more often than not, individual differences in reaction to treatment emerge, evidencing little effect or even totally intractable cases of non-responders, most typically falling into the category of the poorest-achieving, lowest-performing and, at the same time, most severely disordered children. Hence, the suggestion that assessing treatments in terms of their overall effectiveness requires going beyond group mean differences.

In fact, Whiteley *et al.* (2007) report that about 30% of young children identified as at-risk for literacy difficulties fail to take advantage of early conventional, phonologically based intervention, even in the context of one-to-one tuition. Those non-respondents or non-beneficiaries are predicted by particularly below-standard letter knowledge and low level of expressive vocabulary. Naturally, they require intensive special instruction in these aspects of knowledge in addition to phonological training.

In a similar vein, Gustafson *et al.* (2007) note that phonological training, notwithstanding its empirically supported effectiveness with regard to general average improvements in reading skill, tends not to be equally effective for all participants. Children with dyslexia vary with respect to phonological and orthographic word decoding; Gustafson and colleagues indicate that these skills can have critical effect on the intervention results. In fact, they verified the effectiveness of two diverse computerised training programmes for poor readers with predominantly phonological or principally orthographic problems, one programme being phonologically oriented, and the other orthographically focused. Children receiving phonological and orthographic training alike, on average strongly improved their text reading and general word decoding skills. However, the improvement did not prove statistically greater than that evidenced by children from the comparison groups, namely, regular readers and children who received ordinary special instruction (run by teacher-therapists, accommodating reading instruction to individual needs and abilities of children). All in all, phonologically deficient readers improved their general word decoding skills more from phonological than from orthographic training. The opposite was demonstrated for children with poor orthographic skills. Thus, in the cases of children showing a considerable gap between their phonological and orthographic word decoding abilities, reading interventions and training programmes should focus on their relative weakness rather than strength in word decoding. Similarly, White *et al.* (2006) strongly suggest that treatments for dyslexia should deal with observed individual deficits rather than claim to constitute a solution to all dyslexic problems.

Naturally, the problem of denoting effective reading intervention also applies to bilingual and multilingual context, for example, with regard to ESL/EAL. It seems that research data on reading instruction for reading-disabled ESL learners is indeed sparse (Lovett *et al.*, 2008).

In fact, as is the case with early screening procedures designed primarily for monolingual children, the critical components of reading intervention programmes prepared with monolinguals in mind can most probably benefit bilinguals. Lovett *et al.* (2008) report no overall differences between reading-disabled native English-speaking children and ESL school-age students in response to systematic, explicit, phonologically based reading intervention. The training proves effective irrespective of the primary language background of poor readers, however, it seems to be conditioned by the former achievement of the basic level of English language competence.

As for some alternative types of treatment, let us begin with methods of therapy for dyslexia type P (perceptual) and L (linguistic) compiled by Bakker.[2] This intervention programme is based on the assumption that the normal developmental process of literacy acquisition, either in a first or a subsequent language, begins with more substantial involvement of the right hemisphere and then transfers to the left (Robertson, 2000b; Robertson & Bakker, 2008; Stamboltzis & Pumfrey, 2000). Reading difficulties manifest themselves if, during the process of learning to read, the shift of dominance from the right to the left hemisphere takes place either too late (P-type dyslexia) or too early (L-type dyslexia), bringing about the lack of balance between the perceptual and linguistic strategies used for reading. P-type and L-type can be treated by stimulation of the left and right hemispheres, respectively, with the use of various sensory modalities – tactile, auditory and visual. Such an activity should presumably result in alterations in the use of the reading strategies and, consequently, in changes in the reading performance.

Two remedial techniques have been proposed: *hemisphere-specific stimulation* (HSS) and *hemisphere-alluding stimulation* (HAS). The HSS technique involves direct unilateral presentation of the reading material to the right or left visual field, to the right or left ear and/or to the fingers of the right or left hand in P-type and L-type dyslexics, respectively. The right visual field and the right hand project onto the left hemisphere; the left visual field and the left hand project onto the right hemisphere. However, as far as the auditory channel is concerned, the dissociation in hemispheric projection is not total. Although contralateral projections dominate, ipsilateral ones also exist. Still, the activity of the ipsilateral hemisphere may be reduced during listening tasks through the simultaneous presentation of verbal information to one ear and non-verbal information to the other ear.

HAS provides for indirect bilateral presentation of the reading material to stimulate the left or right hemisphere. The stimulus is perceived by both hemispheres, but HAS engages each of the hemispheres by specifically manipulating the nature of the reading task. For example, a perceptually difficult text (atypical fonts, pictures), which necessitates greater involvement of the right hemisphere, should be presented to L-type dyslexics. It is further recommended that reading materials for P-type dyslexics, to activate the left hemisphere, be perceptually simple and require the use of linguistic strategies (e.g. filling the missing words in a text, recognising and forming rhymes, forming sentences from the given words). HAS is transferable to the classroom situation, while, unsurprisingly, HSS is not transferable because sophisticated equipment is required for carrying out the tasks.

A substantial bulk of behavioural and electrophysiological research has been conducted to validate Bakker's balance theory, particularly relating to classifying dyslexics into P and L types in line with the pattern of reading errors and reading speed and to the efficiency of therapy (Bakker, 1984, 1990, 1995; Bakker *et al.*, 1995; Bogdanowicz & Krasowicz, 1995, 1996/1997; Kappers, 1997; Robertson, 2000a, 2000b). Bakker *et al.* (1995) argue that electrophysiological studies indicate different patterns of hemispheric activation during reading and processing of letters in P- and L-type dyslexics, thus supporting the argument about diverse involvement of the left and right brain areas. Additionally, left versus right hemisphere stimulation results in different effects on reading accuracy and speed. More precisely, greater effects of direct and indirect hemispheric stimulation, irrespective of sensory modality, have been obtained with reference to the right hemisphere in L-type dyslexia. Some positive influence of HSS and HAS has also been observed with regard to the left hemisphere in P-type dyslexia. Nevertheless, despite the apparently high efficiency of hemispheric stimulation, unfortunately it cannot change a dyslexic reader into a non-dyslexic reader (Bakker, 1990). Still, as Kappers (1997) and Robertson (2000a) claim, it has brought about considerable improvements in the reading ability of many severely disordered children with dyslexia.

However, as reported by other studies (Dryer *et al.*, 1999), treatment aimed at stimulating the underactive hemisphere when compared to treatment aimed at stimulating the overactive hemisphere, did not result in greater reading gains. Admittedly, these findings seem to run counter to the predictions based on the balance model. They suggest that the gains made during the intervention programme may have been attributable to other variables rather than to the specific nature of remedial methods. In addition, the reliability of dyslexia types proposed by Bakker has been questioned by Dryer *et al.* (1999).

According to Bogdanowicz and Krasowicz (1995, 1996/1997), the efficiency of the therapy proposed by Bakker is, to some extent, guaranteed by the multimodal activity, and the controversies referred to earlier may result from inadequate identification of dyslexia type. Consequently, a given kind of therapy may not bring about the anticipated results. It is further argued that the application of HSS and

HAS could be linked to the diagnosis of the cognitive functioning, namely, visual-spatial functions deficits would be treated by the right hemisphere stimulation, while language deficits would require the activation of the left hemisphere.

Another suggestion for therapeutic activities can be traced back to the visual and auditory magnocellular hypothesis. The fact that monocular occlusion (blanking the vision of one eye) can improve the reading ability of children with visual binocular instability has been confirmed (Stein, 2001; Stein et al., 2000a). In the cases of such children, reading with one eye (the right one), with the other blanked, reduces their binocular perceptual confusion and allows improvement in their reading performance. The effects are claimed to be dramatic and progress is far greater than in other remediation methods for dyslexics (Stein, 2001; Stein et al., 2001).

Yet another therapeutic proposition touches on the sensory training in detection of rapidly presented acoustic stimuli, which leads to better phonological processing and therefore to reading improvement (Bower, 2000; Stein, 2001). Highly accurate processing of temporal change by the auditory system is important for proper development of the phonological skills (Talcott et al., 2000b; Tallal et al., 1996). It has been found (Bogdanowicz, 1999; Horgan, 1997; Merzenich et al., 1996; Stein, 2001) that training children with language learning impairment, using a computer program in which the sound frequency changes can be slowed down and amplitude changes can be increased (stretched speech), greatly ameliorated their performance. In all likelihood, individuals with dyslexia undergoing similar training would display analogous results (Stein, 2001), namely, greater ability to distinguish between rapidly occurring acoustic stimuli and their sequence, leading to better phonological processing, which presupposes the improvement in the reading skill.

Another kind of therapy for children with dyslexia suffering from *scotopic sensitivity syndrome* (SSS) was introduced by Irlen. SSS is connected with sensitivity to light. Students report the perception of a glare from white paper, which makes it hard to decipher a text, and difficulty seeing the print clearly, let alone an impression that it moves around the page. SSS is additionally connected with eyestrain – eyes often water, itch or burn (Jameson, 2000; Jędrzejowska & Jurek, 2003; Ott, 1997). It has been suggested that coloured overlays or tinted lenses can help. Children's responses to colour filters for viewing the text are measured by an apparatus called the Intuitive Colorimeter and then adequate coloured lenses can be prescribed. However, the nature of the treatment seems to be controversial and there is no conclusive evidence that it can improve poor reading performance. Coloured lenses or filters are likely to reduce the feeling of sore, tired eyes, headaches and, consequently, enhance the child's motivation to read, but they are not likely to change a dyslexic reader into a good reader (Ott, 1997). However, some accommodation of classroom materials may prove beneficial for children with dyslexia, for example, large, widely spaced print, clear text on an uncluttered page tend to decrease the visual perceptual impression of the letters and words moving around the page, blurring or spinning. On the other hand, small, newspaper-like grey print, fancy or unusual fonts, capitalisation of whole words and phrases can intensify the disturbances (Jameson, 2000; Levinson, 1980).

Summing up, I will share the sceptical view expressed by Kirk *et al.* (2001: 293) with reference to the proposed effectiveness and alleviating effect on the reading ability of the 'almost weekly addition of dyslexia cures', such as fish oil capsules, massage therapy, vitamins, coloured lenses, neurolinguistic programming, reorientation of the brain and others. Apparently, sensational media reports about wonderful cures for dyslexia certainly do no good, quite the opposite, they are unhelpful both for the professionals and individuals with dyslexia. Dyslexia is a lifetime and diversifying condition in terms of types and severity of impairment. Bearing that fact in mind, in the construction of therapeutic programmes, allowances should be made for the educational needs and abilities of individuals with dyslexia. All in all, dyslexia is not a disease – it cannot be cured, however, its negative effects certainly can be reduced or even sometimes completely eliminated due to intensive, adequate and regular educational efforts, focusing on reading and spelling skills enhancement.

In a similar vein, White *et al.* (2006: 252) suggest: 'There is no point training the auditory abilities of children who have no auditory deficit, the binocular control of children who have no visual impairment, the balance of children who have no balance problem, and the phonological skills who have no phonological deficit'. White *et al.* (2006) strongly advise against indiscriminately applying a given type of treatment to all children with dyslexia in the hope of ameliorating their impairments. In fact, they claim that the majority of dyslexics with definite phonological deficit should receive phonological treatment, while much fewer children with dyslexia who suffer from various types of visual disorders would benefit most from visual interventions, tailored to a given kind of visual deficit. They also voice a claim that it is unreasonable to expect any auditory or motor treatment to have advantageous results with regard to reading. In fact, White *et al.* (2006) initiated an intense debate on the role of the sensorimotor impairments in dyslexia (including implications for clinical practice) among researchers, receiving some bitter criticism from their opponents and advocates of the abovementioned treatment methods.

In sum, highly structured phonic reading instruction, paired with phonemic awareness training seems to be a sound, theoretically based intervention whose effectiveness in alleviating reading difficulties in dyslexia has been repeatedly shown. Impressive effects of the equivalent approach (involving explicit phonemic awareness training, coupled with letter-sound training) in preventing reading failure in children at-risk for dyslexia have also been reported. Still, ameliorating reading difficulties does not necessarily equal eliminating them, what is more, it usually requires great investment in terms of effort and time. Thus, preventing and overcoming reading difficulties heavily depends on intensive and specialist teaching, often extending over long periods of time.

Principles of the Multisensory Structured Learning Approach

Pedagogical therapy is defined as an intervention employing special forms of educational and didactic help, undertaken in order to minimise or eliminate disorders, stimulate learning and induce positive changes in the cognitive and emotional-motivational functioning of a given child. Thus, the main aim of pedagogical therapy is to create opportunities for all-round mental, psychological and social development, through levelling disharmonies and deficits, and reducing scholastic failure, and, in the long run, its emotional and social consequences (Czajkowska & Herda, 1998). Therapeutic activities are realised in the form of correction-compensation/special instruction classes, concentrating on the correction of developmental deficits as well as on compensation, defined as further improvement of the functions that are not disordered, so that they can support or replace the disordered ones (Czajkowska & Herda, 1998; Jędrzejowska & Jurek, 2003; Kaja, 2001b).

The introduction of systematic remedial work, run by a teacher-therapist at school or on a one-to-one basis, can be further continued by parents at home or, if necessary, by specialists at a psychological-pedagogical clinic. Such a line of conduct typically allows decreasing or suppressing developmental disorders, thus facilitating a successful beginning of school career (Bogdanowicz, 2002a). Unsurprisingly, the later the therapeutic activities are undertaken, the more difficult and effortful they are, because reading difficulties routinely become increasingly intractable with age (Jędrzejowska & Jurek, 2003; Zakrzewska, 1999).

As already pointed out, a starting point for the construction of the remedial teaching programme are recommendations drawing on a detailed assessment. Individual plans of therapeutic activities are naturally subject to verifications and modifications, applied depending on the ongoing identification of the needs and achievements (Reid, 1998; Tod, 2008; Zakrzewska, 1999).

In general, several principles regulate the course of organisation of the remedial teaching process. Individualisation of measures and methods is particularly important due to considerable differentiation as to the type, range and intensity of developmental disorders and learning difficulties. Graduation of the complexity of tasks and activities is aimed at developing reading and spelling skills in proportion to the capabilities of a given child. Thus, after completing elementary, simple exercises, we can move towards more complicated tasks. Appropriate matching of the perplexity of a task to the abilities of a child with dyslexia conditions successful completion of the assignment (Czajkowska & Herda, 1998). Reid (1998) stresses the need for the application of a structured approach, so that learning can appear in a linear developmental manner, which enables learners to grasp a particular skill before advancing to a subsequent one. A sequential and cumulative approach may help to make the learning process more meaningful and effective. Needless to say, the choice of materials relevant for students' interests as well as employment of diverse and attractive teaching techniques and exercises exerts positive influence on the way the tasks are executed by students. Additionally, children with dyslexia require plenty of reinforcement, repetition and overlearning, which are meant to eventually lead to automaticity (Deponio *et al.*, 2000; Reid, 1998; Thomson & Watkins; 1990). Frequent recapitulation inevitably is a must for students with dyslexia because they usually find it abnormally troublesome to anchor information in memory, moreover intensive rehearsal invites more complete mastery of a certain part of material before the new information is introduced.

The most poorly acquired skills require the most intense practice, realised through multiple diverse activities. Another crucial aspect is regularity and relatively high frequency of special education activities. Systematic and recurrent practice provides the most welcome results, while long intervals tend to bring about partial or total regress.

Continuous psychotherapeutic efforts to prevent neurotic behaviour, negative attitudes towards school and learning, and emotional-motivational problems from developing and intensifying are inescapable. Teachers strive not only to make children with dyslexia able to learn, but also to make them want to do so. The fulfilment of such a goal is conditioned by creating the success-oriented tasks, noticing and appreciating the smallest attainments and, last but not least, refraining from comparing the results of dyslexic students' work with the achievements of their peers, but rather evaluating dyslexics' progress measured commensurate with their previous scores (Czajkowska & Herda, 1998; Gąsowska & Pietrzak-Stępowska, 1994; Juszczyk & Zając, 1997; Kaja, 2001b; Zakrzewska, 1999).

The direct multisensory structured approach is advocated for teaching reading and spelling in the native language to children with dyslexia. The *multisensory structured learning* (MSL) style has been found effective with regard to foreign language instruction as well (Crombie & McColl, 2000; Jameson, 2000; Miller & Bussman Gillis, 2000). Originally, Gillingham and Stillman devised the multisensory teaching programme, based on the pioneering work of Orton. The programme became known as the *Orton-Gillingham* (OG) *instructional approach* (Gillingham & Stillman, 1997) and has since been successfully used to teach reading and spelling to students with native language learning problems.

Numerous remedial programmes for teaching reading and writing are based on the fundamental principles of the multisensory method (Sparks et al., 1992a). For example, *Alpha to Omega, the A–Z of Teaching Reading Writing and Spelling* (Hornsby et al., 1999) or *The Bangor Dyslexia Teaching System* by Miles, *The Hickey Multi-sensory Language Course* by Augur and Briggs, as well as the *Units of Sound* by Bramley (Ott, 1997). Richey and Goeke (2006) enumerate the following: *Alphabetic Phonics, Wilson Reading System, The Herman Method, Project ASSIST, The Slingerland Approach, The Spalding Method, Starting Over and Project Read*, which by no means constitute an exhaustive list. Reid (1998) provides a comprehensive and thorough review of programmes for students with dyslexia, dividing them into four groups: individualised programmes, support approaches and strategies, assisted learning techniques and whole-school approaches. All the programmes mentioned above relate to teaching English as a native language. In Poland, for example, the *Method of the Good Start* compiled by Bogdanowicz (1985b) is based on the visual–auditory–kinaesthetic–tactile (VAKT) approach and is used both in prevention and in therapy (Bogdanowicz, 1997a). In the training programme for teaching German as a foreign/second language to at-risk learners, Schneider (1999) introduced the *multisensory structured metacognitive language instruction* (MSML). She additionally addressed the metacognitive component more directly than in the traditional MSL approach. According to Schneider (1999), the training of matacognitive skills is necessary for students with language learning disabilities because of their poor ability to recognise and understand the rule system of a foreign/second language.

The fact that children with dyslexia require a multisensory approach in teaching and learning is nowadays widely known and commonly accepted (Ganschow & Sparks, 1995; Jędrzejowska & Jurek, 2003; Johnson, 1978; Ott, 1997; Sparks & Ganschow, 1993; Sparks et al., 1991; 1998c; Thomson & Watkins, 1990). Schneider (1999), Szczerbiński (2007), Sparks and Miller (2000), Ritchey and Goeke (2006) enumerate the following general features of teaching methods with regard to print processing (reading and spelling) that children with dyslexia find beneficial – multisensory, direct and explicit (rules do not have to be guessed or inferred by students), systematic, highly structured, sequential, cumulative, synthetic, phonetic, phonics-driven and, finally, giving sufficient practice and consolidation, and preferably conducted in small groups or individually.

More precisely, simultaneous activation of the auditory, tactile, visual and kinaesthetic pathways, which supports compensation, makes up a basic component of the MSL. Thus, in other words, the information integrated via unaffected routes can lead to the development of written language skills. The multimodal perception is usually more advantageous than mono-modal with regard to both the amount of remembered material and the pace of learning (Włodarski, 1998). The simultaneous presentation of linguistic material with the use of as many sensory channels as possible benefit individuals with dyslexia, in fact, it is assumed that the more modalities involved in the learning process, the more effective it appears to be. Teaching reading and spelling with the help of multisensory methods is realised by the integration of visual, auditory, kinaesthetic and tactile stimuli and involves simultaneous presentation of information coming from various senses. Thus, multisensory teaching is based on the constant use of the following: what a letter or a word looks like, how it sounds and how the speech organs and hand feel when producing it (Bogdanowicz, 1997a; Ott, 1997). A person with dyslexia learns how to read and spell words by hearing, seeing and pronouncing them, by making models of plasticine, forming them from wooden, sponge or plastic letters; finally, by tracing them on various surfaces, such as paper, carpet, floor, sand and by writing them. The more the perceptual channels are open, the greater the possibility of forming associations between the graphic (visual) and phonological aspects of a word as well as its meaning. If a stimulus is complex, it activates several receptors and perception of information is realised simultaneously through several sensory channels.

Another rule pertains to the direct and explicit familiarising of students with the phonological (phonological awareness), alphabetic (letter-sound correspondences), morphemic (roots, prefixes, suffixes) as well as syntactic structure of language. Thus, for example, children with dyslexia are specifically made aware of the individual phonemes in words and how to relate them to their written representations (graphemes), and they also learn how to sequence them in words. Children with dyslexia require carefully planned (in terms of scope and sequence), direct and explicit instruction, as opposed to implicit and incidental. Philips *et al.* (2008) see the backbone of the explicit instruction in the way the teacher participates in the classroom interaction, namely, he/she issues statements and behaves in a way that clarifies the task's demands to students and gives a model of the task outcome that is expected. Thus, defining, modelling and explaining are the most commonly referred to instructional techniques in explicit teaching. In order to successfully complete a task, children with dyslexia require a lot of repetition and practice until they are ready to come up with the answer unaided. Self-dependence is achieved in a step-by-step fashion, beginning with guided practice, through supported practice to independent practice. Importantly, children get constant support taking the form of scaffolding (verbal prompts, modelling, additional examples), accommodated to individual needs. Last but not least, frequent, immediate, positive and specific feedback characterises explicit instruction.

The effective instruction should also be synthetic/analytic, where students are taught how to break down larger units into their constituent components as well as how to put the parts back in the proper sequence. Sight words, which do not follow any rule patterns, are taught as whole units. Furthermore, MSL teaching is structured, which means that it is organised into small units with logical and straightforward presentation and practice of the rules. It is also sequential – in the course of training we move from the simple and regular patterns to more complex and irregular ones, and cumulative – new information is built on what is already thoroughly integrated. Thus, only a small amount of material is presented at a time, with a full mastery of the content via multisensory techniques (simultaneous saying, seeing, hearing and writing) before advancing to new components. The crucial component of the MSL is repetition and overlearning, employed in order to ensure automaticity as well as to increase memory and rate of access. The teaching process is individualised with ongoing assessment and diagnostic information as to progress and needs.

Ritchey and Goeke (2006) review literature on the effectiveness of the OG and OG-based reading instruction programmes in contrast to other instructional approaches. The overall conclusion is that OG and OG-based instruction brings about positive effects in terms of word reading, word attack/decoding, spelling and comprehension. Moreover, it proves valid across age groups, settings and populations. However, some studies reported the lack of statistically significant differences favouring any of the analysed programmes or found the OG and OG-based programmes inferior in the results they produced to alternative programmes. All in all, the small number of studies selected for investigation and their apparent methodological diversity and faults makes the undertaken task of comparing them and generalising as to their overall effectiveness extremely difficult. Notwithstanding this, the OG and OG-based programmes have been widely accepted and used for five decades, and repeatedly reported as overwhelmingly efficient (also across settings, age groups and languages) by practitioners and teachers. Again, Ritchey and Goeke (2006) stress the mismatch or a gap between research and practice and suggest the need for more thorough and comprehensive research on the OG and OG-based instructional programmes.

As much as the MSL approach proved to be widely valued across educational settings and ages, still Wearmouth and Reid (2008) voice an opinion that it seemingly lacks certain elements they consider crucial in learning and teaching. Such aspects as metacognition, learning styles and reasoning abilities should be given more attention, as students with dyslexia quite often insufficiently realise their own thinking and reasoning processes and find it troublesome to control them. In view of the above, a teacher's role would also involve evaluation and reinforcement of the development of matacognitive awareness. Knowing how to learn and being able to reflect on and analyse the process of learning as such, not only its content and final outcome, are the skills that need to be incorporated into the course of training designed to overcome dyslexic difficulties.

Multisensory Structured Learning Approach and Foreign Language Study

Adaptation of the multisensory structured learning approach to foreign language teaching

Currently, the emphasis in foreign language instruction has been on the communicative approaches, in which the aspect of inferring meaning from the context is highlighted, while the direct teaching of sound, sound-symbol and grammatical rule system is de-emphasized. However, there seems to exist limited evidence confirming the success of the natural approaches in teaching foreign languages to students with learning difficulties (Ganschow *et al.*, 1998; Ganschow & Sparks, 2000; Sparks *et al.*, 1992b). On the other hand, efficient lower-level verbal processing operations (letter identification and word recognition) are claimed to play a crucial role in successful foreign language reading comprehension (Koda, 1992). What is more, early direct and explicit instruction in the orthographic (sound-symbol) system of a foreign language as well as increased exposure to print is highly recommended, particularly for learners with relatively weak native language skills (Sparks *et al.*, 2006; Kahn-Horwitz *et al.*, 2006). Still, as maintained by Sparks *et al.* (1997c, 1998c), it is likely to benefit all foreign language learners. Naturally, for literate students, reading is likely to enhance foreign language learning (FLL), which seems in accord with the finding in the native language research concerning the 'Matthew effects' in reading – good readers, unsurprisingly, further improve their reading skills through the sheer activity of reading, whereas poor readers become even poorer (Stanovich, 1986; Kahn-Horwitz *et al.*, 2006).

Sparks *et al.* (1998c) hypothesised that since oral native language skills are enhanced by exposure to written language, then, logically, early and frequent presentation of print in a foreign language, combined with listening to and speaking, is potentially profitable for at-risk foreign language learners because it provides a multisensory input. Even though for good native and foreign language learners such an approach may seem a bit unnatural, it is necessary for the students with weak language skills, who are unable to intuitively grasp the knowledge as to how spoken words are composed of smaller segments and represented by letters.

Sparks *et al.* (Ganschow & Sparks, 2000) transferred the OG methodology, a specialised approach to teaching basic literacy skills to individuals with dyslexia in their native language, into the field of FLL. At that time, neither special needs educators nor foreign language teachers, who, as a matter of fact, were hardly familiar with the approach in question, had considered such a transfer of instructional philosophy and practice across languages feasible.

Adaptation of the multisensory (MSL) methodology to teaching foreign languages to at-risk foreign language learners resulted in improvement of both the oral and written aspects of the student's native language performance as well as foreign language aptitude (on the modern language aptitude test; MLAT) (Ganschow *et al.*, 1998; Ganschow & Sparks, 1995; Sparks *et al.*, 1991, 1997a). The most desirable option for learning disabled (LD) students would entail the application of the MSL approach to foreign language teaching, with reference to all components of language learning, with special emphasis put on phonology. Additionally, it proves advantageous to employ a foreign language as a language of classroom instruction, with the native language reserved for clarification of areas of special difficulty. Finally, frequent review is a must (Sparks *et al.*, 1991).

The research findings that at-risk foreign language learners experience hindrance expressly with the phonological code of language constitute the instructional rationale (Ganschow *et al.*, 1991; Sparks *et al.*, 1989, 1992a). It has been demonstrated that students with FLL difficulties who receive direct multisensory instruction in the phonology/orthography of a foreign language make significant gains and maintain them over time (Ganschow & Sparks, 1995; Sparks *et al.*, 1992b). Nevertheless, despite the undeniable progress in development of the phonological/orthographic competence that at-risk learners make, it is possible that they keep lagging behind good foreign language learners (Sparks *et al.*, 1991, 1997a).

Interestingly, any improvement in the sound and sound-symbol performance as regards the native language is frequently reflected in enhanced foreign language performance. This idea is clearly supported by research outcome, showing that students with stronger native language reading and spelling skills obtain higher grades in foreign language courses and are more verbally proficient in a foreign language

(Sparks et al., 1995b). Sparks et al. (1992b) conducted a preliminary investigation of the effects of the multisensory structured learning (MSL) approach on native and foreign language performance over one year. The pre- and post-test scores on the native language and foreign language aptitude tests of three groups of at-risk high school students, enrolled in special sections of a first-year Spanish course, were compared. Two groups were instructed with the use of the MSL approach, one was taught in both English (native language) and Spanish (foreign language) (MSL/ES), the other only in Spanish (MSL/S), while the remaining group (NO-MSL) was under the influence of the traditional foreign language teaching methodology. The hypothesis that both the native language phonological skills as well as foreign language aptitude of the students receiving the MSL instruction in a foreign language will improve was supported. However, the two MSL groups differed in the gains they achieved. More precisely, the MSL/ES group made significant progress on all the native language phonological measures and the long and short forms of the modern language aptitude test (MLAT) as well as its subtests. On the other hand, the MSL/S group demonstrated vital attainment only with reference to the long and short forms of the MLAT and not its subtests and did not show any noticeable procurement as far as the native language phonological measures were concerned. Additionally, the MSL/ES group were critically superior in the matter of receptive vocabulary and verbal short-term memory measures. By contrast, the NO-MSL group made no significant gains on the native language and foreign language aptitude measures. It clearly follows from the abovementioned findings that students with weak native language skills find it helpful and beneficial to use their native language in order to support foreign language instruction with respect to phonological and syntactical systems. In addition, it may seem rather unreasonable to expect students with weak phonological processing skills to succeed in FLL, which starts out with listening to a foreign language and assumes students to learn to comprehend and speak a foreign language similar to the way they acquired their native language. Thus, logically, the instruction should rely more on the simultaneous oral (listening and speaking) and written (reading and spelling) practice in learning the sound/symbol system in a foreign language in the cases of at-risk foreign language learners.

The above study was replicated with the same students (cohort 1) and a new group of students (cohort 2) to further scrutinise the effectiveness of the MSL/ES instruction on native and foreign language performance. Students from cohort 2 made significant gains on the native language phonological test and foreign language aptitude test. Students from cohort 1 were followed over the second year of foreign language instruction in order to more precisely determine the efficacy of the

MSL tutoring. The group maintained their initial acquirement on all the native and foreign language aptitude measures over the second year of foreign language study (Sparks & Ganschow, 1993). Evidence from these studies suggests that the at-risk foreign language students are able to display and maintain the acquisition in a foreign language as well as improve their foreign language aptitude due to the effect of the direct MSL/ES instruction.

In another study, Ganschow and Sparks (1995) analysed the results of direct tutoring in foreign language phonology (Spanish) on the native language skills and foreign language aptitude of at-risk foreign language learners. The multisensory approach to teaching phonological/orthographic aspects of a foreign language again resulted in improvement in the native language performance, thus allowing the at-risk foreign language learners to catch up with not-at-risk learners in at least some aspects of the phonological/orthographic measures. Furthermore, foreign language coaching (multisensory structured language instruction for at-risk learners and traditional for not-at-risk learners) resulted in amelioration, touching on foreign language aptitude as regards both at-risk and not-at-risk learners. It is indicated in this study that foreign language instruction alone is powerful enough to amend one's phonological/orthographic, syntactic and semantic skills as well as rote memory as measured by the MLAT. The odds are that it is indeed the specific instruction in the phonology/orthography that makes the difference for the at-risk foreign language learners, who show no improvement in either foreign language aptitude or in any native language skill after one year of foreign language traditional instruction (without direct and explicit teaching of the sound system of a foreign language) (Sparks *et al.*, 1992b).

Still, despite substantial native language and foreign language aptitude upgrading, the at-risk learners repeatedly and significantly evidence falling behind the not-at-risk students, relevant to foreign language aptitude measured by the MLAT (Ganschow & Sparks, 1995). Thus, direct instruction in phonology/orthography, even though apparently beneficial for at-risk learners, tends not to guarantee the equalising of the scores for the at-risk and not-at-risk students on the foreign language aptitude test.

Sparks *et al.* (1997a) obtained similar results, consistent with the findings of the previous study (Ganschow & Sparks, 1995), with regard to the performance on the native language and foreign language aptitude measures of the at-risk and not-at-risk learners, after two years of foreign language (Spanish) tutoring. Again, the at-risk group underwent multisensory structured language training, while the not-at-risk group received instruction via traditional methodology. Additionally, the experiment aimed at answering the question, whether the two-year multisensory structured study in Spanish phonology/orthography exerted a positive influence on the native language abilities and foreign language aptitude of the at-risk learners. The outcome of the research suggests that both the at-risk and not-at-risk students achieved decent gains in foreign language aptitude over one year of foreign language teaching. Moreover, the at-risk learners managed to maintain their gains over the second year of direct multisensory structured instruction, however, they were unable to increase them, unlike the not-at-risk learners. What follows is that the multisensory structured language coaching again proves particularly salient and efficient for the at-risk individuals; nevertheless, despite explicit training they repeatedly tend to fall behind the not-at-risk students with respect to phonological/ orthographic competence.

The benefits of MSL instruction in Spanish as a foreign language were also examined in another study by Sparks *et al.* (1998c). Four groups of high school at-risk and not-at-risk students participated in this study. The at-risk students were assigned to three groups: MSL – multisensory Spanish training in self-contained classrooms, SC – traditional teaching of Spanish, provided in self-contained classrooms, and NSC – traditional tutoring in Spanish, in regular (not self-contained) classes. The at-risk groups varied in terms of both the type of foreign language classroom (self-contained versus not self-contained) and the type of foreign language instruction (MSL versus traditional with instructional accommodations). Not-at-risk students constituted the fourth group (NAR) and received traditional lessons in Spanish in regular classes, similar to the instruction provided to the NSC group. The three different at-risk groups were compared on native language, foreign language aptitude, and foreign language oral and written proficiency measures. The performance of the not-at-risk group on the same measures was compared to the three at-risk groups. In light of the previously mentioned research findings, it is unsurprising that the MSL group evidenced significant gains in the foreign language aptitude as measured by the MLAT, while the SC and NSC groups did not. Thus, the proposition of the superiority of MSL for at-risk students over the traditional textbook-based instruction gained clear support. Similarly, the NAR group manifested vital gains on the MLAT. Again, consistently with the outcome of other studies, this time, even though the MSL group improved their scores on the MLAT, they again appeared to be unable to keep pace with the NAR group. It needs stressing that all four groups demonstrated noticeable achievements over time on some native language skills. Still, expectedly, the scores of the at-risk foreign language learners on these measures usually fell behind the scores of the not-at-risk students. The MSL and NAR groups obtained substantially greater gains on the foreign language aptitude and native language tests (reading comprehension, word recognition and pseudo-word reading). In addition, they scored significantly higher on the measure of oral and written foreign language proficiency than SC and NSC groups; intriguingly, no differences relating to this particular measure were indicated between the MSL and NAR groups. Seemingly, such a finding constitutes a strong piece of evidence for the efficacy of the MSL instruction for teaching a foreign language to at-risk foreign language learners. All in all, even though the at-risk students from the SC and NSC groups achieved certain levels of foreign language proficiency, which eventually allowed them to pass the foreign language courses, the learners who received MSL instruction appeared to be more competent in the foreign language than SC and NSC students. Thus, drawing on the abovementioned research findings, a conclusion can be put forward that, apparently, at-risk foreign language learners are capable of acquiring specific levels of foreign language capacity and that it is most effectively realised when MSL techniques are employed. The application of the MSL techniques comparatively frequently enables foreign language at-risk students to attain the levels of foreign language ability commensurate with those reached by the not-at-risk foreign language learners.

Descriptive and empirical studies pertaining to the effectiveness of the MSL approach in teaching a foreign language to at-risk foreign language learners have also been reported in languages other than Spanish. Sparks *et al.* (1996) report an attempt they undertook to determine the effect of the study of Latin by means of MSL instruction on the native language skills and foreign language aptitude of LD students. Three groups of foreign language learners were selected for the comparisons: non-LD learners – who were taught Latin with the use of traditional methodology (NLD group), LD students – who received MSL tutoring in Latin (LD-MSL group), and LD individuals – who experienced a study of Latin via traditional method (LD-NO/MSL group). Ostensibly, the findings of this study generally support the conclusions of the previously cited research on students learning Spanish as a foreign language. As expected, the training in Latin enhanced the scores on one or more of the native language phonological measures and foreign language aptitude test of the NLD and LD/MSL groups, but not the LD/NO-MSL group. Furthermore, in spite of the fact that the LD-MSL group showed substantial improvements on some of the phonological/orthographic measures, they kept scoring well below the NLD students, who, in addition, were superior to the LD groups as regards the foreign language aptitude test. To sum up, the at-risk foreign language learners' native language faculty and foreign language aptitude can improve with foreign language study. Unfortunately, they are unlikely to be comparable to the language skills of the not-at-risk foreign language learners.

Schneider (1999) successfully adapted the MSL approach to teach German as a foreign language by expanding the native language MSL principles to the training in foreign language phonology/orthography, grammar and vocabulary/morphology. The author referred to her adaptations of the MSL as MSML, which stands for multisensory structured metacognitive instruction, because she explicitly addressed the development of metacognitive processing skills. Similarly, Downey et al. (2000) demonstrated that Latin classes conducted in accordance with instructional modifications introduced in order to cater to the needs of college students with dyslexia proved successful.

The findings of the studies described above yield several implications for teaching foreign languages to students with dyslexia. They support the effectiveness of direct multisensory instruction in the phonology/orthography of foreign languages. As already mentioned, an accumulating body of evidence indicates that difficulties, whether subtle or overt, experienced by a great majority of poor foreign language learners are of phonological nature (Sparks & Ganschow, 1993). Thus, learners with dyslexia, who hardly benefit from methodologies that force them to intuitively discover the phonological structure of a new language, will most probably take advantage of the direct instruction in the phonology of the target language.

The reluctance of foreign language educators to accept the importance of explicit multisensory instruction in phonology and grammar is, presumably, a natural consequence of their being good language learners themselves (Sparks et al., 1991). Arguably, more attention should be given to acquainting pre-service and in-service teachers of foreign languages with the constitutional nature of dyslexic difficulties in the first place, as well as with the effective teaching methods and the techniques that could be employed while working with students with dyslexia.

To further benefit students with dyslexia, there should be more collaboration between special educators and foreign language teachers. Since native and foreign language skills are interrelated, consequently, weak native language skills, especially phonological, have a natural impact on FLL. Direct multisensory instruction in a foreign language not only substantially improves FLL, but also has a potential to increase native language phonology (Ganschow & Sparks, 1995; Sparks et al., 1992b). Moreover, the improvement in the performance on the sound identification and manipulation tasks, and in the awareness of the spelling choices of students in their native language may have a positive effect on their foreign language skills – it has been shown that students with stronger native language reading and spelling skills achieve higher grades in foreign language courses and are more verbally proficient in a foreign language (Sparks et al., 1995).

Small-scale intervention study in dyslexia and foreign language learning

Introduction and method

This subsection presents the outcome of research conducted in the field of teaching English as a foreign language to Polish students with dyslexia. The study concerned the effectiveness of the direct multi-sensory instruction in improving word reading and spelling skills in English, through the systematic study of selected grapheme-phoneme relations, spelling patterns and rules.[3] Three groups of learners participated in the study, one experimental and two control groups. Progress was measured by a set of reading and spelling pre- and post-tests. Within- and between-group comparisons concerning the scores on pre-tests and post-tests were used. After six months of training, significant improvement in the ability to relate phonemes to graphemes was shown in the experimental group, which outperformed non-dyslexics. Even though the results are very promising, they must be treated with caution due to the small number of participants and absence of the comparison treatment.

In languages with deep orthographies, like English, the grapheme-phoneme relations are especially difficult to learn. The following characteristics of these relations seem particularly troublesome, first, the capacity of a single sound to be graphically represented by more than one letter; second, the fact that a single sound may be represented by different letters or letter combinations in different words (inconsistent spelling); and third, the fact that a given letter or a combination of letters may represent more than one sound and that there is a great number of exceptions and irregular words.

To elucidate the operation of the MSL, and, specifically, to show the rationale for the explicit teaching of the grapheme-phoneme conversion rules, three groups of English language learners were selected. One group, defined as the experimental, consisted of five individuals with dyslexia. The remaining two groups were labelled the control groups: the first was made up of 10 individuals with dyslexia, and the second was composed of 10 students without dyslexia.

The study took place in a secondary school in one of the major cities in Poland, where 15 students were randomly chosen from a dyslexic group of 100 – the number amounting to about 12% of the school population – and assigned to two groups. Five students (two males, three females, mean age 17.6) formed the experimental group and ten students (eight males, two females, mean age 17) formed one of the control groups. In a further selection, ten students (five males, five females, mean age 17) from the non-dyslexic part of the school population were assigned to the second control group. All the students from the experimental group and the control group with dyslexia had an up-to-date assessment, indicating specific difficulties in learning to read and write. They had clearly non-general learning difficulties, but limited and specific difficulties in learning to read and spell. Their development was normal, as was their intelligence, which ranked average or above average. There were no emotional or personality disorders, nor any hearing or sight deficits. Finally, no environmental or educational negligence was observed. All students with dyslexia were receiving compensatory teaching services in their native language, in the form of self-contained classes, run by the school teacher-therapist. However, no compensatory teaching to minimise foreign language difficulties was officially granted. All three groups were enrolled in their regular English classes at school, conducted with the use of traditional foreign language methodology by the same teacher, who refrained from devoting time to explicit presentation of phoneme-grapheme conversion rules. Students were expected to infer these relations naturally and spontaneously from the input they received in the language classroom. The author provided tutorial MSL sessions for the experimental group, whereas the control group with dyslexia and the control group without dyslexia attended no such classes. No tutoring sessions with the application of any comparison approach (alternative to MSL) were introduced in the study.

As far as their ability to read and spell in the native language is concerned, no additional tests were given to the participants with dyslexia apart from the formal assessment of these skills that they had undergone in the pedagogical-psychological dispensary. Interviews with the teacher of Polish and the teacher-therapist, who run the correction-compensation classes, were conducted in order to collect qualitative data on the estimated level of the participants' skills in Polish. The dyslexics' native language skills were described as considerably poorer than the skills of the non-dyslexic participants of the study, in most cases lower than satisfactory.

Prior to the introduction of training in the experimental group, skills in English as a foreign language of all the students participating in the study were evaluated by their teacher of English on the 6-point scale, where 1 denoted unsatisfactory, while 6 stood for excellent. Additionally, all the students were asked for self-assessment, applying the same criteria. The following aspects were assessed: reading aloud, reading silently with comprehension, listening comprehension, speaking, written assignments, pronunciation, vocabulary, spelling and grammar. Students with dyslexia were assessed by their teacher of English as very poor learners of English, usually representing the level lower than satisfactory. Students with dyslexia perceived themselves as poor foreign language learners as well. Generally, learners with dyslexia were assessed by the teacher of English as much poorer learners of English than their non-dyslexic peers participating in the study.

The study sought answers to the following research questions: Do Polish learners with dyslexia experience greater difficulties in learning the English phonological-orthographic systems than their non-dyslexic peers? Does direct, multisensory and structured instruction in selected grapheme-phoneme correspondences and spelling rules improve dyslexic learners' ability to decode and encode the language? The proposed hypotheses for the present study assumed that:

(1) Polish learners with dyslexia experienced greater difficulties in learning the English phonological-orthographic system with the use of traditional instruction than their non-dyslexic peers.
(2) Direct, multisensory and structured instruction in selected English grapheme-phoneme correspondences and spelling rules would improve dyslexic learners' ability to decode and encode the language (read and spell).
(3) Pre- and post-test comparisons in the experimental group would reveal significant differences between the results of pre- and post-tests, indicating a considerable gain.
(4) Pre- and post-test comparisons in the control group with dyslexia would not reveal significant differences between the results of pre- and post-tests, indicating no considerable gain.
(5) Pre- and post-test comparisons in the control group without dyslexia would reveal significant differences between the results of pre- and post-tests, indicating a considerable gain.
(6) There would not be significant differences between the results of the spelling and reading pre-tests in the experimental group and the control group with dyslexia. Significant differences between the results of the spelling and reading post-tests in the experimental group and the control group with dyslexia would be found. The experimental group would show greater pre- and post-test gains than the control group with dyslexia.
(7) Significant differences between the results of the spelling and reading pre- and post-tests in the experimental group and the control group without dyslexia would be found. Despite considerable progress and gain in the knowledge of English grapheme-phoneme correspondences, the experimental group would still lag slightly behind the control group without dyslexia or, in other words, would not show greater pre- or post-test gains.
(8) Significant differences between the results of the spelling and reading pre- and post-tests in the control group with dyslexia and the control group without dyslexia would be found. The control

group without dyslexia would show greater pre- and post-test gains than the control group with dyslexia.

In order to verify the proposed hypotheses, the research was conducted with the use of the experimental procedure, aiming to produce an observable gain in the experimental group, stemming from the introduction of an innovative factor, responsible for improvement of learning and teaching (Komorowska, 1982). The independent variable in the present study is the direct multisensory language instruction in the English phonological/orthographic system. The dependent variable is made up of the results of teaching the English grapheme/phoneme correspondence using the MSL approach. Thus, the dependent variable is operationalised as the test scores after training in the experimental group.

The design of the study departs slightly from the experimental scheme of the classic type, which normally involves a pre-test, a post-test and a control group (Komorowska, 1982). The present research employed two different control groups and two post-tests, as shown in Table 5.1.

In Table 5.1, PRE-S denotes a spelling pre-test, PRE-R – reading pre-test, POST-S1 – first spelling post-test and POST-R1 – first reading post-test administered immediately after the treatment and, finally, POST-S2 stands for the second spelling post-test and POST-R2 – for the second reading post-test, administered two weeks after the treatment.

The pre-test (PRE-S and PRE-R) and the post-test 1 (POST-S1 and POST-R1), as well as the post-test 2 (POST-S2 and POST-R2), consisted of a word level reading and spelling task. The pre-test and post-test 1 comprised exactly the same words, whereas the post-test 2 featured a different list (see Appendix 1). The words included in the pre- and the post-tests were carefully selected to contain all the phoneme/grapheme regularities and spelling choices covered in the programme (see Appendix 2). Furthermore, the number of words with the same spelling patterns was equal across the tests.

Before the introduction of the experimental factor in the experimental group, spelling and reading pre-tests were administered to all three

Table 5.1 The design of the study

Experimental group	→	PRE-S, PRE-R	→	Treatment	→	POST-S1, POST-R1	→	POST-S2, POST-R2
Control group with dyslexia	→	PRE-S, PRE-R	→	–	→	POST-S1, POST-R1	→	POST-S2, POST-R2
Control group without dyslexia	→	PRE-S, PRE-R	→	–	→	POST-S1, POST-R1	→	POST-S2, POST-R2

groups. Each group was tested separately: the spelling test had a written form and was conducted with the whole group. The reading test was administered individually and students were recorded. A list of 63 words was first dictated to the students; then, after a break, a recording was made of the students reading the same list of words. Each word was dictated in isolation twice, interspersing the dictation with a single reading of the word in a sentence. The students were to write down individual words onto the form provided. There was no difference between the groups regarding the time allotted for testing, and no time limits were set. A special education teacher, who works at the school where the study took place, assisted in the administration of the pre-test. In the assessment of the students' performance, only the words that were spelled and read correctly were accepted. One point was given for each correctly spelt or read word. The handwriting of all the students participating in the study was intelligible enough, so there were no dubious cases. The students scored a point for every read word as long as they could make themselves understood. Even though 63 words make up a long list, testing did not seem to tire the students, on the contrary, they were eager to co-operate all through.

In the next stage of the research, the experimental group was exposed to the operation of the experimental variable (MSL instruction), which was not applied to the control groups. The classes for the experimental group were conducted by the author herself. They were all 90-minute contact sessions, which took place once a week, over a period of six months. During the treatment in the experimental group, direct multisensory teaching of the phoneme/grapheme relations and spelling rules in English was conducted in a structured and step-by-step fashion. The specific problem areas covered during the training were the same as in the pre- and post-tests. The instructional style followed the principles of the direct multisensory structured instruction, described earlier in this chapter. Sample tasks, teaching aids and worksheets used in the programme can be found in Chapter 6.

Immediately after the treatment had ended, the spelling post-test 1 and the reading post-test 1 were administered to all three groups. Two weeks later, the spelling post-test 2 and the reading post-test 2 were administered to all participants. Analogous procedure to that used during pre-test administration was applied.

The current data analysis consists of the pre- and post-test comparisons both within and between the groups. The pre- and post-tests comparisons for each group were generated by determining the means and standard deviations. The differences between the pre- and post-tests' means were analysed using the Wilcoxon Test. The pre- and post-tests comparisons between groups were generated by determining the means and standard deviations. The Mann–Whitney U-test was used to

Table 5.2 Results of the spelling and reading pre- and post-tests in the experimental group, the control group with dyslexia and the control group without dyslexia

Test	Experimental group Mean%	SD	Control group with dyslexia Mean%	SD	Control group without dyslexia Mean%	SD
PRE-S	27.62	6.47	24.60	8.06	38.41	8.13
PRE-R	57.46	7.16	59.21	7.83	76.51	6.73
POST-S1	71.74	13.54	26.19	8.10	46.35	9.54
POST-S2	87.62	6.76	62.38	5.85	79.37	6.31
POST-R1	82.86	7.85	27.78	8.58	48.73	11.62
POST-R2	83.81	3.56	57.46	8.97	74.76	5.76

determine the possible existence of any significant differences between the experimental group, the control group with dyslexia and the control group without dyslexia (Jóźwiak & Podgórski, 1994; Luszniewicz & Słaby, 2001; Stanisz, 1998).

Table 5.2 gives the results of all the tests in all three groups. The pre-test results were low in all three groups, but it can also be seen that the non-dyslexic group performed better, in both spelling and reading tasks, than their dyslexic peers. It is also observable that spelling posed more severe difficulties for learners with dyslexia than reading: the experimental and the dyslexic control group achieved 27.62 and 24.60%, respectively on spelling, but approximately 60% each on reading. Figures 5.1 and 5.2 illustrate the results of the spelling and reading pre- and post-tests in the experimental group, the control group with dyslexia and the control group without dyslexia, respectively.

Pre- and post-test comparisons within and between groups

In the experimental group, the POST-R1 resulted in the highest mean score (87.62%). The low mean score of the PRE-S (27.62%) and the relatively high mean scores of the POST-S1 (71.74%) and the POST-S2 (82.86%) indicated an improvement in spelling skills in the experimental group. Analogously, the low mean score of the PRE-R (57.46%) and the relatively high mean scores of the POST-R1 (87.62%) and POST-R2 (83.81%) marked an improvement in reading skills in the experimental group. Statistically significant differences emerged between the results of the following pairs of variables: PRE-S and POST-S1, PRE-S and POST-S2, PRE-R and POST-R1, as well as PRE-R and POST-R2 (in all cases $T = 0.0$, $p = 0.04$). Conversely, no significant differences were found between the

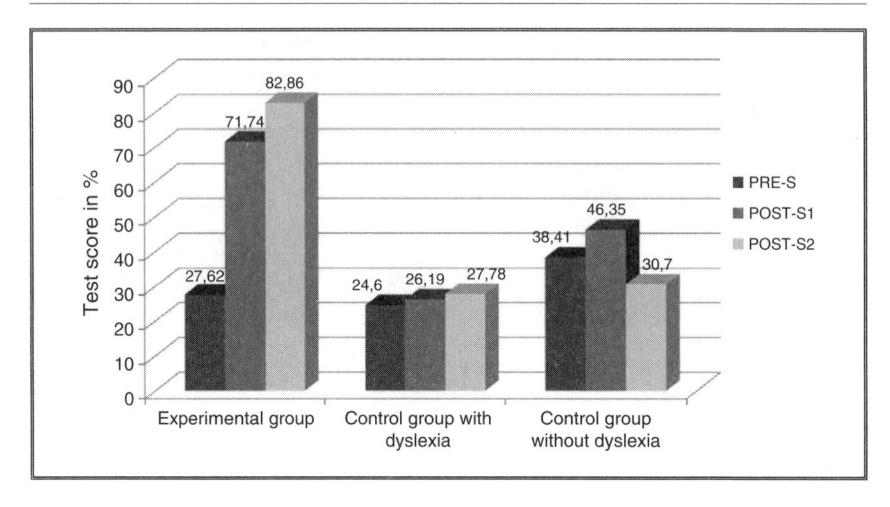

Figure 5.1 Results of the spelling pre- and post-tests in the experimental group, the control group with dyslexia and the control group without dyslexia

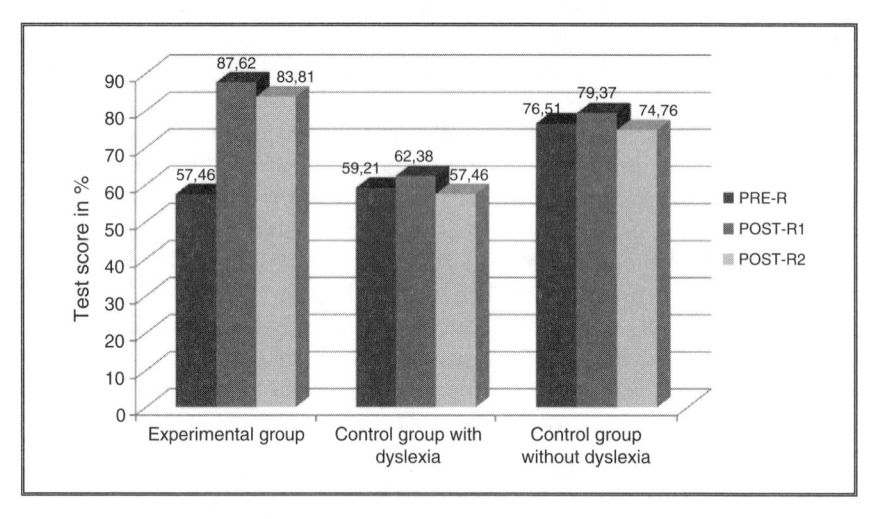

Figure 5.2 Results of the reading pre- and post-tests in the experimental group, the control group with dyslexia and the control group without dyslexia

results of the following pairs of tests: POST-S1 and POST-S2 ($T = 0.0$, $p = 0.07$), POST-R1 and POST-R2 ($T = 2.0$, $p = 0.14$).

Students in the control group with dyslexia achieved the highest mean score on the POST-R1 (62.38%) and the lowest on the PRE-S (24.60%). The mean scores of all the spelling tests – PRE-S (24.60%), POST-S1 (26.19%) and POST-S2 (27.78%) – had similar values, which indicated no improvement in spelling skills in the control group with dyslexia. The mean scores of all the reading tests – PRE-R (59.21%), POST-R1 (62.38%) and POST-R2 (57.46%) – had similar values, which again shows no improvement in reading skills in the control group with dyslexia. In contrast to what was observed in the experimental group, there were no statistically significant differences between the results of the following pairs of tests in the control group with dyslexia: PRE-S and POST-S1 ($T = 11.5$, $p = 0.36$), PRE-S and POST-S2 ($T = 9.0$, $p = 0.21$), PRE-R and POST-R1 ($T = 12.0$, $p = 0.21$), as well as PRE-R and POST-R2 ($T = 13.0$, $p = 0.26$).

In the control group without dyslexia, the highest mean score was yielded by the POST-R1 (79.37%), while the lowest by the PRE-S (38.41%). The mean score of the PRE-S (38.41%) was lower than the mean scores of the POST-S1 (46.35%) and the POST-S2 (48.73%), which might indicate some enhancement of the spelling skills in the control group without dyslexia. Even though the differences were not as considerable as in the experimental group, they were still significant in statistical terms. The mean scores of all the reading tests – PRE-R (76.51%), POST-R1 (79.37%) and POST-R2 (74.76%) – had similar values, which showed that the reading skills in the control group without dyslexia underwent no improvement. There were statistically significant differences between the results of the PRE-S and POST-S1 ($T = 0.0$, $p = 0.007$), as well as the PRE-S and POST-S2 ($T = 1.0$, $p = 0.01$). No statistically significant differences between the PRE-R and POST-R1 ($T = 5.0$, $p = 0.07$) or between the PRE-R and POST-R2 ($T = 11.0$, $p = 0.33$) emerged in the control group without dyslexia.

The results of the PRE-S ($U = 23.5$, $p = 0.85$) and PRE-R ($U = 20.0$, $p = 0.54$) indicated no differences between the experimental group and the control group with dyslexia. By contrast, statistically significant differences were observed between the results of all post-tests, with the experimental group outperforming the control group with dyslexia (POST-S1 ($U = 2.0$, $p = 0.005$), POST-S2 ($U = 0.0$, $p = 0.002$), POST-R1 ($U = 2.5$, $p = 0.006$) and POST-R2 ($U = 1.0$, $p = 0.003$)).

As regards the comparison between the experimental and the control group without dyslexia, significant differences were yielded on three measures: PRE-R ($U = 4.0$, $p = 0.01$) in favour of the control group without dyslexia, POST-S1 ($U = 8.0$, $p = 0.04$) and POST-S2 ($U = 3.5$, $p = 0.008$) both in favour of the experimental group. The observable differences between the means of the other tests were small and of no statistical significance: PRE-S ($U = 18.0$, $p = 0.39$), POST-R1 ($U = 11.0$, $p = 0.09$), POST-R2 ($U = 9.5$, $p = 0.06$).

As anticipated, the control group without dyslexia performed better on all measures than the control group with dyslexia. The differences were statistically significant between the results of the PRE-R ($U = 12.5$, $p = 0.005$), POST-S1 ($U = 15.0$, $p = 0.008$), POST-S2 ($U = 18.0$, $p = 0.015$), POST-R1 ($U = 10.5$, $p = 0.003$) and POST-R2 ($U = 18.5$, $p = 0.02$).

However, there were no statistically significant differences between these two groups as far as the result of PRE-S ($U = 27.5$, $p = 0.09$) is concerned.

Discussion of results

Polish learners with dyslexia experience greater problems in learning the English phonological-orthographic system than their non-dyslexic peers, as was revealed by the poorer results of the word spelling and reading pre-tests in the experimental group and the control group with dyslexia in comparison to the control group without dyslexia. This has been further confirmed by the poor achievement in the spelling post-test of the dyslexic control group (Hypothesis 1).

Hypothesis 3 was also supported as the pre- and post-test comparisons within the experimental group revealed significant differences between the results of the pre- and post-tests, which indicated a considerable gain. A very low mean score of the PRE-S (27.62%) and relatively high mean scores of the POST-S1 (71.74%) and POST-S2 (82.86%) indicated an improvement of spelling skills in the experimental group. A similar situation was found for the reading tasks – a low mean score of the PRE-R (57.46%) and relatively high mean scores of the POST-R1 (87.62%) and POST-R2 (83.81%) meant enhanced reading skills in the experimental group. Moreover, the above differences were all statistically significant. Thus, the experimental group performed significantly better on completion of the training than at the onset of the instructional programme. Hence, the increased efficiency of the students in the experimental group on the spelling and reading tasks after the training, as compared to their scores before, can be attributed predominantly to the MSL intervention rather than to other factors (Hypothesis 2).

The above assertion is strengthened by the fact that no significant differences between the mean scores on the spelling and reading pre- and post-tests were found in the control group with dyslexia. Such finding had been anticipated in view of the absence of MSL instruction. The mean scores of all the spelling tests had similar values, which indicated no improvement in the spelling skills in this group. Likewise, the values of the mean scores of all the reading tests were similar, which, again, indicated no improvement. Finally, no statistically significant differences emerged between the following pairs of variables: PRE-S and POST-S1, PRE-S and POST-S2, PRE-R and POST-R1, as well as PRE-R and POST-R2. Thus, it can be concluded that, despite the traditional instruction the group received at school, they did not make any progress in terms of their word spelling and reading skills (Hypothesis 4).

In the control group without dyslexia, statistically significant differences were found between the results of the PRE-S and the POST-S1, as well as the PRE-S and the POST-S2, which indicates some improvement in the spelling skills in this group. However, one should not lose sight of the fact that they were, from the start, in a much more beneficial position than the other groups, since they demonstrated no specific developmental reading or spelling disorders. It could then be assumed that in their case the traditional instruction was successful. Interestingly, the mean scores on all their reading tests had similar values, with no statistically significant differences, which indicated no improvement in the reading skills of this group after six months of regular instruction. The control group without dyslexia did not achieve any progress in their word reading skills. Hence, Hypothesis 5 that the pre- and post-test comparisons in the control group without dyslexia would reveal significant differences between the results of the pre- and post-tests was only partially supported.

The results of the spelling and reading pre-tests were poor in the case of the experimental group and the control group with dyslexia, and the scores did not differ significantly between these two groups. By contrast, Hypothesis 6, stating that there would be significant differences between the results of the spelling and reading post-tests, received clear confirmation, as did the comparative postulate that the experimental group would show greater pre-and post-test gains than the control group with dyslexia. Both groups received traditional instruction in English as a foreign language during the experiment, but the control group with dyslexia, unlike the experimental group, did not undergo MSL training, which could be the reason why they did not make any progress on the spelling and reading post-test. Apparently, the experimental group demonstrated enormous progress in acquiring the relationships between the graphemes and phonemes and, consequently, in the word reading and spelling (Hypothesis 2). The role of the direct multisensory instruction in the success of the experimental group cannot thus be overestimated.

Surprisingly, Hypothesis 7, stating that significant differences would occur between the results of the spelling and reading pre- and post-tests in the experimental group and control group without dyslexia – the scores favouring the control group, was only partially validated. To even greater surprise, the ensuing hypothesis that, despite considerable progress, the experimental group would still be slightly lagging behind the control group without dyslexia, was not verified either. The latter hypothesis was based on recent empirical findings suggesting that, in spite of explicit instruction in phonological/orthographic skills, at-risk learners are still likely to continue to lag behind good foreign language learners in terms of their phonological/orthographic skills (Sparks *et al.*, 1991, 1997a). However, as can be seen from the present study, students with dyslexia (experimental group) may be no worse than their non-dyslexic peers; in fact, they may well be capable of achieving better scores in spelling and reading tests. It needs stressing that the experimental group's scores on the post-tests after the implementation of direct multisensory training, a performance markedly better than that of the control group without dyslexia, was the most surprising outcome of the study. Even allowing for a considerable gain, the experimental group was still expected to situate itself on the achievement scale slightly behind the non-dyslexic students.

Hypothesis 8 that there would be significant differences between the control group with dyslexia and the control group without dyslexia was confirmed by the results of all the spelling and reading pre- and post-tests. The control group without dyslexia received much higher scores. There were statistically significant differences between the results of all the tests, apart from the spelling pre-test. These findings prove that students with developmental dyslexia experience greater difficulties in learning English as a foreign language with the use of traditional instruction than their non-dyslexic peers, as supposed in Hypothesis 1.

Although originally weaker, the students from the experimental group showed considerable improvement in their performance on all the spelling and reading tests. The calibre of their academic growth as well as its rapidity indicate the effectiveness of direct multisensory instruction in the area of grapheme/phoneme correspondences and spelling rules in English, contributing to an enhanced performance of Polish students on the word spelling and reading tests.

The results of the study yield several implications for teaching foreign languages to students with dyslexia. They support the effectiveness of direct multisensory instruction in the phonology/orthography of the English language. Learners with dyslexia, who hardly benefit from methodologies that force them to intuitively discover the phonological structure of a new language, will most probably take advantage of direct instruction in the phonology of the target language. Nevertheless, however promising a start, the outcome of the study must be treated cautiously because of the small sample size and the absence of a comparison approach in tutoring sessions. These restrictions definitely limit the generalisability of the results, which should be considered tentative and subject to further investigation. Even though there are several sound theoretical reasons for believing that the MSL approach applied in tutoring sessions contributed significantly to the progress observed in the experimental group, this supposition remains just that. What can be safely inferred from the findings of the study is that intervention itself exerted a causal effect, however similar inferences as to the nature of the intervention cannot be applied at this stage.

Another issue concerning the degree of difficulty that the individual students had in Polish reading and spelling would certainly require more thorough investigation, as this might have been a relevant factor determining the outcome of the study. Moreover, it would have been interesting to find out whether the multisensory direct instruction in English phonology had any influence on the native language skills of the students with dyslexia from the experimental group. Furthermore, it would be necessary to carry out longitudinal research upon dyslexic versus non-dyslexic students, to study the effects – regarding both native and foreign language skills – of direct multisensory instruction as opposed to the traditional approach. Comparing the efficacy of the MSL structured instruction with other than traditional instructional practices in foreign language teaching, including the alternative comparison approach applied in tutoring sessions, with regard to their effects on word reading and spelling skills would yield some interesting results. It also has to be noted that the results of the study indicate that, perhaps, direct multisensory instruction in English as a foreign language would also be beneficial for non-dyslexic students, as it would allow them to achieve even greater success in their spelling and reading skills. While it was beyond the scope of this study to check out such a possibility, the specific effects of MSL instruction on non-dyslexic students should still be determined in future research. This study has been an attempt to inspire further experimentation with the use of the direct multisensory approach, an activity promising, in the long run, a more successful foreign language instruction offered to learners with dyslexia and potentially non-LD students as well.

Educational Accommodations Towards Learners with Dyslexia

The fundamental issue seems to be raising awareness of dyslexia among all parties involved in the creation and functioning of the educational environment. It appears particularly important in light of the multiple formal regulations, which have been introduced in many countries, concerning the conditions and ways of assessing, classifying, promoting and conducting examinations for students with special educational needs. Children with special educational needs can benefit from the type of schooling available to the majority of children, usually through a set of special educational arrangements, which adapt the system towards their needs and abilities – it is referred to as *inclusion education* or *mainstreaming*. The prevailing positive attitude of the educational stakeholders towards inclusive education for children with dyslexia needs to be translated into significant changes implemented into the existing educational systems if these children are to be truly included.

Unique, diverse abilities, needs, interests and ways of learning reflect individual differences between children, and these attributes require understanding, support and incorporating into the educational systems that aspire to be inclusive. Principally, inclusion policy involves rearrangements at the level of school management and those introduced by the individual teachers in order to address the special needs of children with dyslexia (e.g. individual education plans). Teachers' and parents' awareness and alertness can trigger early identification of learning difficulties, ideally followed by the offer of a wide range of supporting activities and services, matched to the severity of the disorder.

As much as the appropriate inclusion essentially does its job in supporting educational endeavours in most cases, the most severely disordered children with dyslexia may still require a more individualised, exclusive approach to help them overcome their impairments. Dyslexic problems are of varying degrees of severity, and the disorder is probably best illustrated as a continuum of difficulties, ranging from subtle through mild to severe. Thus, it seems that there is enough logic behind viewing the intensity and range of educational intervention and help as parallel to the continuum of difficulties. Some children with dyslexia can be included in the educational system with ease, given the fact that minimum alterations and accommodations are incorporated into it; however, for other children more individualised, small group or one-to-one treatment seems a must (Bogdanowicz & Sayles, 2004).

The legal status of the special rights – defined as specific enabling solutions and arrangements – offered to children with dyslexia varies considerably across countries, schools and teachers. Thus, the availability of particular accommodations, influencing the actual everyday school life of children with dyslexia, may be regulated by a national policy, school policy or can be entirely at a teacher's discretion. Indeed, this last option seems to be the case in the majority of instances. The aforementioned special rights may cover the areas of assessment, alternative ways of performing at school, special conditions during examinations and foreign language study (the data for the analysis were collected in 20 countries; Bogdanowicz & Sayles, 2004).

The legislation concerning the principles of provision and organisation of psychological-pedagogical help in public kindergartens, schools and institutions, suggests that any special, more individualised help for students with specific learning difficulties should be organised in the form of correction-compensation classes. However, there is usually no mention of foreign language instruction, whereby, as it stands, students with dyslexia do not receive any specialised help in FLL. To offset the negative consequences of the above, quite often a regulation is implemented to the effect that students with deep dyslexia be exempted from learning a second foreign language (L3), temporarily or even permanently. As a result, facing the uninviting alternative of their children's failure in learning another foreign language, rather unsurprisingly, parents of learners with dyslexia would most probably take advantage of this option.

Since the reception of a standard educational programme by children with dyslexia is usually hindered, their abilities and needs ought to be catered for through the implementation of specially adapted, more or less individualised (depending on the severity of difficulties) conditions. These would involve the appropriate pace of work, individual learning plans, special teaching techniques and activities, preferably conducted by well-qualified teachers (Bogdanowicz, 1995; Tomaszewska, 2001). In general, teachers are obliged to adjust their educational practices, requirements as well as conditions and forms of external examinations to suit the individual needs and abilities of students with dyslexia, however, how exactly this translates into practical applications significantly differs across schools and teachers.

Ensuring the active participation of students with dyslexia in classroom activities can be successfully executed by adjusting, altering and differentiating teaching practices. It needs stressing though that accommodating does not necessarily mean lowering the requirements, but rather teaching children with dyslexia the way they learn best and devise conditions for them to demonstrate their knowledge and full potential. Because of their underlying impairment, children with dyslexia get slowed down in the course of processing new information, especially in the printed form, and retrieving knowledge from memory. Much can be done to make their learning a less painful experience. It can be achieved through creating a supporting atmosphere and a generally positive learning environment. What they need is more time for completing tasks and help in sustaining concentration so that they can show their strengths and attainment. Signalling that we would like them to respond and securing enough time for preparation as well as providing in advance the questions and issues we want to discuss in a lesson, rather than calling on students for spontaneous responses, markedly mitigates their anxiety and fear. Teachers' teaching style, flexibility, openness, readiness to implement changes in their teaching routines in order to foster scholastic attainment in children with dyslexia greatly influences the way they function at school. Regular consultations and feedback from students makes it possible for teachers to tailor their teaching accommodations most accurately towards the needs and abilities of children with dyslexia.

When we take students' performance in the classroom into account, a set of alterations, the description of which follows, can successfully create a more fertile ground for active and more efficient functioning of children with dyslexia. Students with dyslexia can be released from reading aloud in front of the whole class. Instead, they can provide the teacher with a recording of their reading aloud at home. They work with a selection of texts agreed upon by the teacher, including some texts of their own choice, on topics relevant and interesting to them. Poor handwriting should not disqualify children's work along with poor spelling. Accepting the use of laptop computers (typewriters) for editing, note-taking and generally typing in class instead of hand writing is of great help, together with automated spellers (spellcheckers) and dictionaries.

The use of technology indeed seems invaluable in supporting classroom procedures. Computers, spellcheckers, books on tape, overhead projectors, PowerPoint presentations, tape recorders, the internet, websites, e-mail, let alone more sophisticated assistive technological support, which includes specialised computer software, speech-control tape recorders, reading machines with optical character recognition, listening aids that use a microphone and headset, and voice output systems that read back texts displayed on a computer screen (Ganschow et al., 2000: 188), can considerably aid the efforts of teachers and students alike (cf. Schneider & Crombie, 2003). Even if access to the abovementioned equipment is limited, simply allowing oral instead of a written performance as well as involving a reader, who would read the material aloud, and/or a scribe, who would do the writing part for the children with dyslexia, aids efficiency of work and saves time. This idea can be easily put into practice in the classroom through pair and group work, where students are allocated different tasks and roles. With reference to homework, learners can be encouraged to hand in various assignments prepared in the form of a tape recording or a multimedia presentation rather than in written form.

Frequent repetition and overlearning, being a must for children with dyslexia, brings a danger of boredom and decreasing motivation. Schneider and Crombie (2003) advocate avoiding it through practicing a given learning step in a variety of contexts and incorporating tasks that involve the use of movable teaching aids. Diverse, more or less guided activities using coloured cards, blackboard, picture-to-text matching activities are followed by regular paper-pencil tasks. Moreover, a gradual change from larger to smaller print, coloured to black and white print on cards is suggested, eventually giving up card-sorting tasks in favour of paper and pencil activities. A similar rule, moving from easier to more difficult, is also applied to the character of the task – receptive before productive.

Colour coding and shape coding (cf. Schneider, 1999; Schneider & Crombie, 2003) of various linguistic concepts (e.g. parts of speech; roots, prefixes, suffixes) proves helpful in anchoring them in memory. Numerous movable devices (e.g. illustrating letter-sound patterns, word formation processes or orthographic regularities), for instance orthographic slides, sentence strips, flashcards[4] or tracing pads with varying surfaces, can be designed to enhance learning and remembering. All of the abovementioned aids can be laminated (with the exception of tracing pads of course) for the sake of durability, collected and kept by students in special boxes/files to be easily accessed for reference, review and interactive language games, involving the kinaesthetic-tactile elements of learning.

Kinaesthetic-tactile experience can be easily reinforced by students practicing the position of the mouth and tongue when producing particular sounds and modelling the sound-letter structure of words with the use of tokens; finger tracing of letters and words on various surfaces; colour- and shape-coded card sorting with simultaneous modelling and verbalising language concepts they represent; using tokens, cards with letters and body movements to illustrate linguistic processes (word formation, grammar structures[5]). Also mnemonic teaching aids (Jurek, 2008), which enhance the ability to remember and retrieve information through unique, sometimes humorous, surprising or even nonsensical associations (e.g. a sentence with a picture and demonstration to illustrate its meaning – 'I keep my elb*ow* on a yell*ow* pill*ow* under the wind*ow*' – to remember the spelling choice '-ow' for the /əʊ/ sound), are students' favourite choice. Such activities allow unlimited practice and repetition, aimed at reaching automaticity in a multisensory, boredom- and stress-free fashion. Moreover, engaging students in producing their own sets of such teaching aids proves a valuable learning experience in itself due to the kinaesthetic-tactile learning opportunities it provides.

Importantly, as noted by Schneider and Crombie (2003), kinaesthetic-tactile context can be successfully applied to producing longer texts. Paper outlines are written in keywords on coloured cards. Basic paragraph features – topic sentence with the main idea of the paragraph; supporting details, facts and reasons; examples that support each detail – when colour coded are much more easily understood and manipulated by students, who finally get ready to write texts of several paragraphs. Additionally, conjunction words are provided on separate cards.

The multimodal/multisensory structured input (characterised earlier in this chapter), divided into digestible, logically sequenced (from easier to more difficult) chunks, can be summarised in figures, charts, tables, graphs and illustrations. It is also worth encouraging students to organise and represent the information in mindmaps and spidergrams. Handouts prepared by teachers, containing well-organised notes, summaries, crucial points and conclusions of the lesson, constitute an invaluable help for students with dyslexia as regards later study and consolidation of the material as well as a model that they can follow while preparing notes themselves. However, pages cluttered with information in a rather unclear and chaotic way should be avoided; instead, highlighting salient points together with using larger fonts would most certainly be appreciated. Students are responsible for filing all the handouts together with notes, assignments, projects and homework in portfolios (electronic forms being possible as well). The plan of the lesson, given to students at the beginning of the lesson, together with clear sets of instructions and modelled responses preceding particular tasks back up and direct the successful completion of the tasks and allow the students to concentrate better on the content of the lesson.

The need to develop stronger metacognitive skills, reasoning abilities and self-correction strategies is often highlighted with regard to students with dyslexia (Schneider, 1999; Schneider & Crombie, 2003; Wearmouth & Reid, 2008). Gaining awareness of the nature of the learning process as such and being able to reflect on it requires undertaking a series of small steps, including the application of the verbalisation strategy. At the beginning, students can be encouraged to simply comment on what exactly they are doing and how, while completing various tasks. Teachers stimulate and elicit responses through mime, gesture and thought-provoking questions (e.g. Why would you spell it this way? Where would you insert this word and why? Can you see the pattern? What are you thinking?). This ability to identify the mechanisms and strategies underlying the actions we take extends to verbalising (out aloud) the discovery course of linguistic processing in the area of reading, spelling, pronunciation, grammar structures, vocabulary and writing (expressing thoughts on paper). Schneider and Crombie (2003) claim the need to enhance development of the following skills in learners with dyslexia: the ability to identify a problem (e.g. a spelling mistake), knowledge of a set of strategies to solve it, the ability to choose and apply the most suitable strategy to solve the problem quickly and successfully, and, last but not least, the ability to double check (to ask check questions) the outcome of the applied strategy. The role of the teacher in developing the matacognitive strategies in students with dyslexia involves, firstly, explicit modelling of a variety of strategies to aid self-reflection and self-correction, and secondly, providing multiple opportunities for students to extensively practice these strategies in a stress-free environment.

Schneider and Crombie (2003) mention several actions that can be undertaken with regard to creating opportunities for obtaining satisfactory test results. They highlight the influential role of an explicit instruction in preparation strategies, such as the use of mnemonic devices, multisensory structured studying, summary information charts, mock examinations, time management and task organisation. Apart from the test preparation strategies, also test-taking strategies, which refer to behaviour during the test/examination, should be plainly taught to dyslexics. Still, by far the most important seems to be the introduction of the proper test-taking modifications, such as, for instance, extending time and providing a separate, distraction-free room. Another option constitutes the alternative test modes, such as take-home tests, which can be applied to the whole examination or only parts of it, or tests prepared to be completed with the use of a computer. Securing a scribe or a reader in a language test-taking situation also requires a separate room so that other test takers are not disturbed. Finally, careful selection of test tasks seems crucial, for instance, cloze procedure tasks should be avoided, as they prevent learners with dyslexia, who tend to rely heavily on the contextual clues, from demonstrating their actual knowledge. In addition, matching tasks may prove difficult, especially for students with impaired visual processing. During oral examinations, it is best to avoid immediate forced responses, but rather distribute questions in advance, in that way giving enough time for retrieving information from memory.

When correcting the written work of learners with dyslexia, only certain aspects of it can undergo assessment, for instance, the arguments presented, the vocabulary use, the choice of grammatical structures or spelling. As far as spelling mistakes are concerned, it is recommended (Jurek, 2008) not to highlight or circle them (especially with a red pen) or otherwise expose them, in order to prevent students from concentrating their attention on and consolidating the erroneous forms. It seems more justified to cross the misspelled word and provide the correct spelling above or next to it so that it is the correct form that is focused on and integrated. Such an approach proved more effective than, for instance, writing the words on the blackboard and asking students to compare with their own spelling attempts. Teachers also often indicate in the margin the occurrence of a mistake in a given line of the text, however, they do not specify where exactly it is, expecting the students to do so, or they simply count down the mistakes and provide the total number at the bottom of the text, again with no indication of the position of the mistakes. Unfortunately, such expectations expressed towards children with dyslexia are bound to produce rather negative results. Even very careful and intensive looking at words and searching for mistakes cannot guarantee spotting the misspelled words. What is more, frequently, words that are perfectly well spelled get corrected. Thus, it seems more time wise and effect wise to cross misspellings and provide correct forms for students. Naturally, decent practice with regard to words which do not seem well integrated yet is a must, however, mere mechanical rewriting is useless and monotonous, it kills motivation and enthusiasm. Instead, teachers may find the multisensory techniques and movable devices described earlier useful. Students can also be asked to colour the troublesome spelling patterns in words, to verbalise orthographic rules, to provide other examples of words where the rules apply, to form word families for the misspelled words, to form negations, to form sentences with the words, to design mnemonics that would help to remember the correct spelling (especially in the cases of irregular words and exceptions).

Students with dyslexia can greatly benefit from frequent feedback on their educational progress from teachers, both oral and written as well as quantitative and qualitative. Especially relevant is that they compare what they have already learned with their own previous achievements rather than with the attainments of their peers. It is important that they see how they advance in their study, consequently realising their individual teaching plans, and that they can count on the attention, understanding and help of their teachers.

Notes

1. See Chapter 2: 'Brain mechanisms in dyslexia' for a discussion of brain abnormalities in dyslexia.
2. See Chapter 1: 'Reading strategies and stages of reading development' for more information on the *balance model of reading* by Bakker.
3. For a more thorough discussion see Nijakowska (2008).
4. See Chapter 6 for examples.
5. See Chapter 6 for examples.

Chapter 6
Sample Activities for Learners with Dyslexia Learning English as a Foreign Language

Activities for Developing Phonological Awareness and Awareness of Sound-letter Relations

As already indicated, explicit phonological awareness training is believed to be necessary for children with dyslexia, who fail to sufficiently develop phonological awareness skills. It has also been stressed that such training needs to follow a developmental sequence, starting from bigger chunks within words and subsequently moving to individual phonemes. Thus, finally, individuals should be able to hear and discriminate between sounds, to identify them in various positions in words (initial, final, medial) and to manipulate them. Mastering these abilities in an auditory context translates into more rapid success in spelling and reading (written context).

Pure phonemic awareness activities are based on spoken words and are responded to orally. However, it is recommended to use auditory (clapping) and visual (boxes, blocks, tokens, cards) cues to help children understand that the sounds in words are separate entities. Apparently, visible, movable representations of sounds help to clarify and guide counting, segmenting and blending tasks and children should be encouraged to use auditory and visual cues.

In all phonological awareness activities, the visual representations of sounds (boxes, blocks, tokens, cards) can be substituted with letters. The aim of such training is to eventually make the letter-to-sound relations definite. Letters corresponding to the sounds being mastered can be introduced and placed on the tokens. It has been demonstrated that there is an advantage to combining phoneme awareness with letter knowledge training, over the phonological awareness training without the letter-to-sound relations, as well as over the letter knowledge training without phonological awareness instruction (Maurer, 2003). The aim of teaching phonics is predominantly to gain the knowledge that written words are built of letters or clusters of letters that represent the sounds of spoken words and to acquire those systematic relations between letters and sounds. Not until sounding out letters and spelling patterns is automatic can readers naturally concentrate on meaning rather than on decoding while reading. Skilful and automatic decoding allows a shift of focus from recognition of letters and words to comprehension, which, in turn, leads to a critical assessment and creative use of the content of the text. The time and effort allotted to decoding should be gradually reduced during the course of learning to read. Summing up, a truly effective reading programme should comprise a direct and explicit instruction in both the phonological awareness and letter/sound correspondences.

In addition, there is a debate on what grain sizes are optimal for teaching rather inconsistent English letter-sound correspondences. Should the instruction concentrate on small or larger units of sound? It has been suggested that English is relatively more consistent with regard to larger units such as rimes or syllables, while grapheme-phoneme relations tend to be irregular. Thus, English-speaking children need both small- and large-size decoding strategies. All in all, Ziegler and Goswami (2006) suggest that combining phonics-based methods with regard to small and large units with whole word teaching, hence forming a kind of complementary balanced approach, is important in developing high-grade word recognition ability in English. Some English words have to be learned as distinct patterns (e.g. 'choir', 'people'), other words have rich orthographic neighbours and share consistent rime spellings and pronunciations with numerous words (e.g. 'light'), finally, there are words with relatively consistent grapheme-phoneme relations, which can be easily decoded at this small grain size level (e.g. 'cat', 'hen').

The following is a sequence of activities for developing phonological awareness and the awareness of sound-letter relations, based on word, syllable, onset-rime and phoneme-level manipulations, all of which can be easily incorporated into classroom procedures. In all the following tasks, tokens are used to represent phonological units, and later, letters can be introduced – printed on tokens to make the phonology-orthography relations more explicit.

Sample Activities for Learners with Dyslexia Learning English 155

Activities for Developing Phonological Awareness and the Awareness of Sound-letter Relations

Type of task	Procedure
1. Segmenting compound words and sentences into words.	a) ◆ Students say 'toothbrush' without a 'tooth,' 'rainbow' without 'bow,' 'girlfriend' without 'girl.' b) ◆ Students listen to the teacher reading a sentence and place a marker from the left to the right for each word heard. 'Ben had a hen' 'Ben....had......a......hen' ◆ To make the boundaries between words clear teachers can use a device made of tokens fastened to the elastic band; they simply need to stretch the band. ◆ Later, the words can be put on the tokens. The / fat / cat / is / on / the / mat The	fat	cat	is	on	the	mat

156   Dyslexia in the Foreign Language Classroom

Type of task	Procedure
2. Segmenting and blending syllables.	◆ Students listen to the teacher saying words, count the syllables and place a marker from the left to the right for each syllable heard. The procedure with an elastic band can be used here as well. For example: 'en-list,' 'per-form,' 'dis-em-bark,' 'en-joy-ing.' ⇩ ⇩ ⇩ [en	list] ⇩ ⇧ ⇩ [en] [ ] [list]
3. Recognizing and creating rhymes.	a) ◆ Recognizing rhymes. Students name the objects that are in the pictures and say their names aloud. Then they listen to the teacher saying pairs of words and if they rhyme students raise their thumbs up, circle the pictures and colour them. 'bat' – 'cat' 'rat' – 'men'

Sample Activities for Learners with Dyslexia Learning English 157

Type of task	Procedure
	b) ◆ Students name the objects in each row and say their names aloud. They circle the picture whose name does not rhyme with the other names. 'ten' 'men' 'cat' 'hen' 'rat' 'ten' c) ◆ Creating rhymes. Students name the pictures in each row and say their names aloud. In each row they draw a picture whose name rhymes with the names of the other two pictures.
4. Segmenting and blending onsets and rimes.	◆ Flashcards with pictures, tokens as well as flashcards with onsets, rimes and words are needed. Colour coding is used to help students distinguish between the onsets and rimes. Movable devices – slides are used to manipulate letters to form words. First students are shown three pictures and provide the names for them e.g. 'men,' 'ten,' 'hen' or 'cat,' 'hat,' 'rat.' They listen to the teacher saying the words and are asked if they can hear any common parts in all of the words. They use tokens to represent onsets and rimes. They are given flashcards with the 'en' rime and with the onsets 'm,' 't,' 'h' and are asked to form words. They match the

Type of task	Procedure
	pictures to the words. The procedure is then repeated with other examples of rimes and onsets. Students manipulate slides to form words.

Sample Activities for Learners with Dyslexia Learning English 159

Type of task	Procedure
5. Identifying initial and final sounds in words.	a) ◆ Students name the objects in the pictures in each row; say their names aloud. Then they listen to the teacher saying them; if the words start with the same sound students raise their thumbs up, circle them and colour them. 'pig' 'pen' 'car' 'rat' 'key' 'cat'

Type of task	Procedure
	b) ◆ Students say aloud the names of the objects in each row and choose a picture whose name doesn't start with the same sound as the other names.

'car'   'cat'   'pig'

'pig'   'ten'   'pen'

c) ◆ Students listen to the words and identify the sounds at the beginning.
Do 'cup' and 'cake' begin the same?
Do 'sun' and 'ship' begin the same?
Do 'shop,' 'ship,' 'sheep,' 'shoe' start with the same sound?
Do 'shop,' 'cheap,' 'shoe,' 'ship' start with the same sound?
Do 'pen,' 'pet,' 'pill,' 'pot' start with the same sound?

d) ◆ Students listen to the words and identify the sounds at the end?
Do 'pet,' 'pot,' 'cat,' 'mat' end with the same sound?
Do 'sun,' 'man,' 'gone,' 'goat' end with the same sound? |

Sample Activities for Learners with Dyslexia Learning English 161

Type of task	Procedure
6. Segmenting and blending individual sounds in words.	a) ◆ Students look at the pictures, listen to the teacher saying words, count the phonemes and place a marker from the left to the right for each phoneme heard. Later letters can be put on tokens. 'hen' 'bat' b) ◆ Students look at the pictures, listen to the teacher saying words, count the phonemes and cut the pictures into the number of pieces corresponding to the number of phonemes.

Type of task	Procedure
	c) ◆ Students listen to the teacher saying words, count the phonemes and place a marker from the left to the right for each phoneme heard. Then they blend them to make a word again. The procedure with an elastic band can be used here as well. For example: 'rat'.

⇩ ☐ ☐ ☐

⇩ | r | a | t |

⇩ ☐ ☐ ☐ ☐

⇩ | r | a | t |

d) ◆ Students listen to the sets of words and decide whether they have the same sound in the middle. Tokens are used to represent sounds in words. For example: 'lip,' 'rib,' 'flip,' 'chick' or 'pet,' 'pin,' 'sun,' 'bun' or 'sun,' 'bun,' 'cup,' 'nut'.

e) ◆ Students listen to the words and identify the sounds they hear at the beginning, end and in the middle of these words. Tokens are used to represent sounds in words.

f) ◆ Students listen to the words first, then to individual sounds and signal whether they are heard at the beginning, end or in the middle of the word. Tokens are used to represent sounds in words. |
| 7. Manipulating sounds (deleting, adding, substituting). | a) ◆ Leave off the beginning sound of a given word to make a new word.

| p | a | t | ⇩ | p | a | t | |

Sample Activities for Learners with Dyslexia Learning English   163

Type of task	Procedure
	For example: 'pat' – it starts with /p/ and ends with /æt/, take the first sound away and it says /æt/. Take /k/ out of 'cat' and it says /æt/. Say 'mat' without /m/. What word will be left if you take /p/ off pat? What is missing in 'eat' that you can hear in 'meat'? b) ◆ Leave off the end sound of a given word to make a new word. The procedure is similar to the one used with initial sounds. c) ◆ Listen to the word and substitute the initial sound. What is the beginning sound in 'cat'? Say 'cat' with /h/ instead of /k/. What is the beginning sound in 'hen'? Say 'hen' with /p/ instead of /h/. | c	a	t
---	---	---
h	a	t	

Type of task	Procedure
	d) ◆ Listen to a word and substitute the final sound. What is the end/final sound in 'bet'? Say 'bet' with /l/ instead of /t/. 	b	e	t
b	e	ll | | b	e	ll | e) ◆ Listen to a word and substitute the middle sound. What is the middle sound of 'met'? Say 'met' with /æ/ instead of /e/. | m	e	t
m	a	t	 	m	a	t	 f) ◆ Listen to a word and change one sound to form a new word. eg. 'met' – 'mat' – 'sat' – 'sit' – 'sin' – 'bin' – 'bun' – 'nun' – 'nut' – 'hut'

Orthographic Awareness Activities[1]

English orthography is widely perceived as non-transparent and difficult, however, Kessler and Treiman (2003) provide convincing evidence that it is in fact more regular than one would think. There are several productive spelling patterns and principles whose exploration can aid the effectiveness of teaching. Position (initial, final) and environment (surrounding sounds) have an effect on the spelling of a given sound. English vowels tend to be notoriously misspelled. The analysis of syllables in words, involving the division of syllables into onsets and rimes (consisting of vowels and codas), supports spelling. Rimes prove to play the most crucial role here. Presenting words in sets classified according to the rimes they share is very useful, and this also applies to onsets with multiple spellings (e.g. /k/) in words grouped by the following vowel. Obviously, several patterns have exceptions, for instance certain rimes have varying spellings in different words. Kessler and Treiman (2003) demonstrated that adults rely on the environmental characteristics (onset and coda) of a word when attempting to spell vowels, thus children learning spelling patterns at school later resort to them in adulthood.

The following is a set of sample activities selected from the programme used in the small-scale intervention study described in Chapter 5. The study concerned the effectiveness of direct multisensory instruction for improving word reading and spelling skills in English through the systematic study of selected grapheme-phoneme relations, spelling patterns and rules.

The following activities predominantly concern practicing the spelling choices for the /ai/ sound, namely 'i-e' in single-syllable words, '-y' at the end of a word and 'igh' in the middle of a single-syllable word.

Orthographic Awareness Activities	
Type of task	*Procedure*
1. Short and long vowels – comparison.	◆ Teacher asks the students to give the key words to unlock the sounds of short vowel sounds. The words: 'apple,' 'egg,' 'Indian,' 'octopus,' 'umbrella' are written on the board. Students are asked to read the words and say what the beginning sound in each of them is. Teacher stresses that they are short vowel sounds and writes the corresponding symbols of phonetic transcription-/æ/, /e/, /I/, /ɒ/ and /ʌ/. Students are asked to provide some examples of words containing short vowel sounds, e.g. 'hat,' 'hen,' 'zip,' 'hot,' 'nut'. ◆ Teacher elicits from the students the vowels's names (they revise the alphabet if necessary). The teacher writes the following on the board: 'a'-/ei/, 'e'-/i:/, 'i'-/ai/, 'o'-/ðʊ/, 'u'-/ju:/ or /u:/.

Type of task	Procedure
2. Auditory differentiation between short and long vowel sounds – minimal pairs.	◆ It is explained to the students that a minimal pair is a pair of words that differ only in one sound. Here they differ in a vowel sound. Students listen to teacher reading minimal pairs of words and decide in which word they hear a short vowel sound and in which one a long vowel sound. ◆ e.g. a) 'ship - sheep', b) 'note - not', c) 'bed - bead', d) 'fit - fight', e) 'read-red', f) 'cut-cute', g) 'bat-bait' 	Minimal pair	Short vowel sound	Long vowel sound
---	---	---
a	1	2
b	2	1
c	1	2
d	1	2	
3. Auditory differentiation between short and long vowels – odd one out.	◆ Students listen to teacher reading sets of one-syllable words containing either short or long vowels and choose the odd one out. Each set consists of four words. The students mark their answers in the chart, e.g. a) 'cut', 'sun', 'nut', 'cute'; b) 'wine', 'five', 'win', 'nice'; c) 'hop', 'hot', 'hope', 'cot' | Nr	1	2	3	4
---	---	---	---	---
a				v
b			v	
c			v		
4. 'Magic, silent or lengthening e' rule.	◆ It is made explicit to students that there are several ways of spelling long vowel sounds but we will concentrate on one of them. Teacher draws the chart* on the board with the headings and the first column filled up. Then she says the words 'mad', 'met', 'win', 'hop', 'cut' and asks students whether they contain short or long vowel sounds. Students indicate in which row of the second column they should be written down. Next teacher asks students to write these words again adding the 'e' at the end of each of them in the corresponding rows of the third column. Teacher reads the words from the third column, then the minimal pairs and asks the students what spelling pattern they can see in the words from the third column. We add the 'e' after the final consonant and this makes the vowel long (or say its name).

Sample Activities for Learners with Dyslexia Learning English

Type of task	Procedure
✓	◆ Rule card: *Adding the 'e' after the single final consonant of a one-syllable word makes the vowel in the middle of that word long (or say its name).* * |	1	2	3 | |---|---|---|---| | Vowel | Short sound | Long sound | | a | mad | made | | e | met | mete | | i | win | wine | | o | hop | hope | | u | cut | cute |
5. The /ai/ sound spelled with 'i-e.'	◆ Teacher writes the following words on the board: 'white', 'time', 'write', 'five', 'nice', 'pine', 'like' and reads them. Students are asked what spelling pattern they can see in these words. Teacher highlights the 'i-e' pattern in all the words and writes the 'i-e' rule on the board. ◆ Rule card 'i-e': *When we hear the sound /ai/ ('i' saying its name) in the middle of a one-syllable word followed by a single consonant sound ('e' is silent), we <u>most frequently</u> spell it with the letters 'i-e'.*
6. Reading drill – 'i-e.'	◆ Students are given flash cards with 'i-e' words for reading practice. They look at the underlined letter, say the sound it makes and read a word. There is the sound /ai/ printed at the left top corner and a word in the middle of a flash card. The letters used to spell a given sound are printed in bold type, e.g.: | /ai/	/ai/	/ai/ | |---|---|---| | t**i**m**e** | n**i**c**e** | sm**i**l**e** |
7. Hands on activity – 'i-e.'	◆ Students are given movable devices – slides. The task is to form and read words with the /ai/ sound. Later they write the words into the chart. The consonants are already filled in, the missing element in all words is the 'i-e' pattern.

Type of task	Procedure
	'i-e' - /ai/
			1	t	**i**	m	**e**	
		2	s		z		
		3	n		c		
	◆ Students are provided with a movable device comprising four piles of flash cards joined at the top with a spring. The first pile consists of white cards with consonants or initial consonant blends or digraphs, the second pile consists of a grey card with the letter 'i,' the third pile includes white cards with consonants and the forth pile consists of a grey card with the letter 'e.' Colour coding is used to enhance visual perception. Students are asked to form words by moving the cards, they read and write the words. The words are printed on the reverse side of the white cards so that the students can check whether they have formed a correct word.
8. Auditory/ visual integration.	◆ Students are given charts with the 'i-e' pattern, they listen to the teacher reading the words and fill in the missing consonants, e.g.:
		1	_ i _ e	time	
		2	_ i _ e	wine	
		3	_ i _ e	like	

Sample Activities for Learners with Dyslexia Learning English 169

Type of task	Procedure

9. Grid.	◆ Students are asked to solve the puzzles on the left and write the words in the boxes on the right. To make the exercise easier the list of words can be provided for students. Worksheet adapted from Shemesh and Waller (2000), e.g.:
	
	     A number, half of ten | | i | | e |
	     A colour | | i | | e |
	     Belongs to me | | i | | e |
	     A reward | | i | | e |

10. Letter leads.	◆ Students solve the puzzles and write the letters in the boxes, one letter in each box. The letter in the marked box will be the first letter of the next word. To make the exercise easier the list of words can be provided for students Worksheet adapted from Shemesh and Waller (2000), e.g.: The river of Egypt. | N | I | L | E | A citrus fruit. | L | I | M | E | A measure of distance. | M | | | |
11. Spelling the /ai/ sound at the end of a word with the letter '-y.'	◆ Teacher writes the following words on the board: 'try', 'cry', 'spy', 'fly', 'by', 'why', 'sky', 'rely', 'reply', 'shy', 'my', 'July', 'dry', 'deny' and reads them underlining the ending '-y.' Then she asks students whether they can observe any spelling patterns. Finally, she writes the rule on the board. ◆ Rule card: *When we hear the /ai/ sound ('i' saying its name) at the end of a word, we <u>most frequently</u> spell it with the letter '-y'.* Exceptions: 'high', 'sigh', 'thigh', 'nigh', 'tie', 'lie', 'pie', 'die', 'eye', 'buy', 'bye'. When adding a suffix to a word ending in a consonant + '-y,' change the '-y' into 'i', e.g.: 'sky' – 'skies', 'try' – 'tries', 'spy' – 'spied'.
12. Hands-on activity.	◆ Students are given movable devices – slides and manipulate them to form words. They are asked to read and write the words down. Colour coding is used to enhance visual perception.

Type of task	Procedure
	⇐ /ai/ ⇒ | tr	cr	sp	fl	b	sk	**y**	m | ♦ Students manipulate the movable device comprising two piles of cards joined at the top with a spring to form words containing the /ai/ sound spelled with the letter '-y' at the end. They form, read and spell the words, e.g.: | sk	y	
13. Filling the missing words.	♦ Students are given sentences with the '-y' words missing to fill. The words a provided, e.g.: 'fly', 'by', 'why', 'my', 'sky', 'July'; a) …….. do you want to buy this book?; b) The stars are on the …….; c) In ……. we go for holiday.
14. Consolidating spelling patterns for the /ai/ sound.	♦ Students visually perceive a list of words containing the /ai/ sound and cover them. Then, they listen to the teacher reading the words and decide whether the /ai/ sound is spelled with the letters 'i-e' or '-y'. The students are reminded that the 'i-e' pattern occurs when the /ai/ sound is followed by a single consonant sound, whereas '-y' appears at the end of a word. They fill the chart by writing a tick under the appropriate heading. Finally, they write the whole word, e.g.: 1. 'cry', 2. 'wine', 3. 'time' 	Nr	'i-e'	'-y'	word
---	---	---	---
1		v	cry
2	v		wine
3	v		time	
15. Spelling the /ai/ sound followed by the letter 't' with the letters 'igh'.	♦ Teacher writes the following words on the board: '**night**', '**light**', '**sight**', '**bright**', '**fight**', '**fright**', '**might**', '**right**', '**tight**', '**slight**' and reads them underlining the letters 'igh'. Then she asks the students whether they can observe a common spelling patterns in all the words. Finally, she writes the rule on the board. ♦ Rule card: *When we hear the /ai/ sound ('i' saying its name) followed by the letter 't', we often spell it with the letters 'igh'*. This spelling pattern is most commonly found followed by the letter 't' but it also appears as a final vowel sound in the following words: '**sigh**', '**high**', '**thigh**', '**nigh**'. *The most common spelling pattern of the sound /ai/ ('i' saying its name) in the middle of a one-syllable word followed by the sound of a single consonant is 'i-e'.*

Sample Activities for Learners with Dyslexia Learning English   171

Type of task	Procedure

16. Hands-on activity.	◆ Students manipulate a movable device comprising three piles of cards joined at the top with a spring to form words containing the /ai/ sound spelled with the letters 'igh' in the middle. They read and spell the words.
	
	       n igh t
	
	◆ Students are given movable devices – slides and manipulate them to form words. They read and write the words down.
	
	   r fl fr br s l sl **ight** f t /ai/

17. Consolidating the 'igh' spelling pattern.	◆ Students are given sentences with the 'igh' words missing. They write down the appropriate words into the grid. The number of letters in a word equals the number of boxes in the grid, the 'igh' pattern is already written in, e.g.: 1. Switch on the ...... please; 2. Did you sleep well last ......? 3. It was a ......, sunny day. | 1 | | l | i | g | h | t | | 2 | | | n | i | g | h | t | | 3 | b | r | i | g | h | t |
18. Consolidating spelling patterns for the /ai/ sound.	◆ Students perceive visually a list of words containing the /ai/ sound and cover them. Then, they listen to the teacher reading the words and decide whether the /ai/ sound is spelled with the letters 'igh' or '-y'. The students are reminded that the 'igh' pattern is usually followed by 't', whereas '-y' appears at the end of a word. They fill the chart by writing a tick under the appropriate heading and finally, they write the whole word, e.g.: 1. 'cry', 2. 'light', 3. 'bright' | Nr | 'igh' | '-y' | word | |---|---|---|---| | 1 | | v | cry | | 2 | v | | light | | 3 | v | | bright |

Type of task	Procedure
19. Reading and spelling practice.	◆ Students are given a chart divided into three parts and filled with the words containing the /ai/ sound spelled with the letters 'i-e', 'igh' and '-y'. The words are printed without these letters, instead there are dashes whose number corresponds to the number of the missing letters. Students revise the rules stating when a given spelling pattern should be used, fill the missing letters, say the sound they give and read the whole word, e.g.: 	/ai/	'i-e'	t _ m _, sm _ l _, wh _ t _, s _ z _,
---	---	---
	'igh'	n _ _ _t, f _ _ _ t, r _ _ _ t, br _ _ _ t,
	'-y'	sk _, tr _, fl _, m_,	
20. Reading drill.	◆ Students are given flash cards with words containing the /ai/ sound spelled with the letters 'i-e', '-y' or 'igh' for reading practice. They look at the highlighted letters, say their names and the sound they give. Finally, they read the word. 	/ai/ t**i**me	/ai/ sk**y**	/ai/ n**igh**t
---	---	---	
21. Bingo game – auditory/ visual matching.	◆ Every student is given a different bingo board and a set of little white cards. First students look carefully at their bingo boards and try to remember the position of words, then they listen to the teacher reading a word, find the word on the bingo board and cover it with a card. The first student to cover all words in one column and one row says 'bingo' and wins the game, e.g.: 	white	try	right	time
---	---	---	---
cry	might	my	crime
fright	nice	shy	bright
write	flight	slight	fly	
22. Find the odd one out.	◆ Students are given sets of words, they are asked to listen to teacher reading them, to look at them and to choose the odd one out. They cross out the word that does not belong to the group, write it down and indicate the spelling pattern that all the other words contain, e.g.:

Sample Activities for Learners with Dyslexia Learning English 173

Type of task	Procedure
✓	<table><tr><td>Words</td><td>Odd one out</td><td>Common part</td></tr><tr><td>white time try crime</td><td>try</td><td>'i-e'</td></tr><tr><td>right nice fright bright</td><td>nice</td><td>'igh'</td></tr><tr><td>fly sky cry slight</td><td>slight</td><td>'-y'</td></tr></table>
23. Dominoes. ✓	♦ Each student is given a board for dominoes and a set of cards. On every card there are two words. Students are supposed to match identical words until the board is full. When they are all ready, they are asked to read and write the words down, e.g.: | right | crime | crime | cry |
24. Consolidation – spelling board game – 'Battleships.' ✓	♦ Players choose the words with the /ai/ sound they worked on and put the counters with letters on their boards or write them down into a grid vertically or horizontally. Players are supposed to shoot and immerse the word-ships of their adversary, to read and write them down. The student who manages to immerse all the word-ships of his/her adversary first is the winner. They shoot giving a possible position of the letter, for example, 3B or 9K, and a letter can be either missed or hit. A sample grid: <table><tr><td>1</td><td></td><td></td><td></td><td></td><td></td><td></td><td></td><td></td><td></td></tr><tr><td>2</td><td>l</td><td>i</td><td>g</td><td>h</td><td>t</td><td></td><td></td><td></td><td></td></tr><tr><td>3</td><td></td><td></td><td></td><td></td><td></td><td>c</td><td></td><td></td><td></td></tr><tr><td>4</td><td></td><td>n</td><td></td><td></td><td></td><td>r</td><td></td><td></td><td></td></tr><tr><td>5</td><td></td><td>i</td><td></td><td></td><td></td><td>y</td><td></td><td></td><td></td></tr><tr><td>6</td><td></td><td>c</td><td></td><td></td><td></td><td></td><td></td><td></td><td></td></tr><tr><td>7</td><td>t</td><td>e</td><td></td><td></td><td></td><td></td><td></td><td></td><td></td></tr><tr><td>8</td><td>i</td><td></td><td></td><td>f</td><td>l</td><td>i</td><td>g</td><td>h</td><td>t</td></tr><tr><td>9</td><td>m</td><td></td><td></td><td></td><td></td><td></td><td></td><td></td><td></td></tr><tr><td>10</td><td>e</td><td></td><td></td><td></td><td></td><td></td><td></td><td></td><td></td></tr><tr><td></td><td>A</td><td>B</td><td>C</td><td>D</td><td>E</td><td>F</td><td>G</td><td>H</td><td>I</td><td>J</td></tr></table>

Type of task	Procedure
25. Consolidation – spelling board game – 'Letter maze'.	◆ Players throw a dice ten times in turns and move their counters towards the centre of the maze collecting the letters. They are supposed to form as many words with the /ai/ sound they worked on as they can from the letters they collected. They write and read the words. If the words are correct, the players score one point for every letter that has been used. The one to score the most points is the winner. Players can decide to play for more than one round hence collecting more letters and forming more words. ◆ Each player chooses three words with the /ai/ sound they worked on and writes them down, then they throw a dice in turns and move their counters towards the centre of the maze collecting the letters. The players are supposed to collect all the letters that their words are built of, the first one to do it is the winner. A sample letter maze: | s | x | u | t | m | z | i | w | k | p | | v | f | j | e | k | f | a | k | g | o | | a | h | d | w | i | t | h | e | j | n | | j | r | o | b | c | e | m | v | o | r | | c | i | c | i | p | g | w | s | f | e | | e | p | b | l | z | o | a | l | w | h | | m | d | n | u | s | m | c | a | u | j | | h | g | o | z | b | u | r | n | x | l | | k | o | t | l | i | v | q | a | p | h | | → | d | g | a | z | j | c | u | b | f |
26. Dictation.	◆ Students perceive visually a list of words and cover them. Then, they listen to teacher reading the words with the 'i-e,' 'igh' and '-y' spelling patterns and write them down into the chart under the appropriate heading, e.g.: | | 'i-e'/ai/ | 'igh' /ai/ | '-y' /aï/ | |---|---|---|---| | 1. | | | | | 2. | | | | | 3. | | | |

Morphological Awareness Activities

The supportive role of morphological awareness in spelling English words is stressed by several researchers (Chliounaki & Bryant, 2007; Deacon & Bryant, 2005, 2006; Hurry *et al.*, 2005; Jurek, 2008). Morphology may form a clear basis for the way some words are spelled. Chliounaki and Bryant (2007) give the example of the identical end sounds represented by diverse spellings of the following pairs of words: 'kiss*ed*' and 'list', 'socks' and 'box', 'trees' and 'freeze'. The first word in each pair consists of two morphemes, the final morpheme in each case is either a past tense or plural inflectional morpheme. Hurry *et al.* (2005: 188) claim that 'language is a morphological jigsaw which we manipulate all the time to increase our word power', thus equipping children with the knowledge and understanding of the morphological principles enables them to enhance their performance on spelling and reading tasks.

Basically, morphology focuses on how words are structured from constituent parts. Many words can be divided into smaller units – *morphemes*, which constitute the smallest linguistic units with a meaning (e.g. '*un*happy', '*un*lucky', '*un*satisfied') or a grammatical function (e.g. 'looks', 'look*ed*'). Some words cannot be further broken down (e.g. 'car'), they are *free morphemes* since they can stand alone, while *bound morphemes* (e.g. 'un-', '-s', or '-ed') are always attached to some other morphemes. There are various classes of morphemes (e.g. free and bound) and ways in which certain morphemes can combine with other morphemes (e.g. '*re*take', '*re*write'; 're-' can only be attached to verbs). Bound morphemes (or *affixes*) are classified into *prefixes*, which attach to the beginning of words, and *suffixes*, which attach to the end of words. Bound morphemes can be also divided, according to their function in complex words, into *derivational* and *inflectional* morphemes. When derivational morphemes are added to words, they have a power to derive (create) new words, either by changing the original word's meaning (e.g. 'un-' added to 'happy') or its part of speech (e.g. '-ness' added to 'quick'). Inflectional morphemes do not form new words, but change the existing ones in a different way – by refining and giving extra information (e.g. '-s' added to 'cat'). In English, there are eight inflectional morphemes, and all are suffixes ('-s' third person singular present, '-s' plural, '-ed' past tense, '-ing' progressive, '-en' past participle, '-s' possessive, '-er' comparative and '-est' superlative). They point to a syntactic and semantic relation between words in a given sentence and occur at the end of a word, following derivational morphemes. Each word is composed of at least one morpheme. Complex words consist of a free morpheme, in other words a base, root or stem, and a number of affixes (Jannedy *et al.*, 1994).

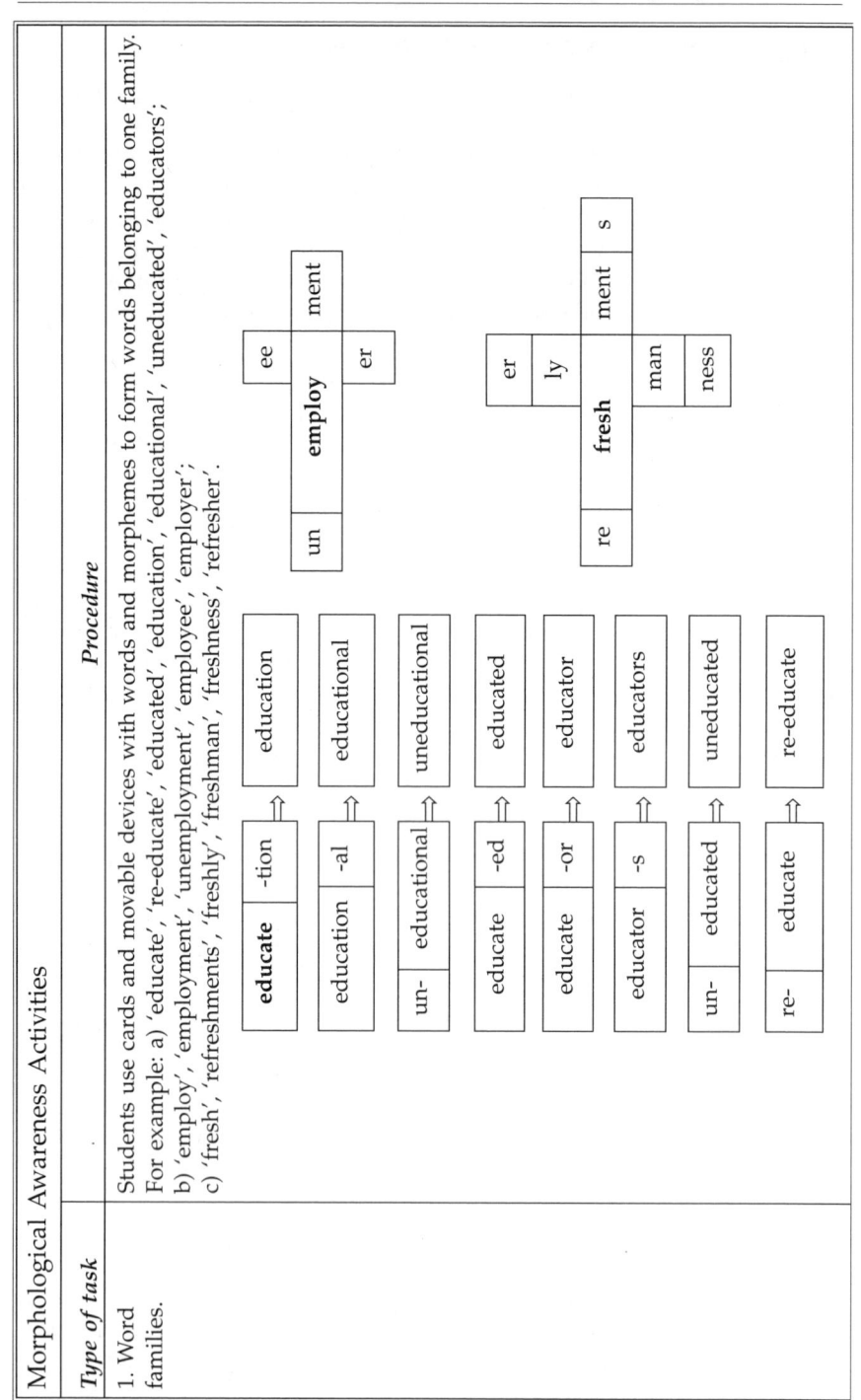

Morphological Awareness Activities

Type of task	Procedure
1. Word families.	Students use cards and movable devices with words and morphemes to form words belonging to one family. For example: a) 'educate', 're-educate', 'educated', 'education', 'educational', 'uneducated', 'educators'; b) 'employ', 'employment', 'unemployment', 'employee', 'employer'; c) 'fresh', 'refreshments', 'freshly', 'freshman', 'freshness', 'refresher'.

educate + -tion ⇒ education
education + -al ⇒ educational
un- + educational ⇒ uneducational
educate + -ed ⇒ educated
educate + -or ⇒ educator
educator + -s ⇒ educators
un- + educated ⇒ uneducated
re- + educate ⇒ re-educate

[Cross diagram with **employ** in center; un (left), ee / ment (top with er below), er (right)]

[Cross diagram with **fresh** in center; re (left), er / ly / man / ness stack, ment / s (right)] |

Sample Activities for Learners with Dyslexia Learning English 177

Type of task	Procedure
	Such activities can help students realize that they do not have to learn the spelling of all the words in a family separately but knowing how to spell the base word and common affixes allows for spelling impressive number of words. Other types of exercises involve analysing groups of words belonging to a given family in order to identify and to split them into the base word and affixes, classifying words into word families, finding the words that do not belong to a given family (Jurek, 2008).
2. Find the words that do not belong to a 'belief' family.	beliefs disbelief believable beautifully disbelieve unbeatable unbelievably believer unbelievable non-believer
3. Choose the odd one out in each line.	| differently | differential | difficult | difference | different | differ | | central | certain | centralize | centrally | center | centralization | | perfect | perfection | prefect | imperfection | perfectionist | imperfect |
4. Sort the cards to form two word families.	friend painfully friendship painful friendly pain painkiller unfriendly painless

Type of task	Procedure
5. Divide the words into two families.	cleaner cleanliness cleanser close closet cleanly cleanest disclosure cleansing closely cleanest enclosed cleaning
6. Do the following pairs of words belong to the same family.	friend/friendliness casual/causal enable/unable praying/playing filing/filling science/scientist

7. Split the words into its constituent morphemes write them on cards.	formalize
	formally
	informal
	                    informally
	                     formalist

8. Split the words into its constituent morphemes.	correct corrective correctional incorrect incorrectly corrections correctly correctness

Grammatical Awareness Activities

A number of activities for developing *grammatical awareness* presented below are helpful in analysing the separate constituent elements of a language (Nijakowska, 2007). Some students do not develop sufficient grammatical awareness along with communicative effectiveness despite fully experiential and meaningful classroom second language learning. These limitations can be reduced by the pedagogical interventions involving raising grammatical awareness or, in other words, focusing on form. Thornbury (1999) stresses the need to point out language items in order to help the learners notice them and, in so doing, support and speed up the acquisition process.

The study of grammar, provided it is not treated as an end in itself but one of the ways to achieve a thorough mastery of a language, helps to learn to use the language, and by no means has to be perceived as a boring, dry and de-motivating experience. Since fun and playing compose a vital part of children's growing and learning, they naturally form a fertile ground for incorporating them into grammar practice activities and create opportunities for multiple repetition and reproduction of grammatical material, which, consequently, leads to automatisation. The abovementioned natural characteristic of children allows teachers to use games, project work, crafts (e.g. various movable teaching devices made by children), surveys (simple repetitive activities but with clear communicative focus), movement and multisensory techniques in order to make children focus on grammatical concepts. This, in turn, allows children to acquire the feeling of what is grammatically accurate and offers chances for integrating language skills as well. Learners become aware of the constituent elements and their proper order as well as the meaning of a given grammatical structure. Stimulating and learner-friendly activities, involving playing, manipulating and moving around, provide an excellent opportunity for practising grammar. What follows is a set of sample grammar activities.

Grammatical Awareness Activities

Type of task	Procedure	Comments
1. Colour parsing.	◆ Language: Present Simple – general questions; materials: coloured chalk, coloured pencils; time: 20–30 min. ◆ Four colours are needed: red for verbs ('like', 'love', 'hate'); blue for subject pronouns ('I', 'you', 'she', 'he', 'etc'.); yellow for auxiliary verbs ('do', 'does') and green for nouns for food ('pizza', 'coffee', 'tea', 'bananas', 'tomatoes'). ◆ Teacher divides the board into two halves. On the left she writes some words that fit into the chosen sentence structure. ◆ Teacher underlines the verb in red and invites children to underline other red words. Teacher does the same with blue, yellow and green words. ◆ Teacher writes her model sentence on the right of the board and asks the children to underline the words in the appropriate colours. ◆ Teacher shows the children how to make other sentences like hers, using the words on the left. Then they make some of their own. They read the sentences and write under the model. ◆ Children do a questionnaire. Before children go around the room, teacher asks the questions and notes down the answers 'Yes' and 'No,' makes them form the questions and writes them on the board as well as makes sure they know how to correctly pronounce the questions.	The activity is an example of a simple language analysis combined with the introduction of matalanguage. Children study sentences such as 'Do you like bananas?' analysing the component parts of the structure *auxiliary + pronoun + verb + noun*. Colour coding is used to help children conduct the analysis. What follows is a controlled practice stage in the form of a spoken task with clear communicative purpose (information gap activity), though with a language scope limited to the target structure only.

Sample Activities for Learners with Dyslexia Learning English 181

Type of task	Procedure	Comments
	Find: 		Name			 		Alice	John	Tom	Jane	 	1. someone who likes bananas	No				 	2. three people who love coffee	No				 	3. two people who like pizza	Yes				 	4. three people who love chocolate	Yes				 	5. someone who hates spinach	No				 	6. two people who hate milk	No				 ◆ As a follow up, children may be asked to analyse the answers and form affirmative sentences (revision), for example, 'John likes bananas'. 'Alice, Tom and Jane like coffee' (idea adapted from Phillips, 1993).	In a communicative drill, such as the one used in the activity, learners are supposed to use given grammar structures several times in order to find out the lacking information. This multiple repetition greatly aids automatisation, while the focus on meaning is exercised through the use of information gap. Learners demonstrate a clear communicative purpose and satisfy the need for real communication by bridging the gap. Furthermore, by nature, the interaction is reciprocal, it requires both, listening and speaking.

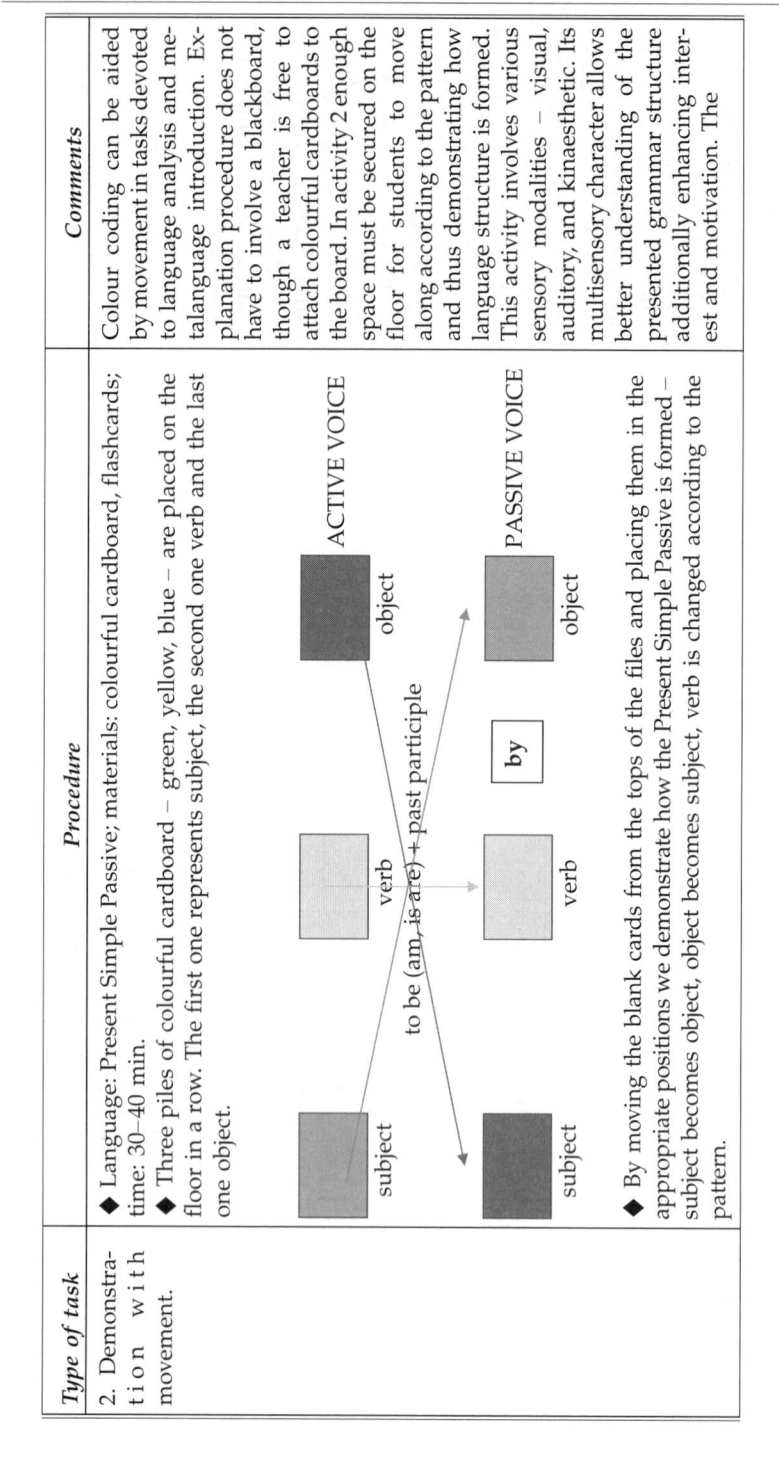

Type of task	Procedure	Comments
2. Demonstration with movement.	◆ Language: Present Simple Passive; time: 30–40 min. ◆ Three piles of colourful cardboard – green, yellow, blue – are placed on the floor in a row. The first one represents subject, the second one verb and the last one object. ACTIVE VOICE: subject — verb — object to be (am, is, are) + past participle PASSIVE VOICE: subject — verb — by — object ◆ By moving the blank cards from the tops of the files and placing them in the appropriate positions we demonstrate how the Present Simple Passive is formed – subject becomes object, object becomes subject, verb is changed according to the pattern.	Colour coding can be aided by movement in tasks devoted to language analysis and metalanguage introduction. Explanation procedure does not have to involve a blackboard, though a teacher is free to attach colourful cardboards to the board. In activity 2 enough space must be secured on the floor for students to move along according to the pattern and thus demonstrating how language structure is formed. This activity involves various sensory modalities – visual, auditory, and kinaesthetic. Its multisensory character allows better understanding of the presented grammar structure additionally enhancing interest and motivation. The

Sample Activities for Learners with Dyslexia Learning English 183

Type of task	Procedure	Comments
	◆ Then we write parts of a sample sentence on the appropriate cards and ask three volunteers to help to demonstrate the example. Each of the volunteers stands behind one pile in the first row, then takes the card with the word, moves towards the appropriate pile in the second row and, finally, puts the card down. ◆ Teacher writes more examples on the cards, asks students to form some sentences in passive voice by moving the cards from the piles in the upper row and placing them in the appropriate positions in the lower row. Next, he or she makes them draw slips of paper with sentences in active voice and then transform the sentence into passive voice. This time they only move according to the pattern while pronouncing the sentences. John loves Mary Mary ACTIVE VOICE by Mary is loved John PASSIVE VOICE	drill performed in the activity is far from dull and boring.

Type of task	Procedure	Comments
3. Stepping stones.	◆ Real-life-size game or a board game; language: any grammar structure; materials: two pieces of ribbon to mark the banks of the river on the floor; some cardboard stones across it; cardboard frogs for each team; one pile of cards with questions and, optionally, piles of cards with answers for each team; time: 20–30min. ◆ Students are divided into teams. Teams take turns in drawing cards with questions, they read questions aloud and try to give the answer (or match the answer). If the answer is correct, the team scores one point. For each point the frog goes forward one stone. The first team to reach the other side of the river wins the game (idea adapted from Phillips, 1993).	Game is a technique that has been repeatedly proved to work well with children. Ur (1988) argues that it is a pleasurable tension felt by the participants that makes up the success of the game-like grammar practice procedures. Game-like activities 3, 4, 5 and 6 can be successfully incorporated into grammar practice procedures and used as templates accommodated towards the requirements of the program and needs of students. Various simple and more sophisticated grammar patters can be practiced this way.

Sample Activities for Learners with Dyslexia Learning English 185

Type of task	Procedure	Comments
4. Board game.	♦ Language: any aspect of grammar; materials: boards – snakes and ladders; a pile of cards with questions on one side and answers on the reverse side; a pile of cards with forfeits and risks; a dice; counters; time: 20–30min. ♦ The first player throws a dice and moves the counter. If he or she lands on a square with a question mark on it, he/she takes a card from the pile and tries to answer it and then checks the answer on the reverse side of the card. ♦ If the student gets it wrong, he/she goes to the previous position. If the student gets it right, he/she moves forward the same number of squares again. If students land on the squares with the snakes or leathers, they climb up or slide down. The winner is the player who reaches the last square first. ♦ Forfeits and risk spaces are included along the game path. If children land on a square with a star, they must take a card from a special pile and do whatever is written on it, for example, jump, sing, say a poem, wait a turn, move two squares back, roll a dice once again, spell their name, move forward three spaces, etc. (idea adapted from Rinvolucri, 1985).	

Type of task	Procedure	Comments
5. Playing cards.	◆ Language: any aspect of grammar, e.g. Present Simple Passive, materials: one set of cards (12 pairs + one additional card) for each group of four students; time: 15–20min. ◆ Teacher prepares sets of 12 pairs of cards consisting of one card with a sentence in an active voice and the corresponding card with the sentence transformed into passive voice. One card without a pair is added. ◆ Teacher shuffles the cards and deals between the players. They cannot show their cards to the other players. ◆ Students take turns in drawing cards from each other clockwise. If they find any pairs, they put them on the table face up, so that other players can check, whether they are correctly matched or not. ◆ The first person to get rid of all of the cards is the winner, other students continue the game until one of them stays with a single card which cannot be matched to any other card.	

Sample Activities for Learners with Dyslexia Learning English   187

Type of task	Procedure	Comments
	Question cards / *Answer cards* / *Question cards* / *Answer cards* Mrs Harris cooks our meals. / Our meals are cooked by Mrs Harris. / Policemen help old ladies. / Old ladies are helped by policemen. Ann loves dogs. / Dogs are loved by Ann. / My brother writes books. / Books are written by my brother. People drive cars. / Cars are driven by people. / They make delicious cakes. / Delicious cakes are made by them. He grows beautiful plants. / Beautiful plants are grown by him. / Millions of people watch this program. / This program is watched by millions of people. Our mum cleans the house. / The house is cleaned by our mum. / A lot of people speak English. / English is spoken by a lot of people. My sister studies history. / History is studied by my sister. / John kissed Mary. / Marry was kissed by John. You lose the game☺ This sentence does not have a pair.	

Type of task	Procedure	Comments
6. Playing cards – Snap.	◆ Language: any grammar structure, e.g. Present Simple Passive; materials: one set of cards (20 pairs) for each pair of students; the cards from the previous game can be used here; time: 15–20min. ◆ Teacher prepares sets of 20 pairs of cards consisting of one card with a sentence in an active voice and the corresponding card with the sentence transformed into passive voice. Teacher shuffles the cards and deals between the players. ◆ Students keep their cards on a pile face down. Each of them takes a card from the top of their files and puts it on the table face up. If the cards do not match, they leave them on the table. However, if they constitute a pair, the students are to say 'Snap!' and cover them with a hand. The first one to do it takes all the cards that are on the table. The student who collects all the cards is the winner.	

Sample Activities for Learners with Dyslexia Learning English   189

Note
1. Sample task types, teaching aids and worksheets used in the small-scale intervention study in dyslexia and EFL described in Chapter 5.

Afterword

Developmental dyslexia can bring about serious educational consequences, which leave their imprint on the broadly perceived well-being – comprising social, emotional and also economic aspects – of an individual, during school years and later on in adulthood. Thorough understanding of this cognitive disorder constitutes a prerequisite for undertaking any action aimed at reducing the impact that dyslexia can exert on one's functioning in the school environment, which too often reduces future choices with regard to a professional career. To prevent such consequences through creating a dyslexia-friendly approach, fair attention and effort of all the stakeholders involved in the process of upbringing on different levels – home, school, government – seems a must.

However, understanding dyslexia is an extremely difficult task in itself, especially in light of the complex, and, in many aspects, conflicting outcome of a massive research, conducted in an attempt to delineate the mechanisms underlying specific reading disorders. As such, the study of dyslexia is very much interdisciplinary in nature; it invites expertise and appreciates knowledge in such scientific disciplines as neurobiology, genetics, cognitive psychology, linguistics and pedagogy. Searching these fields for converging pathways, hopefully allowing the creation of a more complete picture of the phenomenon in question, is constantly in the course of action, with new bits and pieces added regularly. For instance, the advances in technology greatly enhance the grasp of dyslexia; in particular, the use of non-invasive brain imaging techniques for the examination of regularities and abnormalities in the brain structure and functioning is of significant help in understanding the disorder. This neurobiological insight into the mechanisms of dyslexia uncovers new details and facts, which could not have been unveiled previously.

Nevertheless, however promising a start such an interdisciplinary and intensive research approach may seem, it can well turn out to be a blessing in disguise, producing more questions and controversies than answers. Indeed, this seems the case with dyslexia. Clashing research findings are piling up, particularly with reference to the underlying causes of the disorder, the interpretation of which poses considerable problems – some see the evidence as complementary, some as rather contradicting perspectives.

Apparently, dyslexia has become one of the most intensively investigated and best known cognitive disorders; still, the remaining controversy and uncertainty is also mirrored in teachers' hesitation and doubtfulness as to how they can most successfully deal with children with dyslexia (e.g. dyslexia diagnosis in a bilingual setting). Several prevailing misconceptions about the mechanisms, symptoms and teaching approaches are at large, which, most probably, can be attributed to the gap – the mismatch between the contemporary sophisticated scientific knowledge and practice. From the practitioner's standpoint, the outcome of the prolific multidirectional research on dyslexia needs translating into practical applications in the school setting and, vice versa, research can also be informed by the findings of the invaluable teacher classroom observation. In fact, it nicely matches the idea of the three different levels of explanation – biological, cognitive and behavioural – and the dynamic, bidirectional interaction between them, with no one level of greater importance than the remaining levels.

How does this idea affect practitioners – teachers, who confront various behavioural facets of dyslexia every day? It does, even though neuroscience seems so distant from didactics, it lends considerable support in bringing answers to the questions about the most effective treatments, tutoring and teaching approaches. It serves well in assessing and verifying the environmental influences (e.g. the effects of teaching and learning) on brain functioning. The neurobiological foundations are, in turn, claimed to underlie and determine the cognitive functioning of an individual, hence an in-depth investigation of the cognitive processes and their disorders, to which dyslexia can be traced. The link between biology, cognition and behaviour, all of which undergo environmental influences, in the study of dyslexia seems most apparent. A thorough understanding of the processes specific to each of the three levels is necessary to build up a complete image of the phenomenon (Frith, 1999). This is so because a single symptom at the behavioural level may equally follow from different impairments at the biological and cognitive levels. The picture becomes even more complicated because a particular impairment at the cognitive or biological level is well capable of contributing to more than one deficit at the behavioural level (Helland, 2007). Nicolson (2001) uses a medical model to illustrate the situation. Such a model comprises three elements: a cause, a symptom and a treatment. Obviously, several diseases may have similar symptoms, but they markedly differ as to causes and treatments, which is why the use of further, more sensitive tests, administered by specialists, constitutes a necessary condition to determine the true underlying cause and thus the proper treatment.

The complexity of the phenomenon of dyslexia, largely brought about by its multiple behavioural manifestations, has given rise to numerous and, indeed, at times controversial etiological theories of the disorder. Nevertheless, they have gained substantial interest and generated a great deal of research, inviting intense academic debates in recent years. In order to avoid confusion in dyslexia research, a need for consensus is highlighted, since, quite naturally, the understanding of such a complicated condition would require a complex, interdisciplinary cooperation, leading to the formulation of a causal theory of dyslexia. Such a theory, as it stands, should be capable of explaining the symptoms, their underlying causes as well as an optimal therapeutic and support system (Fawcett & Nicolson, 2001; Nicolson, 2001; Reid & Fawcett, 2004).

Dyslexia is a neurodevelopmental disorder. Adopting the developmental perspective in an approach to investigate dyslexia requires deep awareness of the typical development of the reading skill first and then comparing it to what can be observed in children with dyslexia. From such a standpoint, dyslexia can be described as a delay in reading development, hence perceiving it in dimensional terms seems most justified. It means that reading ability can be illustrated in a form of continuum, thus considerable individual differences in acquiring the skill come into play. Individuals may suffer from dyslexia to varying degrees; still, they would occupy the bottom end of the proposed continuum. However, categorical descriptions of the disorder apparently are in use, despite an obvious difficulty to decide on the arbitrary cut-off point on the continuum, after reaching which, one would qualify to be diagnosed as having dyslexia (Hulme & Snowling, 2009).

Perceiving dyslexia as a dimensional construct, as a delay, alters the way we look at the improvement in the reading skill. Development is dynamic and characterised by change; quite naturally, the same holds true for the symptoms of dyslexia. Some of the symptoms are observable at the onset of formal schooling and reading instruction and, later, can reduce or disappear, which by no means implies that the underlying impairment, most probably in the form of phonological processing deficit, vanishes (Frith, 2008). Other signs, i.e. spelling difficulty, seem to persist into adulthood. So, the behavioural manifestations of dyslexia change over the course of time and development. Does this mean that one can grow out of dyslexia? This is where the categorical labels become problematic, while a dimensional description offers a more plausible explanation – dyslexia is a life-long condition, with considerable inter- and intra-variation with reference to behavioural facets. Once diagnosed, one remains dyslexic; however, as a result of compensation activities and learning, one becomes able to successfully handle tasks that used to pose great demand and moves up along the continuum of the reading ability.

As for the characteristic symptoms, the fundamental difficulty lies in the acquisition of skilful word decoding (reading) and encoding (spelling), leaving the child behind his/her peers with regard to literacy development. The language processing system is selectively impaired in children with dyslexia, mainly with reference to phonological processing, while other aspects of language are rather normal. Thus, the characteristic deficit in dyslexia seems to pertain to poor quality of phonological representations of speech sounds, which are to support spoken word recognition and production. Dyslexic phonological representations tend to be inaccurately specified and deprived of distinctness, which is how the phonological processing difficulties in individuals with dyslexia arise (Goswami, 2000; Snowling, 2001a). Additionally, learning to read requires the capacity to map letter strings of printed words (orthography) on phonemic sequences that spoken words are built of (phonology). Normally developing children are able to grasp the relations between the spelling patterns and their pronunciations (the alphabetic principle) and acquire a powerful tool that allows them to further explore the print (Lundberg & Hoien, 2001; Shaywitz, 1997; Snowling, 2001a). On the contrary, children with dyslexia are claimed to have noticeable trouble in establishing the connections between phonemes and their graphic representations as well as in generalising their knowledge in order to read unfamiliar words.

In fact, across numerous studies, poor readers consistently demonstrate significantly worse performances on phonological awareness and letter-to-sound decoding tasks in comparison to good readers. In addition, the most interesting and exciting evidence for poor phonological skills constituting a manifest cause of reading failure in beginning readers comes from training and intervention studies (Vellutino et al., 2004), where direct instruction in phonological awareness and letter-sound correspondences repeatedly proved highly effective in enhancing word identification facility as well as spelling and reading skills. The strongest effects on reading acquisition are noticed when phonological training is combined with the instruction in letter-sound mappings.

Thinking about the time and course of development of the reading skill, one cannot ignore the multitude of factors influencing it, among which a prominent position is held by the language-specific factors. Differences in literacy acquisition – reading accuracy and speed – depend to a great extent on the orthographic system of a given language. Thus, we can expect that typical development of a reading skill differs across languages and so do the behavioural manifestations of dyslexia. The more transparent the phoneme-grapheme mapping system of a language, the fewer difficulties it poses on individuals with dyslexia learning to read in it, irrespective of whether it is a native, a second or a foreign language. This is so because the underlying core phonological deficit, causing delay in reading development in one's native language, exerts substantial influence on the acquisition of the consecutive languages.

Hardly anyone would argue against a decent command of a foreign language, or even languages, constituting a tremendous asset in the contemporary world. Foreign language faculty is no longer perceived a luxury and an extra quality enhancing job prospects, quite the opposite, foreign language requirement has become a regular, compulsory part of educational systems and one of the elementary skills expected of candidates for many professional positions. How does such expectations relate to dyslexia? Individuals with dyslexia are prone to encounter difficulties in foreign language study, varying in scope and intensity, because foreign language learning is built upon native language skills. Strong native language competence fosters foreign language acquisition, while poor native language codes significantly determine the degree of proficiency in a foreign language. Most poor foreign language learners seem to find the phonological/orthographic processing particularly troublesome (Sparks *et al.*, 1989).

An intriguing question arises whether all poor foreign language learners are dyslexic and, more importantly, whether individuals with dyslexia can achieve average or above average competence in a foreign language. Similar to reading ability, also in the case of foreign language proficiency, a dimensional rather that categorical perspective is adopted. Foreign language ability, with regard to individuals with dyslexia as well as low-achieving but non-disabled learners, can be represented on a continuum, with the foreign language learning difficulties ranging from mild to severe. It seems reasonable to expect that most students with dyslexia would occupy the bottom part – the more severe end of the continuum. We can tentatively expect that the degree to which the placement of a given individual with dyslexia on the continuum of reading development in the native and foreign language parallel would depend on numerous factors. Among these factors, the type and severity of the disorder, in particular the strength of the phonological skills, and the characteristics of the phonological/orthographic system of a language can be listed. So, it seems a theoretically sound assumption that, even though the majority of students with dyslexia would be expected to show varying degrees of difficulty in a foreign language study, they are capable of achieving average results, provided an adequate teaching approach is adopted. Still, despite undeniable progress, they would still slightly lag behind the non-dyslexic individuals. However, there would also be learners with dyslexia reaching above-average foreign language competence.

As much as there is a wide consensus on the need for early diagnosis and intervention in the monolingual settings, it is lacking with respect to multilingual backgrounds. It is true that interest and sensitivity is constantly growing on the issue of diagnosing dyslexia in children being brought up in bilingual, multilingual and multicultural contexts, which is reflected in research findings. The situation concerns children from ethnic and linguistic minorities, who use their native language at home and second language at school. Frequently, it is the case that they possess rather limited competence in the second language prior to the commencement of formal instruction at school. The controversy that arises here is mainly whether we should wait for these children to acquire an acceptable level of spoken proficiency in the second language before they can become liable to the valid identification towards dyslexia in that language. This assumption is apparently based on the commonly shared view that in order to develop skilful reading, one needs to have adequate speaking skills in the second language. However, the crucial effect that oral proficiency in the second language exerts on reading comprehension does not seem to apply with regard to word and pseudo-word decoding abilities. Thus, the early assessment of these skills is highly recommended. What is more, since phonological processing skills in one language are capable of predicting word recognition ability within and across languages, it means that phonological processing abilities in one language, no matter whether native or second, can predict individual differences in word decoding in another language, even in view of not yet fully developed proficiency in the second language (Geva, 2000). Beyond doubt, whether conducted in the monolingual or bilingual setting, timely diagnosis ensures greater opportunities for effective intervention and reading success, while postponing assessment can bring about the far-reaching damaging effects of cumulative scholastic failure.

Recommendations drawn from the detailed identification constitute a foundation for designing remedial activities and intervention programmes for students with dyslexia. Such an approach should most preferably apply in the context of the native, second and foreign language learning. In principle, tutoring in dyslexia should be individualised and tailored to the particular needs and abilities of the students, especially with regard to the teaching approach, pace of presentation and work, as well as the intensity and frequency of repetition and consolidation. Regularity, reinforcement and overlearning are to lead to automaticity, which, nevertheless, needs the back up of the explicit development of the metacognitive skills.

With regard to treatment, teaching methods and techniques in dyslexia, the aforementioned alliance of research and practice is most welcome. The noticeable reluctance of teachers, especially foreign language teachers, towards accepting and applying research-based interventions is most probably triggered by the often controversial and conflicting research outcomes, let alone the confusion induced by the frequent occurrence of the miracle cures for dyslexia on the market. However, it seems especially important to distinguish between issues that are still intensely debated and those well verified, widely accepted and agreed upon. There is no doubt that translating and disseminating the confirmed and replicated findings concerning research-based treatments among teachers and implementing them into school practice is worth every effort. For instance, research-validated educational activities recommended for widespread use involve direct instruction in phonological awareness and letter-sound correspondences, which typically brings highly positive effects in terms of enhanced word identification, spelling and reading ability (Vellutino et al., 2004). Phonological training combined with instruction in letter-sound mappings is claimed to exert the most pronounced facilitating effect on reading acquisition (Bogdanowicz, 2002a; Gustafson et al., 2007; Reid, 1998; Wise et al., 2007). In addition, the direct multisensory structured approach has repeatedly been shown to be effective and is advocated for teaching reading and spelling to children with dyslexia in the native and foreign language alike.

All in all, individuals with dyslexia can become regular beneficiaries of the educational system available to the majority of children in a given cultural context, as long as certain provisions are introduced into the system. Successful mainstreaming or inclusion education for individuals with dyslexia requires the understanding, engagement and collective effort of all parties involved – parents, teachers, policy makers and, last but not least, students with dyslexia themselves. Educational provisions that can be applied in order to reduce and soften the dyslexic difficulties and allow them to demonstrate their potential would vary depending on the severity of the disorder, which is basically consistent with the idea of individualisation. What follows from the above is that some students with dyslexia require minimal alterations to feel relatively comfortably in the educational system, while other learners with dyslexia might need a much more individualised, for example one-to-one teaching approach.

The teacher's role cannot be overestimated in the all-embracing dyslexic educational endeavour. Teachers can form the fertile ground for the overall mental, psychological and social development through reducing disharmonies, lessening scholastic failure as well as lowering emotional tension. Preventing the devastating consequences of the extensive encounter with non-success and disappointment is essential. Rebuilding confidence and restoring self-image can be achieved through noticing even the smallest educational advances and encouraging further effort in students with dyslexia.

Appendix 1

Words Used in the Pre-test, Post-test 1 and Post-test 2

Nr	*Pre-test and post-test 1*	*Problem area*	*Post-test 2*
1	tag	Short vowel sounds, CVC words	fan
2	fix		bin
3	mug		rug
4	shift	Initial and final consonant blends and digraphs	shed
5	crush		blush
6	such		much
7	whip		when
8	chick		chin
9	flint		cloth
10	froth		twist
11	slick		crisp
12	thin		theft
13	clamp	Nasal sounds, assimilation	plump
14	trench		clench
15	shunt		print
16	frond		brand
17	clink		blink
18	prong		cling

Appendix 1 (*Continued*)

Nr	Pre-test and post-test 1	Problem area	Post-test 2
19	thrust	Initial triple consonant blends	strung
20	strand		shrimp
21	sprung		spring
22	shrink		splash
23	miss	Doubling rule – single vowel followers	spill
24	fuzz		buzz
25	stiff		sniff
26	swan	'W' rules	swamp
27	wharf		ward
28	word		worm
29	lark	Vowel/consonant digraphs	smart
30	cord		north
31	fern		verb
32	have	'V' rules	live
33	cover		glove
34	cane	'Magic e' rule	flame
35	cube		duke
36	pine		kite
37	dole		rope
38	pick	Spelling of the /k/ sound	track
39	milk		bark
40	kilt		kettle
41	cactus		clip
42	clinic		basic
43	quit		quest

Appendix 1 (*Continued*)

Nr	Pre-test and post-test 1	Problem area	Post-test 2
44	mix		fax
45	gypsy	Spelling of the /dʒ/ and /tʃ/ sounds	gender
46	jug		junk
47	edge		lodge
48	large		wage
49	fetch		stretch
50	fry	Spelling of the long vowel sounds /ai/, /ei/, /ðʊ/, /ju:/, /u:/, /i:/	spy
51	sight		flight
52	tray		bay
53	brain		fail
54	grow		blow
55	moan		soak
56	glue		clue
57	grew		flew
58	boot		broom
59	keep		wheel
60	east		meal
61	copy		windy
62	niece		piece
63	receive		ceiling

Appendix 2

List of Words Used in the Programme

Sound	Letters	Words
/æ/	'a'	bad, Dad, had, lad, mad, pad, sad, bag, rag, tag, ham, jam, Pam, ram, Sam, can, fan, man, pan, ran, cap, map, nap, tap, at, bat, cat, fat, hat, mat, pat, rat, sat
/e/	'e'	bed, fed, led, Ned, red, Ted, wed, beg, keg, leg, Meg, peg, Ben, hen, men, pen, ten, bet, get, jet, let, met, net, pet, set, wet, yet, yes
/I/	'i'	bid, did, hid, lid, rid, big, dig, fig, pig, wig, him, bin, pin, tin, win, dip, pip, rip, tip, zip, is, his, it, bit, fit, hit, lit, pit, sit, wit, six
/ɒ/	'o'	rob, cod, nod, rod, bog, dog, fog, hog, log, on, Ron, hop, mop, pop, top, cot, dot, got, hot, jot, lot, not, pot, rot, tot, box, fox
/ʌ/	'u'	cub, mud, tub, bug, hug, jug, mug, rug, hum, Mum, rum, sum, bun, fun, gun, run, sun, up, but, cup, cut, gut, hut, jut, nut, pup, us, bus
Initial consonant blends and digraphs		blob, crab, fret, plug, scab, smog, step, chin, blot, cram, frog, plus, smug, stop, chop, brag, drip, glad, pram, skin, snap, swim, ship, brim, drum, glum, prop, skip, snip, swot, shop, clap, flag, gran, tram, slim, spin, twig, thug, clip, flap, grin, trip, slot, spot, twin, thin
Final consonant blends and digraphs		gift, soft, camp, lamp, bank, dust, pink, must, milk, hand, mint, bench, silk, land, rent, lunch, belt, long, desk, felt, song, risk

Appendix 2 (*Continued*)

Sound	Letters	Words
	Initial and final consonant blends and digraphs	brush, crisp, frost, chest, drink, grand, cloth, flint, shift, think, trust, twist, slang, spend, stamp
/aː/	'ar'	car, bar, far, scar, star, arm, farm, harm, charm, march, dark, bark, park, shark, art, chart, part, smart, start, card, hard, sharp
/ɔː/	'or'	or, for, born, corn, form, storm, port, sort, short, sport, fork, lord, forth, north, horse
/ɜː/	'er'	her, herd, herb, verb, nerve, serve, sister, silver, expert, letter, mother, butter, father
/wɒ/	'wa'; 'wha'	what, water, watch, swab, swat, swap, wasp, wand, wad, swamp, swan, was, want, wash, wander
/wɔː/	'war'; 'whar'	warrant, wharf, ward, swarm, dwarf, war, warm, warn, toward, reward
/wɜː/	'wor'	word, work, world, worth, worship, worse, worm, worst, worthy, worthless
/l/	'll'	*all, *ball, *call, *doll, *fall, *hall, *small, *tall, *wall, shall, bell, fell, hell, sell, shell, smell, spell, tell, well, ill, bill, fill, grill, hill, pill, spill, still, till, will, thrill, doll, dull, gull, hull, *bull, *pull, *full
/s/	'ss'	mass, *brass, *glass, *class, *grass, *pass, chess, dress, press, stress, miss, boss, cross, loss, fuss, kiss
/z/	'zz'	jazz, fizz, whizz, buzz, fuzz
/f/	'ff'	cliff, sniff, stiff, whiff, cuff, puff, bluff, *staff
/v/	've'	have, live, give, five, serve, nerve
/ʌv/	'ov'	love, dove, oven, above, cover, glove

Appendix 2 (*Continued*)

Sound	Letters	Words
/k/	'c'	clip, cream, correct, crazy, carpet, coffee, cloud, curtain, cactus, cup, cold, candle, computer, cream, clown, calendar, canary, clock, cat, cage, crown, cable, corn, car, curtain, cap
	'k'	keep, kettle, kind, ketchup, key, kid, kite, killer, kiss, kennel, kitten, kind, kilt, kick, kiss, king
	'-k'	speak, week, book, ask, bank, desk, talk, work, think, look, cloak, hook, croak, took, shook, beak, Greek, cheek, cook, pink, mask, sink, tank, talk, shark, fork, bark, walk, break, park, mark, thank, milk, break, risk
	'-ck'	back, black, neck, stick, luck, clock, quick, duck, sick, lock, suck, trick, sock, block, check, rock, track, click
/kw/	'qu'	question, quite, square, quit, quick, queen, equip, quiz, quake, quest, aquarium, equator, aqua, squeeze, quarrel, equal, quiet, quarter, quack, quality
/ks/	'x'	fox, six, mix, fax, taxi, sixty, text, extra, example, excellent, relax, expert, complex, box, next, wax, fix, exam, exit
/ik/	'ic'	clinic, classic, traffic, basic, plastic, logic, magic, electric, genetic, public, music, cosmetic, linguistic, pediatric, fantastic, scientific, graphic, analytic, panic, comic, problematic, athletic

Appendix 2 (*Continued*)

Sound	Letters	Words
/dʒ/	'-dge'	judge, fridge, sledge, badge, bridge, ledge, lodge, edge, ridge, fudge
	'-ge'	age, change, huge, large, orange, page, stage, wage, cage, charge
	'j'	jail, jazz, job, join, joke, judge, jump, junk, just, jacket
	'g'	gender, general, genetic, gentle, gin, ginger, giant, gym, gypsy, gesture
/g/	'-g'	dog, frog, big, jug, leg, pig
	'g'	girl, go, give, game, get, great
/tʃ/	'ch'	chance, change, check, child, choice, China, chop, chapter, chain, chapel, channel, charm, charge, cheap, choose, cheese, charity, chest, church
	'-ch'	beach, each, reach, speech, teach, touch, bench, lunch, march, coach, peach, French, branch, crunch, punch, search, church
	'-tch'	witch, catch, sketch, stitch, Dutch, match, fetch, switch, watch, stretch, scratch
/ai/	'igh'	night, light, sight, bright, fight, fright, might, right, tight, slight, flight
	'-y'	try, cry, spy, fly, by, why, sky, rely, reply, shy, my, July, dry, deny
	'i-e'	time, ride, mine, fine, side, mile, kite, nine, bite, pipe, like, hide, life, size, wine, white, quite, bride, nice, five, pride, drive, smile, prize, crime

Appendix 2 (*Continued*)

Sound	Letters	Words
/ei/	'ai'	train, sail, jail, brain, rain, fail, paint, afraid, wait, mail, raise, plain, maid, main, tail, stain, pain, nail, faint
	'-ay'	say, may, play, tray, way, day, May, stay, holiday, Friday, subway, replay, yesterday, pay, gray, bay, today, delay, Sunday
	'a-e'	place, shake, grape, brake, plane, flame, shame, snake, bake, name, cake, make, cage, race, late, face, hate, take, rate, tape, made, male, mate, same, pale
/ôʊ/	'oa'	coast, load, float, toast, coal, goat, toad, throat, soak, soap, coach, goal, road, coat, moan, boat
	'-ow'	snow, grow, row, blow, know, show, slow, low, below, elbow, shadow, arrow, window, follow, pillow, throw, yellow, borrow
	'o-e'	home, bone, globe, hope, stone, nose, rope, tone, smoke, close, phone, joke, code, note, clone, spoke, drove, wrote, hole, choke, froze, chose, stole, woke, broke
/uː/, /juː/	'ue'	blue, glue, true, clue, due, value, rescue, issue, continue, argue, statue, sue, cue, avenue, barbecue, tissue
	'-ew'	new, grew, nephew, few, view, blew, crew, knew, flew, threw, screw, stew, dew
	'oo'	moon, root, boot, shoot, afternoon, noon, spoon, soon, room, broom, food, mood, fool, school, tool, cool, pool, gloom, stool
	'u-e'	cube, cute, huge, use, tune, mule, fuse, tube, duke, mute, nude, June, rule, Luke, rude, flute, crude, plume, lute, prune, prude

Appendix 2 (*Continued*)

Sound	Letters	Words
/iː/	'ee'	teeth, green, seem, speech, sweet, wheel, feel, keep, sleep, week, cheese, need, queen, speed, feet, street, meet, feed, free, knee, see, three, tree, agree, bee, coffee, degree
	'ea'	please, peach, speak, peace, mean, leave, cheap, reach, beat, read, dream, teach, stream, team, beach, real, meal, meat, clean, eat, easy, eagle, ear, eager, east, tea, sea
	'-y'	happy, funny, sleepy, lucky, sorry, angry, snowy, cloudy, windy, sunny, rainy, city, family, lady, daddy, baby, granny, mummy, twenty, thirty, forty, chemistry, biology, history, anatomy, Billy, Teddy, Sally
	'-ey'	chimney, donkey, hockey, honey, jockey, journey, kidney, money, monkey, valley, alley, attorney, turkey
	'ie'	piece, niece, field, cashier, believe, priest, chief, thief, relief
	'ei'	ceiling, receive, deceive, receipt, conceive, perceive
	'e-e'	mete, complete, athlete, extreme, recede

Appendix 3

Sample of writing (two pages from the English language notebook; personal details were removed) of a 12-year-old Polish boy with dyslexia, who learns English as a foreign language in a regular primary classroom setting. The two pages differ noticeably in the quality of the graphic level of writing and organisation of the notes on the page. The difference arises from the fact that the left-hand side page contains the homework assignment, on which a considerable amount of time was spent at home, while the right-hand side page contains the notes from the lesson, where the learner was under time pressure, which in turn resulted in poorer handwriting. In addition, mistakes specific to dyslexia occur, for instance: 'slreet' for 'street', 'havean' for 'have an', 'compuler' for 'computer', 'somenlimes' for 'sometimes', 'competitiom' for 'competition', 'ald' for 'old', 'mammols' for 'mammals', 'aninols' for 'animals', 'Engl' for 'English', 'ejght' for 'eight'.

Appendix 4

Sample of writing (two pages from the English language notebook) of a 15-year-old Polish boy with dyslexia, who learns English as a foreign language in a regular classroom setting of a secondary school. Several mistakes can be spotted, such as: *inconsistent spelling* (several spelling attempts of a given word in one piece of writing): 'dolls'/'dols', 'wyth'/ 'with', 'Holiwood'/'Hollywooa', 'thanks'/'thinks', 'story'/'stoy', 'ending'/ 'endring', 'natulal'/'natural'; *phonetic spelling*: 'ajs rink' for 'ice rink', 'koton' for 'cotton'; *adding parts of words*: 'ekspresioning' for 'expressing'; *skipping letters and diacritical marks*: 'stoy' for 'story', 'anxıous' for 'anxious'; *changing the position of letters*: 'trheat' for 'threat', 'trhead' for 'thread'; *difficulty discriminating letters of similar shape, differing in tiny details*: 'aninal' for 'animal', 'habilat' for 'habitat', 'fife' for 'life', 'comnested' for 'connected'; *poorly integrated spelling/incorrect spelling choices*: 'distroyd' for 'destroyed', 'terible' for 'terrible'; 'impresion' for 'impression', 'woryy' for 'worry', 'mowies' for 'movies', 'discower' for 'discover' ('w' is pronounced as /v/ in Polish), 'dols' for 'dolls', 'wyth' for 'with', 'trhead/trheat' for 'threat'; 'trheatd/trhead' for 'thread'; *bizarre spelling*: 'witol' for 'vehicle', 'endangires' for 'endangered', 'edrything' for 'everything'. In addition, letters are poorly formed, rather wobbly and drifting off the intended angles.

Appendix 5

Sample of writing (two pages from the English language notebook) of a 15-year-old Polish boy with dyslexia, who learns English as a foreign language in a regular classroom setting of a secondary school. Even though the handwriting is rather poor, still it is possible to decode, unlike in the sample presented in Appendix 6. Still, numerous spelling mistakes of various types occur, together with corrections and crossings. This piece of writing lacks graphic precision. It took a long time (as compared to non-dyslexic peers) and considerable effort to produce it because of keeping a tight grip on the pen and pressing down too strongly.

Appendix 6

Sample of unintelligible handwriting (two pages from the English language notebook) of a Polish 19-year-old college student with dyslexia, who learns English as a foreign language.

References

Adams, M. (1990) *Beginning to Read: Thinking and Learning about Print*. Cambridge, MA: MIT Press.
Aro, M. (2006) Learning to read: The effect of orthography. In R.M. Joshi and P.G. Aaron (eds) *Handbook of Orthography and Literacy* (pp. 531–550). Hillsdale, NJ: Lawrence Erlbaum.
Atwill, K., Blanchard, J., Gorin, J.S. and Burstein, K. (2007) Receptive vocabulary and cross-language transfer of phonemic awareness in kindergarten children. *The Journal of Educational Research* 100 (6), 336–345.
Aylward, E.H., Richards, T.L., Berninger, V.W., Nagy, W.E., Field, K.M., Grimme, A.C., Richards, A.L., Thomson, J.B. and Cramer, S.C. (2003) Instructional treatment associated with changes in brain activation in children with dyslexia. *Neurology* 61, 212–219.
Bakker, D.J. (1984) The brain as a dependent variable. *Journal of Clinical Neuropsychology* 6 (1), 1–16.
Bakker, D.J. (1990) *Neuropsychological Treatment of Dyslexia*. Oxford: Oxford University Press.
Bakker, D.J. (1995) The willing brain of dyslexic children. In C.K. Leong and R.M. Joshi (eds) *Developmental and Acquired Dyslexia* (pp. 33–39). The Netherlands: Kluwer Academic.
Bakker, D.J., Licht, R. and van Strien, J. (1991) Biopsychological validation of L- and P- type dyslexia. In B.P. Rourke (ed.) *Neuropsychological Validation of Learning Disability Subtypes* (pp. 124–139). New York: The Guilford Press.
Bakker, D.J., Licht, R. and Kappers, E.J. (1995) Hemispheric stimulation techniques in children with dyslexia. In M.G. Tramontana and S.R. Hooper (eds) *Advances in Child Neuropsychology* (Vol. 3) (pp. 144–177). New York: Springer-Verlag.
Bednarek, D. (1999) Neurobiologiczne podłoże dysleksji [Neurobiological basis of dyslexia]. *Przegląd Psychologiczny* 42 (1–2), 17–26.
Bednarek, D. (2003) Dysleksja a zaburzenia słuchu fonematycznego oraz kanału wielkokomórkowego w układzie wzrokowym [Dyslexia and phonological and magnocellular impairments]. In B. Kaja (ed.) *Diagnoza dysleksji [Dyslexia Assessment]* (pp. 128–132). Bydgoszcz: Wydawnictwo Akademii Bydgoskiej im. Kazimierza Wielkiego.
Barca, L., Burani, C., di Filippo, G. and Zoccolotti, P. (2007) Italian developmental dyslexic and proficient readers: Where are the differences? *Brain and Language* 98 (3), 347–351.
Benton, A. (1978) Dyslexia: An appraisal of current knowledge. In L. Benton and D. Pearl (eds) *Dyslexia: An Appraisal of Current Knowledge* (pp. 451–476). New York: Oxford University Press.
Biscaldi, M., Gezek, S. and Stuhr, V. (1998) Poor saccadic control correlates with dyslexia. *Neuropsychologia* 36, 1189–1202.

Bishop, D.V.M. (2006) Dyslexia: What's the problem? *Developmental Science* 9 (3), 256–257.
Blachman, B.A., Fletcher, J.M., Schatschneider, C., Francis, D.J., Clonan, S.M., Shaywitz, B.A. and Shaywitz, S.E. (2004) Effects of intensive reading remediation for second and third graders and a 1-year follow-up. *Journal of Educational Psychology* 96, 444–461.
Bloom, J.S. and Hynd, G.W. (2005) The role of the corpus callosum in interhemispheric transfer of information: Excitation or inhibition? *Neuropsychology Review* 15 (2), 59–71.
Boder, E. (1973) Developmental dyslexia: A diagnostic approach based on three atypical reading-spelling patterns. *Developmental Medicine and Child Neurology* 15, 663–687.
Bogdanowicz, M. (1985a) *Psychologia kliniczna dziecka w wieku przedszkolnym* [Clinical Psychology of Pre-school Children]. Warszawa: Wydawnictwa Szkolne i Pedagogiczne.
Bogdanowicz, M. (1985b) *Metoda dobrego startu w pracy z dzieckiem w wieku od 5 do 10 lat* [The Method of the Good Start for Children Aged 5–10]. Warszawa: Wydawnictwa Szkolne i Pedagogiczne.
Bogdanowicz, M. (1989) *Trudności w pisaniu u dzieci* [Writing Difficulties in Children]. Gdańsk: Wydawnictwo Uniwersytetu Gdańskiego.
Bogdanowicz, M. (1995) Uczeń o specjalnych potrzebach edukacyjnych [Students with special educational needs]. *Psychologia Wychowawcza* 3, 216–223.
Bogdanowicz, M. (1997a/2000) *Integracja percepcyjno-motoryczna: Teoria – diagnoza – terapia* [Perceptual-motor Integration: Theory – Diagnosis – Therapy]. Warszawa: Centrum Metodyczne Pomocy Psychologiczno-Pedagogicznej Ministerstwa Edukacji Narodowej.
Bogdanowicz, M. (1997b) Specyficzne trudności w czytaniu i pisaniu w świetle klasyfikacji medycznych, psychologicznych i pedagogicznych [Specific difficulties in reading and spelling in the international medical, psychological and pedagogical classifications]. *Audiofonologia* 10, 145–157.
Bogdanowicz, M. (1997c) Dysleksja rozwojowa – symptomy, patomechanizmy, terapia pedagogiczna [Developmental dyslexia – symptoms, pathomechanisms, pedagogical therapy]. *Terapia Numer Specjalny* (Special issue), 12–16.
Bogdanowicz, M. (1999) Specyficzne trudności w czytaniu i pisaniu [Specific difficulties in reading and spelling]. In T. Gałkowski and G. Jastrzębowska (eds) *Logopedia. Pytania i odpowiedzi* [Logopaedics. Questions and Answers] (pp. 815–859). Opole: Wydawnictwo Uniwersytetu Opolskiego.
Bogdanowicz, M. (2002a) *Ryzyko dysleksji. Problem i diagnozowanie* [Risk for Dyslexia. Definition and Diagnosis]. Gdańsk: Wydawnictwo Harmonia.
Bogdanowicz, M. (2002b) Diagnoza dysleksji rozwojowej [Developmental dyslexia assessment]. In W. Turewicz (ed.) *Zajęcia korekcyjno-kompensacyjne w klasach I–III* [Correction-compensation Classes in Grades I–III] (pp. 5–7). Zielona Góra: Ośrodek Doskonalenia Nauczycieli w Zielonej Górze.
Bogdanowicz, M. (2003a) Specyficzne trudności w czytaniu i pisaniu [Specific difficulties in reading and spelling]. In T. Gałkowski and G. Jastrzębowska (eds) *Logopedia. Pytania i odpowiedzi. Wydanie drugie poprawione i rozszerzone* [Logopaedics. Questions and Answers] (2nd edn) (pp. 491–535). Opole: Wydawnictwo Uniwersytetu Opolskiego.
Bogdanowicz, M. (2003b) Diagnoza dysleksji rozwojowej w Polsce [Developmental dyslexia assessment in Poland]. In B. Kaja (ed.) *Diagnoza dysleksji* [Dyslexia Assessment] (pp. 9–35). Bydgoszcz: Wydawnictwo Akademii Bydgoskiej im. Kazimierza Wielkiego.

Bogdanowicz, M. (2007) Świadomość dysleksji w Polsce – badania porównawcze [The awareness of dyslexia in Poland – comparative studies]. In M. Kostka-Szymańska and G. Krasowicz-Kupis (eds) *Dysleksja. Problem znany czy nieznany?* [*Dyslexia. Familiar or Unfamiliar Problem?*] (pp. 13–35). Lublin: Wydawnictwo Uniwersytetu Marii-Skłodowskiej.
Bogdanowicz, M. and Adryjanek, A. (2004) *Uczeń z dysleksją w szkole. Poradnik nie tylko dla polonistów* [*Dyslexic Student at School. A Guide not only for Polish Language Teachers*]. Gdynia: Wydawnictwo Pedagogiczne Operon.
Bogdanowicz, M. and Krasowicz, G. (1995) Diagnoza i leczenie dysleksji rozwojowej – neuropsychologiczna koncepcja D.J. Bakkera [Assessment and treatment of developmental dyslexia – a neuropsychological conception of D.J. Bakker]. *Psychologia Wychowawcza* 2, 116–130.
Bogdanowicz, M. and Krasowicz, G. (1996/1997) Typy dysleksji rozwojowej. Diagnoza i terapia według koncepcji D.J. Bakkera [Types of developmental dyslexia. Diagnosis and therapy according to D.J. Bakker's conception]. *Annales Universitatis Mariae Curie-Skłodowska* 9/10, 13–26.
Bogdanowicz, M. and Krasowicz-Kupis, G. (2005a) Czytanie i pisanie jako formy komunikacji językowej [Reading and writing as forms of linguistic communication]. In T. Gałkowski, E. Szeląg and G. Jastrzębowska (eds) *Podstawy neurologopedii* [*Introduction to Neurologopaedics*] (pp. 986–1015). Opole: Wydawnictwo Uniwersytetu Opolskiego.
Bogdanowicz, M. and Krasowicz-Kupis, G. (2005b) Diagnoza dysleksji rozwojowej [Developmental dyslexia assessment]. In T. Gałkowski, E. Szeląg and G. Jastrzębowska (eds) *Podstawy neurologopedii* [*Introduction to Neurologopaedics*] (pp. 967–985). Opole: Wydawnictwo Uniwersytetu Opolskiego.
Bogdanowicz, M. and Sayles, H. (2004) *Prawa uczniów z dysleksją w Europie* [*Rights of Dyslexic Children in Europe*]. Gdańsk: Wydawnictwo Harmonia.
Bogdanowicz, M. and Wszeborowska-Lipińska, B. (1992) Rozwój psychomotoryczny. Kariera szkolna i osobowość młodzieży dyslektycznej. [Psychomotor development. School career and personality of dyslexic adolescents]. *Scholasticus* 6, 35–38.
Borkowska, A. (1997) Zaburzenia językowe u dzieci z trudnościami w czytaniu i pisaniu [Language disorders in children with reading and spelling difficulties]. In A. Herzyk and D. Kądzielawa (eds) *Związek mózg – zachowanie w ujęciu neuropsychologii klinicznej* [*The Relation Between the Brain and Behaviour from the Perspective of Clinical Neuropsychology*] (pp. 269–292). Lublin: Wydawnictwo Uniwersytetu Marii Curie-Skłodowskiej.
Borkowska, A. (1998) *Analiza dyskursu narracyjnego u dzieci z dysleksją rozwojową* [*The Analysis of Narrative Discourse in Dyslexic Children*]. Lublin: Wydawnictwo Uniwersytetu Marii Curie-Skłodowskiej.
Borkowska, A. and Tarkowski, Z. (1990) Kompetencja językowa i komunikacyjna dzieci z trudnościami w czytaniu i pisaniu [Linguistic and communicative competence in children with reading and spelling difficulties]. *Logopedia* 17, 35–42.
Bosse, M-L., Tainturier, M.J. and Valdoi, S. (2007) Developmental dyslexia: The visual attention span deficit hypothesis. *Cognition* 104, 198–230.
Bower, B. (2000) Good readers may get perceptual lift. *Science News* 157, 180.
Bowey, J.A. (2005) Predicting individual differences in learning to read. In M.J. Snowling and C. Hulme (eds) *The Science of Reading: A Handbook* (pp. 155–172). Oxford: Blackwell.
Bradley, L. and Bryant, P. (1983) Categorizing sounds and learning to read – a causal connection. *Nature* 301, 419–421.

References

Breznitz, Z. (2003) Speed of phonological and orthographic processing as factors in dyslexia: Electrophysiological evidence. *Genetic, Social and General Psychology Monographs* 129 (2), 183–206.
Brown, H.D. (2000) *Principles of Language Learning and Teaching*. New York: Longman.
Brown, W.E., Eliez, S., Menon, V., Rumsey, J.M., White, C.D. and Reiss, A.L. (2001) Preliminary evidence of widespread morphological variations of the brain in dyslexia. *Neurology* 56, 781–783.
Bryant, P. and Bradley, L. (1980) Why children sometimes write words which they do not read. In U. Frith (ed.) *Cognitive Processes in Spelling* (pp. 355–370). London: Academic Press.
Bryant, P., Maclean, M., Bradley, L. and Crossland, J. (1990) Rhyme, alliteration, phoneme detection, and learning to read. *Developmental Psychology* 26, 429–438.
Brzezińska, A. (1987) *Czytanie i pisanie – nowy język dziecka* [*Reading and Writing – a New Language of a Child*]. Warszawa: Wydawnictwa Szkolne i Pedagogiczne.
Burani, C., Marcolini, S. and Stella, G. (2002) How early does morpho-lexical reading develop in readers of a shallow orthography? *Brain and Language* 81, 568–586.
Caravolas, M. (2006) Refining the psycholinguistic grain size theory: Effects of phonotactics and word formation on the availability of phonemes to preliterate children. *Developmental Science* 9 (5), 445–447.
Carrol, J.B. and Sapon, S.M. (1959) *Modern Language Aptitude Test*. Chicago, IL: The Psychological Corporation. Harcourt Brace Javanovich, Inc.
Carroll, J.M. and Iles, J.E. (2006) An assessment of anxiety levels in dyslexic students in higher education. *British Journal of Educational Psychology* 76, 651–662.
Carroll, J.M. and Snowling, M. (2004) Language and phonological skills in children at high risk of reading difficulties. *Journal of Child Psychology and Psychiatry* 45, 631–640.
Chen, T-Y. (2001) Testing Chinese learners of English for language learning difficulties by the Linguistic Coding Deficit/Difference Hypothesis. *RELC Journal* 32 (1), 34–51.
Chliounaki, K. and Bryant, P. (2007) How children learn about morphological spelling rules. *Child Development* 78 (4), 1360–1373.
Chodkiewicz, H. (1986) *O sprawności czytania w nauczaniu języka obcego* [*A Reading Skill in Foreign Language Teaching*]. Warszawa: Wydawnictwa Szkolne i Pedagogiczne.
Cieszyńska, J. (2001) *Nauka czytania krok po kroku. Jak przeciwdziałać dysleksji?* [*Learning to Read Step by Step. How to Prevent Dyslexia?*]. Kraków: Wydawnictwo Naukowe Akademii Pedagogicznej.
Cirino, P.T., Israelian, M.K., Morris, M.K. and Morris, R.D. (2005) Evaluation of the double-deficit hypothesis in college students referred for learning difficulties. *Journal of Learning Disabilities* 38 (1), 29–43.
Coltheart, M., Rastle, K., Perry, C., Langdon, R. and Ziegler, J. (2001) DRC: A dual route cascaded model of visual word recognition and reading aloud. *Psychological Review* 108 (1), 204–256.
Cornelissen, P., Bradley, L., Fowler, M.S. and Stein, J.F. (1991) What children see affects how they read. *Developmental Medicine & Child Neurology* 33, 755–762.
Critchley, M. (1964) *Developmental Dyslexia*. London: The Whitefriars Press Ltd.
Crombie, M. and McColl, H. (2000) Teaching modern foreign languages to dyslexic learners: A Scottish perspective. In L. Peer and G. Reid (eds)

Multilingualism, Literacy and Dyslexia. A Challenge for Educators (pp. 211–217). London: David Fulton.
Czajkowska, I. and Herda, K. (1998) Zajęcia korekcyjno-kompensacyjne w szkole [Correctio-compensation Classes at School]. Warszawa: Wydawnictwa Szkolne i Pedagogiczne.
Davies, R., Cuetos, F. and Glez-Seijas, R.M. (2007) Reading development and dyslexia in a transparent orthography: Survey of Spanish children. Annals of Dyslexia 57, 179–198.
Davis, C. and Bryant, P. (2006) Causal connections in the acquisition of an orthographic rule: A test of Uta Frith's developmental hypothesis. Journal of Child Psychology and Psychiatry 47 (8), 849–856.
Deacon, S.H. and Bryant, P. (2005) What young children do and do not know about the spelling of inflections and derivations. Developmental Science 8 (6), 583–594.
Deacon, S.H. and Bryant, P. (2006) This turnip's not for turning: Children's morphological awareness and their use of root morphemes in spelling. British Journal of Developmental Psychology 24, 567–575.
DeFries, J.C., Fulker, D.W. and LaBuda, M.C. (1987) Reading disability in twins: Evidence for a genetic aetiology. Nature 329, 537–539.
Deponio, P., Landon, J. and Reid, G. (2000) Dyslexia and bilingualism – implications for assessment, teaching and learning. In L. Peer and G. Reid (eds) Multilingualism, Literacy and Dyslexia. A Challenge for Educators (pp. 52–60). London: David Fulton.
Dockrell, J. and McShane, J. (1993) Children's Learning Difficulties. A Cognitive Approach. Oxford: Blackwell.
Downey, D.M., Snyder, L.E. and Hill, B. (2000) College students with dyslexia: Persistent linguistic deficits and foreign language learning. Dyslexia 6, 101–111.
Dryer, R., Beale, I.L. and Lambert, A.J. (1999) The balance model of dyslexia and remedial training: An evaluative study. Journal of Learning Disabilities 32 (2), 174–187.
Dufva, M. and Voeten, M. (1999) Native language literacy and phonological memory as prerequisites for learning English as a foreign language. Applied Psycholinguistics 20 (3), 329–348.
Durgunoğlu, A.Y. (2006) Learning to read in Turkish. Developmental Science 9 (5), 437–439.
Ehri, L.C. (1995) Phases of development in learning to read words by sight. Journal of Research in Reading 18, 116–125.
Ehri, L.C. (2005) Development of sight word reading: Phasis and findings. In M.J. Snowling and C. Hulme (eds) The Science of Reading: A Handbook (pp. 135–154). Oxford: Blackwell.
Ehri, L.C. (2008) Procesy czytania. Rozwijanie tej umiejętności i konsekwencje dla nauczania [Reading processes, acquisition, and instructional implications]. In G. Reid and J. Wearmouth (eds) Dysleksja. Teoria i praktyka [Dyslexia and Literacy. Theory and Practice] (pp. 235–260). Gdańsk: Gdańskie Wydawnictwo Psychologiczne.
Ehri, L.C. and McCormick, S. (1998) Phases of word learning: Implications for instruction with delayed and disordered readers. Reading and Writing Quarterly 14, 135–163.
Ellis, R. (1994) Understanding Second Language Acquisition. Oxford: Oxford University Press.
Elliott, J. and Place, M. (2000) Dzieci i młodzież w kłopocie. Poradnik nie tylko dla psychologów [Children and Adolescents in Trouble. A Guide not Only for

Psychologists]. Warszawa: Wydawnictwa Szkolne i Pedagogiczne. Spółka Akcyjna.

Everatt, J. (2008) Procesy wzrokowe [Visual processes]. In G. Reid and J. Wearmouth (eds) *Dysleksja. Teoria i praktyka* [*Dyslexia and Literacy. Theory and Practice*] (pp. 121–140). Gdańsk: Gdańskie Wydawnictwo Psychologiczne.

Everatt, J., Adams, E. and Smyth, I. (2000a) Bilingual children's profiles on dyslexia screening measures. In L. Peer and G. Reid (eds) *Multilingualism, Literacy and Dyslexia. A Challenge for Educators* (pp. 36–44). London: David Fulton.

Everatt, J. Smythe, I., Adams, E. and Ocampo, D. (2000b) Dyslexia screening measures and bilingualism. *Dyslexia* 6, 42–56.

Fawcett, A.J. (2008) Dysleksja oraz umiejętność czytania i pisania. Podstawowe zagadnienia [Dyslexia and literacy]. In G. Reid and J. Wearmouth (eds) *Dysleksja. Teoria i praktyka* [*Dyslexia and Literacy. Theory and Practice*] (pp. 25–50). Gdańsk: Gdańskie Wydawnictwo Psychologiczne.

Fawcett, A.J. and Nicolson, R.I. (1999) Performance of dyslexic children on cerebellar and cognitive tests. *Journal of Motor Behaviour* 31, 68–78.

Fawcett, A.J. and Nicolson, R.I. (2001) Dyslexia: The role of the cerebellum. In A.J. Fawcett (ed.) *Dyslexia. Theory and Good Practice* (pp. 89–105). London: Whurr.

Fawcett, A.J. and Nicolson, R.I. (2004) Dyslexia: The role of the cerebellum. In G. Reid and A.J. Fawcett (eds) *Dyslexia in Context. Research, Policy and Practice* (pp. 25–47). London: Whurr.

Fawcett, A.J., Nicolson, R.I. and Dean, P. (1996) Impaired performance of children with dyslexia on a range of cerebellar tasks. *Annals of Dyslexia* 46, 259–283.

Fawcett, A.J., Nicolson, R.I. and Maclagan, F. (2001) Cerebellar tests differentiate between groups of poor readers with and without IQ discrepancy. *Journal of Learning Disabilities* 34, 119–135.

Ferrari, M. and Palladino, P. (2007) Foreign language learning difficulties in Italian children: Are they associated with other learning difficulties? *Journal of Learning Disabilities* 40 (3), 256–269.

Finch, A.J., Nicolson, R.I. and Fawcett, A.J. (2002) Evidence for neuroanatomical difference within the olivo-cerebellar pathway of adults with dyslexia. *Cortex* 38, 529–539.

Fisher, S.E. and Francks, C. (2006) Genes, cognition and dyslexia: Learning to read the genome. *Trends in Cognitive Sciences* 10, 250–257.

Fisher, S.E. and Smith, S.D. (2001) Progress towards the identification of genes influencing developmental dyslexia. In A.J. Fawcett (ed.) *Dyslexia. Theory and Good Practice* (pp. 39–64). London: Whurr.

Frederickson, N., Frith, U. and Reason, R. (1997) *Phonological Assessment Battery*. Windsor: NFER-Nelson.

Frith, U. (1985) Beneath the surface of developmental dyslexia. In K. Patterson, J. Marshall and M. Coltheart (eds) *Surface Dyslexia* (pp. 287–295). Baltimore, MD: University Park Press.

Frith, U. (1999) Paradoxes in the definition of dyslexia. *Dyslexia* 5, 192–214.

Frith, U. (2008) Rozwiązywanie paradoksów dysleksji [Resolving the paradoxes of dyslexia]. In G. Reid and J. Wearmouth (eds) *Dysleksja. Teoria i praktyka* [*Dyslexia and Literacy. Theory and Practice*] (pp. 71–102). Gdańsk: Gdańskie Wydawnictwo Psychologiczne.

Frost, R. (2006) Becoming literate in Hebrew: The grain size hypothesis and semitic orthographic systems. *Developmental Science* 9 (5), 439–440.

Frost, R., Katz, L. and Bentin, S. (1987) Strategies for visual word recognition and orthographical depth: A multilingual comparison. *Journal of Experimental Psychology: Human Perception and Performance* 13 (1), 104–115.

Frost, R. and Ziegler, J.C. (2007) Speech and spelling interaction: The interdependence of visual and auditory word recognition. In M.G. Gaskell (ed.) *The Oxford Handbook of Psycholinguistics* (pp. 107–118). Oxford: Oxford University Press.

Gajar, A.H. (1987) Foreign language learning disabilities; the identification of predictive and diagnostic variables. *Journal of Learning Disabilities* 20 (6), 327–330.

Galaburda, A.M. (1985) Developmental dyslexia: A review of biological interactions. *Annals of Dyslexia* 35, 21–35.

Galaburda, A.M. (1993) Neurology of developmental dyslexia. *Current Opinion in Neurobiology* 3, 237–242.

Galaburda, A.M., Lemay, M., Kemper, T.M. and Geschwind, N. (1978) R/L asymmetries in the brain may underlie cerebral dominance. *Science* 199, 852–856.

Galaburda, A.M. and Livingstone, M. (1993) Evidence for a magnocellular defect in developmental dyslexia. In P. Tallal, A.M. Galaburda, R.R. Llinas and C. von Euler (eds) *Temporal Information Processing in the Nervous System. Annals of the New York Academy of Science* 682 (pp. 70–82). New York: New York Academy of Sciences.

Galaburda, A.M., Lo Turco, L., Ramus, F., Fitch, R.H. and Rosen, G.D. (2006) From genes to behaviour in developmental dyslexia. *Nature Neuroscience* 9 (10), 1213–1217.

Ganschow, L. and Sparks, R. (1986) Learning disabilities and foreign language difficulties: Deficits in listening skills? *Journal of Reading, Writing, and Learning Disabilities International* 2, 306–319.

Ganschow, L. and Sparks, R. (1987) The foreign language requirement. *Learning Disabilities Focus* 2, 115–123.

Ganschow, L. and Sparks, R. (1995) Effects of direct instruction in Spanish phonology on the native-language skills and foreign-language aptitude of at-risk foreign-language learners. *Journal of Learning Disabilities* 28 (2), 107–120.

Ganschow, L. and Sparks, R. (2000) Reflections on foreign language study for students with foreign language learning problems: Research, issues, and challenges. *Dyslexia* 6, 87–100.

Ganschow, L. and Sparks, R. (2001) Learning difficulties and foreign language learning: A review of research and instruction. *Language Teaching* 34, 79–98.

Ganschow, L., Sparks, R., Javorsky, J., Pohlman, J. and Bishop-Marbury, A. (1991) Identifying native language difficulties among foreign language learners in college: A 'foreign' language learning disability? *Journal of Learning Disabilities* 24, 530–541.

Ganschow, L., Sparks, R., Anderson, R., Javorsky, J. and Skinner, S. (1994) Differences in language performance among high and low anxious college foreign language learners. *Modern Language Journal* 78, 41–55.

Ganschow, L., Sparks, R. and Javorsky, J. (1998) Foreign language learning difficulties: A historical perspective. *Journal of Learning Disabilities* 31 (3), 248–258.

Ganschow, L., Schneider, E. and Evers, T. (2000) Difficulties of English as a foreign language (EFL) for students with language-learning disabilities (dyslexia). In L. Peer and G. Reid (eds) *Multilingualism, Literacy and Dyslexia. A Challenge for Educators* (pp. 182–191). London: David Fulton.

Gąsowska, T. and Pietrzak-Stępkowska, Z. (1994) *Praca wyrównawcza z dziećmi mającymi trudności w czytaniu i pisaniu.* [*Remedial Work with Children Encountering Reading and Spelling Difficulties*]. Warszawa: Wydawnictwa Szkolne i Pedagogiczne.
Geva, E. (2000) Issues in the assessment of reading disabilities in L2 children – beliefs and research evidence. *Dyslexia* 6, 13–28.
Gillingham, A. and Stillman, B.W. (1997) *The Gillingham Manual: Remedial Training for Children with Specific Disability in Reading, Spelling and Penmanship* (8th edn). Cambridge, MA: Educators Publishing Service.
Gindrich, P.A. (2002) *Funkcjonowanie psychospołeczne uczniów dyslektycznych* [*Psychosocial Functioning of Dyslexic Students*]. Lublin: Wydawnictwo UMCS.
Goikoetxea, E. (2006) Reading errors in first- and second-grade readers of shallow orthography: Evidence from Spanish. *British Journal of Educational Psychology* 76, 333–350.
Gombert, J.E. (1992) *Metalinguistic Development.* Hemel Hempstead: Havester Wheatsheaf.
Goswami, U. (1999) Causal connections in beginning reading: The importance of rhyme. *Journal of Research in Reading* 22 (3), 217–240.
Goswami, U. (2000) Phonological representations, reading development and dyslexia: Towards a cross-linguistic theoretical framework. *Dyslexia* 6, 133–151.
Goswami, U. (2005) Synthetic phonics and learning to read: A cross-language perspective. *Educational Psychology in Practice* 21 (4), 273–282.
Goswami, U. (2006) Sensorimotor impairments in dyslexia: Getting the beat. *Developmental Science* 9 (3), 257–259.
Goswami, U. and Bryant, P.E. (1990) *Phonological Skills and Learning to Read.* Hillsdale, NJ: Lawrence Erlbaum.
Goswami, U. and Ziegler, J.C. (2006) Fluency, phonology, and morphology: A response to the commentaries on becoming literate in different languages. *Developmental Science* 9 (5), 451–453.
Górniewicz, E. (1998) *Pedagogiczna diagnoza specyficznych trudności w czytaniu i pisaniu* [*Pedagogical Assessment of Specific Difficulties in Reading and Spelling*]. Toruń: Wydawnictwo Adam Marszałek.
Grabowska, A. (1997) Percepcja wzrokowa i jej analogie do innych form percepcji [Visual perception and its analogy to other forms of perception]. In T. Górska, A. Grabowska and J. Zagrodzka (eds) *Mózg a zachowanie* [*Brain vs. Behaviour*] (pp. 147–183). Warszawa: Wydawnictwo Naukowe PWN.
Grant, A.C., Zangaladze, A., Thiagarajah, M. and Saathian, K. (1999) Tactile perception in dyslexics. *Neuropsychologia* 37, 1201–1211.
Gregg, N., Hoy, C., Flaherty, D.A., Norris, P., Coleman, C., Davis, M. and Jordan, M. (2005) Decoding and spelling accommodations for postsecondary students with dyslexia – It's more than processing speed. *Learning Disabilities: A Contemporary Journal* 3 (2), 1–17.
Gustafson, S., Ferreira, J. and Rönnberg, J. (2007) Phonological or orthographic training for children with phonological or orthographic decoding deficits. *Dyslexia* 13, 211–229.
Hadzibeganovic, T., van den Noort, M., Bosch, P., Perc, M., van Kralingen, R., Mondt, K. and Coltheart, M. (in press) Cross-linguistic neuroimaging in dyslexia: A critical view. *Cortex.*
Hanley, J.R., Masterson, J., Spencer, L.H. and Evans, D. (2004) How long do the advantages of learning to read a transparent orthography last? An investigation of the reading skills and reading impairment of Welsh children at 10 years of age. *The Quarterly Journal of Experimental Psychology* 57A (8), 1393–1410.

Hatcher, J. and Snowling, M.J. (2008) Hipoteza reprezentacji fonologicznych jako sposób rozumienia dysleksji: od teorii do praktyki [The phonological representations hypothesis of dyslexia]. In G. Reid and J. Wearmouth (eds) *Dysleksja. Teoria i praktyka* [*Dyslexia and Literacy. Theory and Practice*] (pp. 103–120). Gdańsk: Gdańskie Wydawnictwo Psychologiczne.

Heaton, P. and Winterton, P. (1996) *Dealing with Dyslexia* (2nd edn). London: Whurr.

Heiervang, E., Hugdahl, H., Steinmetz, H., Smievoll, A.I., Stevenson, J., Lund, A., Ersland, L. and Lundervold, A. (2000) Planum temporale, planum parietale and dichotic listening in dyslexia. *Neuropsychologia* 38, 1704–1713.

Helland, T. (2007) Dyslexia at a behavioural and cognitive level. *Dyslexia* 13, 25–41.

Helland, T. (2008) Second language assessment in dyslexia: Principles and practice. In J. Kormos and E.H. Kontra (eds) *Language Learners with Special Needs. An International Perspective* (pp. 68–85). Bristol: Multilingual Matters.

Helland, T., Asbjørnsen, A.E., Hushovd, A.E. and Hugdahl, K. (2008) Dichotic listening and school performance in dyslexia. *Dyslexia* 14, 42–53.

Helland, T. and Kaasa, R. (2005) Dyslexia in English as a second language. *Dyslexia* 11, 41–60.

Ho, C.S-H. and Fong, K-M. (2005) Do Chinese dyslexic children have difficulties learning English as a second language? *Journal of Psycholinguistic Research* 34 (6), 603–618.

Ho, C.S.-H., Law, T.P-S. and Ng, P.M. (2000) The phonological deficit hypothesis in Chinese developmental dyslexia. *Reading and Writing: An Interdisciplinary Journal* 13, 57–79.

Hoien, T. and Lundberg, I (2000) *Dyslexia. From Theory to Intervention*. Dordrecht, Netherlands: Kluwer Academic.

Hoien, T., Lundberg, I., Stanovich, K.E. and Bjaalid, I.K. (1995) Components of phonological awareness. *Reading and Writing* 7, 171–188.

Hogan, T.P., Catts, H.W. and Little T.D. (2005) The relationship between phonological awareness and reading: Implications for the assessment of phonological awareness. *Language, Speech, and Hearing Services in Schools* 36, 285–293.

Horgan, J. (1997) Komputer lekarstwem na trudności w czytaniu [Computer as a cure for reading difficulties]. *Świat Nauki* 1, 62–63.

Hornsby, B., Shear, F. and Pool, J. (1999) *Alpha to Omega. The A–Z Teaching Reading, Writing and Spelling* (5th edn). Oxford: Heinemann Educational.

Hugdahl, K., Heiervang, E., Erland, L., Lundervold, A., Steinmetz, H. and Smievoll, A.I. (2003) Significant relation between MR measures of planum temporale area and dichotic processing of syllables in dyslexic children. *Neuropsychologia* 41, 666–675.

Hulme, C. and Snowling, M. (2009) *Developmental Disorders of Language Learning and Cognition*. Oxford/Malden: Wiley-Blackwell.

Hulme, C., Snowling, M., Caravolas, M. and Carroll, J. (2005) Phonological skills are (probably) one cause of success in learning to read: A comment on Castles and Coltheart. *Scientific Studies of Reading* 9 (4), 351–365.

Hurry, J., Nunes, T., Bryant, P., Pretzlik, U., Parker, M., Curno, T. and Midgley, L. (2005) Transforming research on morphology unto teacher practice. *Research Papers in Education* 20 (2), 187–206.

Hutchinson, J.M., Whiteley, H.E., Smith, C.D. and Connors, L. (2004) The early identification of dyslexia: Children with English as an additional language. *Dyslexia* 10, 179–195.

Jaklewicz, H. (1982) Zaburzenia mowy pisanej i czytanej u dzieci [Disorders of speech and reading in children]. In J. Szumska (ed.) *Zaburzenia mowy u dzieci* [*Speech Disorders in Children*] (pp. 51–57). Warszawa: PZWL.

Jaklewicz, H. (1997) Dysleksja – problemy medyczne [Dyslexia – medical issues]. *Terapia Numer Specjalny* (Special issue), 17–18.

Jameson, M. (2000) Dyslexia and modern foreign language learning – strategies for success. In L. Peer and G. Reid (eds) *Multilingualism, Literacy and Dyslexia. A Challenge for Educators* (pp. 229–234). London: David Fulton.

Javorsky, J., Sparks, R. and Ganschow, L. (1992) Perceptions of college students with and without learning disabilities about foreign language courses. *Learning Disabilities: Research and Practice* 7, 31–44.

Jennedy, S., Poletto, R. and Weldon, T.L. (eds) (1994) *Language Files. Materials for an Introduction to Language & Linguistics*. Columbus, OH: Ohio State University Press.

Jędrzejowska, E. and Jurek, A. (2003) Diagnoza i terapia dysleksji rozwojowej [Assessment and therapy of developmental dyslexia]. In T. Gałkowski and G. Jastrzębowska (eds) *Logopedia. Pytania i odpowiedzi, Wydanie drugie poprawione i rozszerzone* [*Logopaedics. Questions and Answers*] (2nd edn) (pp. 536–608). Opole: Wydawnictwo Uniwersytetu Opolskiego.

Johnson, D.J (1978) Remedial approaches to dyslexia. In A.L. Benton and D. Pearl (eds) *Dyslexia: An Appraisal of Current Knowledge* (pp. 399–423). New York: Oxford University Press.

Johnson, M., Peer, L. and Lee, R. (2001) Pre-school children and dyslexia: Policy, identification and intervention. In A.J. Fawcett (ed.) *Dyslexia. Theory and Good Practice* (pp. 231–255). London: Whurr.

Jorm, A.M. (1985) *The Psychology of Reading and Spelling Disabilities*. London: Routledge and Kegan Paul.

Jurek, A. (2004a) Trudności w nauce języków obcych uczniów z dysleksją rozwojową [Foreign language learning difficulties in dyslexic students]. In M. Bodganowicz and M. Smoleń (eds) *Dysleksja w kontekście nauczania języków obcych* [*Dyslexia and Foreign Language Teaching*] (pp. 98–120). Gdańsk: Wydawnictwo Harmonia.

Jurek, A. (2004b) Języki obce w nauczaniu uczniów z dysleksją rozwojową. Część I [Teaching foreign languages to dyslexic students. Part I]. *Języki Obce w Szkole* 1, 57–72.

Jurek, A. (2004c) Języki obce w nauczaniu uczniów z dysleksją rozwojową. Część II [Teaching foreign languages to dyslexic students. Part II]. *Języki Obce w Szkole* 2, 46–54.

Jurek, A. (2008) *Kształcenie umiejętności ortograficznych uczniów z dysleksją* [*Developing Orthographic Skills in Dyslexic Students*]. Gdańsk: Wydawnictwo Harmonia.

Juszczyk, S. and Zając, W. (1997) *Komputerowa edukacja uczniów z zaburzeniami w czytaniu i pisaniu* [*IT Education for Students with Reading and Spelling Disorders*]. Katowice: Śląsk.

Juul, H. and Sigurdsson, B. (2005) Orthography as a handicap? A direct comparison of spelling acquisition in Danish and Icelandic. *Scandinavian Journal of Psychology* 46, 263–272.

Józwiak, J. and Podgórski, J. (1994) *Statystyka od podstaw* [*Introduction to Statistics*]. Warszawa: Państwowe Wydawnictwo Ekonomiczne.

Kaczmarek, L. (1969) Cybernetyczne podstawy kształtowania się mowy u głuchych [Cybernetic basis of speech development in deaf]. *Logopedia* 8–9, 3–15.

Kahn-Horwitz, J., Shimron, J. and Sparks, R. (2005) Predicting foreign language reading achievement in elementary school students. *Reading and Writing: An Interdisciplinary Journal* 18 (6), 161–185.

Kahn-Horwitz, J., Shimron, J. and Sparks, R. (2006) Weak and strong novice readers of English as a foreign language: Effects of first language and socioeconomic status. *Annals of Dyslexia* 56 (1), 161–185.

Kaja, B. (2001a) Trudności w uczeniu się. Psychopatologia w uczeniu się czy mikrouszkodzenia mózgu? [Learning difficulties. Learning psycho-pathology or minimal brain damage?] In B. Kaja (ed.) *Wspomaganie rozwoju. Psychostymulacja i psychokorekcja. Tom III [Enhancing Development. Psycho-stimulation and Psycho-correction, Vol. III]* (pp. 74–90). Bydgoszcz: Wydawnictwo Uczelniane Akademii Bydgoskiej.

Kaja, B. (2001b) *Zarys terapii dziecka [An Outline of Child Therapy]*. Bydgoszcz: Wydawnictwo Akademii Bydgoskiej.

Kalka, D. (2003) Wartość diagnozy ryzyka dysleksji rozwojowej [The value of developmental dyslexia assessment of the risk for dyslexia]. In B. Kaja (ed.) *Diagnoza dysleksji [Dyslexia Assessment]* (pp. 133–146). Bydgoszcz: Wydawnictwo Akademii Bydgoskiej im. Kazimierza Wielkiego.

Kappers, E.J. (1997) Outpatient treatment of dyslexia through stimulation of the cerebral hemispheres. *Journal of Learning Disabilities* 30 (1), 100–125.

Katz, L. and Frost, R. (1992) The reading process is different for different orthographies: The orthographic depth hypothesis. In R. Frost and L. Katz (eds) *Orthography, Phonology, Morphology, and Meaning* (pp. 67–84). Amsterdam: Elsevier Science.

Katzir, T., Kim, Y-S., Wolf, M., Morris, R. and Lovett, M.W. (2008) The varieties of pathways to dysfluent reading. *Journal of Learning Disabilities* 41 (1), 47–66.

Kessler, B. and Treiman, R. (2003) Is English spelling chaotic? Misconceptions concerning its regularity. *Reading Psychology* 24, 267–289.

Kirk, J., McLoughlin, D. and Reid, G. (2001) Identification and intervention in adults. In A.J. Fawcett (ed.) *Dyslexia. Theory and Good Practice* (pp. 292–308). London: Whurr.

Klingberg, T., Hedehus, M., Temple, E., Salz, T., Gabrieli, J.D.E., Mosely, M.E. and Poldrack, R.A. (2000) Microstructure of temporoparietal white matter as a basis for reading ability; evidence from diffusion tensor magnetic resonance imaging. *Neuron* 25, 493–500.

Knight, D.F. and Hynd, G.W. (2008) Neurobiologia dysleksji [The neurobiology of dyslexia]. In G. Reid and J. Wearmouth (eds) *Dysleksja. Teoria i praktyka [Dyslexia and Literacy. Theory and Practice]* (pp. 51–70). Gdańsk: Gdańskie Wydawnictwo Psychologiczne.

Knobloch-Gala, A. (1995) *Asymetria i integracja półkulowa a mowa i niektóre jej zaburzenia. Problemy diagnozy psychologicznej dzieci z dysleksją [Asymmetry and Hemisphere Integration vs. Speech and Its Selected Disorders. Problems of Psychological Diagnosis in Dyslexia]*. Kraków: Wydawnictwo Uniwersytetu Jagiellońskiego.

Koda, K. (1992) The effects of lower-level processing skills on foreign language reading performance: Implications for instruction. *Modern Language Journal* 76, 502–512.

Komorowska, H. (1982) *Metody badań empirycznych w glottodydaktyce [Research Methods in Glottodidactics]*. Warszawa: Państwowe Wydawnictwo Naukowe.

Krasowicz. G. (1997) *Język, czytanie i dysleksja [Language, Reading and Dyslexia]*. Lublin: Agencja Wydawniczo-Handlowa AD.

Krasowicz-Kupis, G. (1999) *Rozwój metajęzykowy a osiągnięcia w czytaniu u dzieci 6–9-letnich* [*Metalinguistic Development vs. Reading Achievement in 6–9-year-olds*]. Lublin: Wydawnictwo Uniwersytetu Marii Curie-Skłodowskiej.
Krasowicz-Kupis, G. (2003) Językowe, ale nie fonologiczne deficyty w dysleksji [Linguistic but not phonological deficits in dyslexia]. In B. Kaja (ed.) *Diagnoza dysleksji* [*Dyslexia Assessment*] (pp. 95–118). Bydgoszcz: Wydawnictwo Akademii Bydgoskiej im. Kazimierza Wielkiego.
Krasowicz-Kupis, G. (2004) *Rozwój świadomości językowej dziecka. Teoria i praktyka* [*Development of Language Awareness in Children. Theory and Practice*]. Lublin: Wydawnictwo Uniwersytetu Marii Curie-Skłodowskiej.
Krasowicz-Kupis, G. (2006) Dysleksja a rozwój mowy i języka [Dyslexia vs. speech and language development]. In G. Krasowicz-Kupis (ed.) *Dysleksja rozwojowa. Perspektywa psychologiczna* [*Developmental Dyslexia. Psychological Perspective*] (pp. 53–69). Gdańsk: Wydawnictwo Harmonia.
Krasowicz-Kupis, G. (2008) *Psychologia dysleksji* [*Psychology of Dyslexia*]. Warszawa: Wydawnictwo Naukowe PWN.
Krasowicz-Kupis, G. and Bryant, P.E. (2004) Świadomość językowa dzieci polskich i angielskich a czytanie [Linguistic awareness of Polish and English children vs. reading]. In M. Bogdanowicz and M. Smoleń (eds) *Dysleksja w kontekście nauczania języków obcych* [*Dyslexia and Foreign Language Teaching*] (pp. 36–53). Gdańsk: Wydawnictwo Harmonia.
Lavidor, M., Johnson, R. and Snowling, M.J. (2006) When phonology fails: Orthographic neighbourhood effects in dyslexia. *Brain and Language* 96, 318–329.
Ledwoch, B. (1999) Problemy emocjonalne dziecka z dysleksją rozwojową [Emotional problems of dyslexic children]. In A. Herzyk and A. Borkowska (eds) *Neuropsychologia emocji. Poglądy. Badania. Klinika.* [*Neuropsychology of Emotions. Beliefs. Research. Clinical Practice*] (pp. 191–207). Lublin: Wydawnictwo Uniwersytetu Marii Curie-Skłodowskiej.
Leonard, C., Eckert, M., Given, B., Berninger, V. and Eden, G. (2006) Individual differences in anatomy predict reading and oral language impairments in children. *Brain* 129, 3329–3342.
Levinson, H.N. (1980) *A Solution to the Riddle Dyslexia*. New York: Springer-Verlag.
Lindsay, G. (2001) Identification and intervention in the primary school. In A.J. Fawcett (ed.) *Dyslexia. Theory and Good Practice* (pp. 256–280). London: Whurr.
Lindsay, K., Manis, F. and Baily, C. (2003) Prediction of first-grade reading in Spanish-speaking English-language learners. *Journal of Educational Psychology* 95 (3), 482–494.
Lovett, M.W., De Palma, M., Frijters, J., Steinbach, K., Temple, M., Benson, N. and Lacerenza, L. (2008) Interventions for reading difficulties. A comparison of response to intervention by ELL and EFL struggling readers. *Journal of Learning Disabilities* 41 (4), 333–352.
Lovett, M.W., Steinbach, K.A. and Frijters, J.C. (2000) Remediating the core deficits of developmental reading disability: A double deficit perspective. *Journal of Learning Disabilities* 33, 334–358.
Lundberg, I. (2002) Second language learning and reading with additional load of dyslexia. *Annals of Dyslexia* 52, 165–187.
Lundberg, I. and Hoien, T. (2001) Dyslexia and phonology. In A.J. Fawcett (ed.) *Dyslexia. Theory and Good Practice* (pp. 109–123). London: Whurr.

Luszniewicz, A. and Słaby, T. (2001) *Statystyka z pakietem komputerowym STATISTICA PL* [*Statistics with a Computer Program STATISTICA PL*]. Warszawa: Wydawnictwo C.H. Beck.

Lyon, G.R. (1995) Towards a definition of dyslexia. *Annals of Dyslexia* 45, 3–27.

Mabbot, A. (1995) Arguing for multiple perspectives on the issue of learning disabilities and foreign language acquisition: A response to Sparks, Ganschow, and Javorsky. *Foreign Language Annals* 28 (4), 488–494.

Marino, C., Citterio, A., Giorda, R., Facoetti, A., Menozzi, G., Vanzin, L., Lorusso, M.L., Nobile, M. and Molteni, M. (2007) Association of short-term memory with a variant within DYX1C1 in developmental dyslexia. *Genes, Brain and Behavior* 6, 640–646.

Maruszewski, T. (1996) *Psychologia poznawcza* [*Cognitive Psychology*]. Warszawa: Polskie Towarzystwo Semiotyczne.

Maurer, A. (ed.) (2003) *Dźwięki mowy. Program kształtowania świadomości fonologicznej dla dzieci przedszkolnych i szkolnych* [*Speech Sounds. A Program for Developing Phonological Awareness in Pre-school and School Children*]. Kraków: Oficyna Wydawnicza 'Impuls'.

Merzenich, M.M., Jenkins, W.M, Johnson, P., Schreiner, C., Miller, S. and Tallal, P. (1996) Temporal processing deficits of language-learning impaired children ameliorated by stretching speech. *Science* 271, 77–81.

Miązek, D. (2001) *Scenariusze zajęć do pracy z dziećmi ze specyficznymi trudnościami w uczeniu się* [*Lesson Plans for Children with Specific Learning Difficulties*]. Łódź: Wydawnictwo Edukacyjne Res Polona.

Mickiewicz, J. (1997) *Jedynka z ortografii? – Rozpoznawanie dysleksji, dysortografii i dysgrafii w starszym wieku szkolnym* [*Spelling – Failed?: Identifying Dyslexia, Dysorthography and Dysgraphia in Older Children*]. Toruń: Dom Organizatora.

Miles, E. (2000) Dyslexia may show a different face in different languages. *Dyslexia* 6, 193–201.

Miles, T.R. (1996) Do dyslexic children have IQs? *Dyslexia* 2 (3), 175–178.

Miller, S. and Bussman Gillis, M. (2000) The language puzzle: Connecting the study of linguistics with a multisensory language instructional programme in foreign language learning. In L. Peer and G. Reid (eds) *Multilingualism, Literacy and Dyslexia. A Challenge for Educators* (pp. 218–228). London: David Fulton.

Miller-Guron, L. and Lundberg, I. (2000) Dyslexia and second language reading: A second bite at the apple? *Reading and Writing: An Interdisciplinary Journal* 12, 41–61.

Miller-Guron, L. and Lundberg, I. (2004) Error patterns in word reading among primary school children: A cross-orthographic study. *Dyslexia* 10 (1), 44–60.

Morton, J. and Frith, U. (1995) Causal modeling: A structural approach to developmental psychopathology. In D. Cicchetti and D.J. Cohen (eds) *Manual of Developmental Psychopathology* (pp. 357–390). New York: Wiley.

Nicolson, R.I. (2001) Developmental dyslexia: Into the future. In A.J. Fawcett (ed.) *Dyslexia. Theory and Good Practice* (pp. 1–35). London: Whurr.

Nicolson, R.I. and Fawcett, A.J. (1990) Automaticity: A new framework for dyslexia research? *Cognition* 35 (2), 159–182.

Nicolson, R.I. and Fawcett, A.J. (1995) Dyslexia is more than a phonological disability. *Dyslexia* 1, 19–36.

Nicolson, R.I. and Fawcett, A.J. (1996) *The Dyslexia Early Screening Test*. London: The Psychological Corporation.

Nicolson, R.I. and Fawcett, A.J. (2001) Dyslexia as a learning disability. In A.J. Fawcett (ed.) *Dyslexia. Theory and Good Practice* (pp. 141–159). London: Whurr.

References

Nicolson, R.I. and Fawcett, A.J. (2006) Do cerebellar deficits underlie phonological problems in dyslexia? *Developmental Science* 9 (3), 259–262.
Nicolson, R.I., Fawcett, A.J., Berry, E.L., Jenkins, I.H., Dean, P. and Brooks, D.J. (1999) Motor learning difficulties and abnormal cerebellar activation in dyslexic adults. *Lancet* 353, 43–47.
Nijakowska, J. (2004) Usprawnianie umiejętności odczytywania i zapisywania wyrazów w języku angielskim młodzieży z dysleksją rozwojową [Improving an ability to read and spell English words in dyslexic adolescents]. In M. Bodganowicz and M. Smoleń (eds) *Dysleksja w kontekście nauczania języków obcych [Dyslexia and Foreign Language Teaching]* (pp. 144–155). Gdańsk: Wydawnictwo Harmonia.
Nijakowska, J. (2007) Taming grammar. *The Teacher* 8–9 (51), 19–25.
Nijakowska, J. (2008) An experiment with direct multisensory instruction in teaching word reading and spelling to Polish dyslexic learners of English. In J. Kormos and E.H. Kontra (eds) *Language Learners with Special Needs. An International Perspective* (pp. 130–157). Bristol: Multilingual Matters.
Nikolopoulos, D., Goulandris, N., Hulme, C. and Snowling, M. (2006) The cognitive basis of learning to read and spell in Greek: Evidence from a longitudinal study. *Journal of Experimental Child Psychology* 94, 1–17.
Olson, R.K., Wise, B., Conners, F., Rack, J. and Fulker, D. (1989) Specific deficits in component reading and language skills – genetic and environmental influences. *Journal of Learning Disabilities* 22, 339–348.
Opolska, T. (1997) *Pokonujemy trudności w czytaniu i pisaniu. Przegląd metod pracy korekcyjno-kompensacyjnej [Dealing with Reading and Spelling Difficulties. An Overview of Methods of Correction-compensation Work]*. Warszawa: Centrum Metodyczne Pomocy Psychologiczno-Pedagogicznej Ministerstwa Edukacji Narodowej.
Oren, R. and Breznitz, Z. (2005) Reading processes in L1 and L2 among dyslexics compared to regular bilingual readers: Behavioral and electrophysiological evidence. *Journal of Neurolinguistics* 18, 127–151.
Oszwa, U. (2000) Analiza przejawów agramatyzmu u dzieci z dysleksją rozwojową [Analysis of agrammatisms in dyslexic children]. In A. Borkowska and E.M. Szepietowska (eds) *Diagnoza neuropsychologiczna. Metodologia i metodyka [Neuropsychological Assessment. Methodology and Practice]* (pp. 289–306). Lublin: Wydawnictwo Uniwersytetu Marii Curie-Skłodowskiej.
Ott, P. (1997) *How to Detect and Manage Dyslexia. A Reference and Resource Manual*. Oxford: Heinemann Educational.
Pavlidis, G. (1986) The role of eye movements in the diagnosis of dyslexia. In G. Pavlidis and D. Fisher (eds) *Dyslexia: Its Neuropsychology and Treatment* (pp. 97–111). New York: John Wiley & Sons.
Payne, J. (1995) *English Guides 8: Spelling*. London: HarperCollins.
Pennington, B.F. (1989) Using genetics to understand dyslexia. *Annals of Dyslexia* 39, 81–93.
Pennington, B.F. and Smith, S.D. (1988) Genetic influences on learning disability. *Journal of Consulting & Clinical Psychology* 56, 817–823.
Pennington, B.F., McCabe, L.L., Smith, S.D., Lefy, D.L., Bookman, M.O., Kimberling, W.J. and Lubs, H.A. (1986) Spelling errors in adults with a form of familial dyslexia. *Child Development* 57, 1001–1013.
Petrus, P. and Bogdanowicz, M. (2004) Sprawność fonologiczna dzieci w kontekście nauki języka angielskiego [Children's phonological ability in foreign language learning]. In M. Bogdanowicz and M. Smoleń (eds) *Dysleksja*

w kontekście nauczania języków obcych [Dyslexia and Foreign Language Teaching] (pp. 63–77). Gdańsk: Wydawnictwo Harmonia.
Pętlewska, H. (1999) Przezwyciężanie trudności w czytaniu i pisaniu [Overcoming Reading and Spelling Difficulties]. Kraków: Oficyna Wydawnicza 'Impuls'.
Phillips, S. (1993) Young Learners. Oxford: Oxford University Press.
Phillips, B.M., Clancy-Menchetti, J. and Lonigan, C.J. (2008) Successful phonological awareness instruction with preschool children. Lessons from the classroom. Topics in Early Childhood Special Education 28 (1), 3–17.
Piechurska-Kuciel, E. (2008) Input, processing and output anxiety in students with symptoms of developmental dyslexia. In J. Kormos and E.H. Kontra (eds) Language Learners with Special Needs (pp. 86–109). Bristol: Multilingual Matters.
Pietras, I. (2007) O klasifikacji błędów w dysortografii [Classifying errors in dysorthography]. In M. Kostka-Szymańska and G. Krasowicz-Kupis (eds) Dysleksja. Problem znany czy nieznany? [Dyslexia. Familiar or Unfamiliar Problem?] (pp. 81–92). Lublin: Wydawnictwo UMCS.
Pietras, I. (2008) Dysortografia – uwarunkowania psychologiczne [Dysorthography – Psychological Underpinnings]. Gdańsk: Wydawnictwo Harmonia.
Plessen von, K., Lundervold, A., Duta, N., Heiervang, E., Klauschen, F., Smievoll, A.I., Ersland, L. and Hugdahl, K. (2002) Less developed corpus callosum in dyslexic subject – a structural MRI study. Neuropsychologia 40, 1035–1044.
Porter, J.E. and Rourke, B.P. (1985) Socioemotional functioning of learning disabled children: A subtypal analysis of personality patterns. In B.P. Rourke (ed.) Neuropsychology of Learning Disabilities (pp. 257–277). New York: The Guilford Press.
Preis, S., Steinmetz, H., Knorr, U. and Jäncke, L. (2000) Corpus callosum size in children with developmental language disorder. Cognitive Brain Research 10, 37–44.
Pugh, K.R., Sandak, R., Frost, S.J., Moore, D. and Einar Mencl, W. (2005) Examining reading development and reading disability in English language learners: Potential contributions from neuroimaging. Learning Disabilities Research and Practice 20 (1), 24–30.
Puolakanaho, A., Ahonen, T., Aro, M., Eklund, K., Leppänen, P.H.T., Ppikkeus, A-M., Tolvanen, A., Torppa, M. and Lyytinen, H. (2008) Developmental links of very early phonological and language skills to second grade reading outcomes. Strong to accuracy but only minor to fluency. Journal of Learning Disabilities 41 (4), 353–370.
Rae, C., Harasty, J.A., Dzendrowskyj, T.E., Talcott, J.B., Simpson, J.M. and Blamire, A.M. (2002) Cerebellar morphology in developmental dyslexia. Neuropsychologia 40, 1285–1292.
Ramus, F. (2004) Neurobiology of dyslexia: A reinterpretation of the data. Trends in Neurosciences 27 (12), 720–726.
Ramus, F. (2006) Genes, brain, and cognition: A roadmap for the cognitive scientist. Cognition 101, 247–269.
Ramus, F., Rosen, S., Dakin, S.C., Day, B.L., Castellote, J.M., White, S. and Frith, U. (2003) Theories of developmental dyslexia: Insights from a multiple case study of dyslexic adults. Brain 126, 841–865.
Ramus, F., White, S. and Frith, U. (2006) Weighing the evidence between competing theories of dyslexia. Developmental Science 9 (3), 265–269.
Reed, D. and Stansfield, C. (2004) Using the Modern Language Aptitude Test to identify a foreign language learning disability: Is it ethical? Language Assessment Quarterly 1, 161–176.

Reid, G. (1998) *Dyslexia. A Practitioner's Handbook*. Chichester: Wiley.
Reid, G. and Fawcett, A.J. (2004) An overview of developments in dyslexia. In G. Reid and A.J. Fawcett (eds) *Dyslexia in Context. Research, Policy and Practice* (pp. 3–19). London: Whurr.
Richards, T.L. (2001) Functional magnetic resonance imaging and spectroscopic imaging of the brain: Application of the fMRI and fMRS to reading disabilities and education. *Learning Disability Quarterly* 24, 189–203.
Richards, T.L., Cornia, D., Serafini, S., Steury, K., Echelard, D.R., Dager, S.R., Marro, K., Abbott, R.D., Maravilla, K.R. and Berninger, V.W. (2000). The effects of a phonologically driven treatment for dyslexia on lactate levels as measures by proton MRSI. *American Journal of Neuroradiology* 21, 916–922.
Rinvolucri, M. (1985) *Grammar Games*. Cambridge: Cambridge University Press.
Ritchey, K.D. and Goeke, J.L. (2006) Orton-Gillingham and Orton-Gillingham based reading instruction: A review of literature. *The Journal of Special Education* 40 (3), 171–183.
Robertson, J. (2000a) Neuropsychological intervention in dyslexia: Two studies on British pupils. *Journal of Learning Disabilities* 33 (2), 137–149.
Robertson, J. (2000b) The neuropsychology of modern foreign language learning. In L. Peer and G. Reid (eds) *Multilingualism, Literacy and Dyslexia. A Challenge for Educators* (pp. 203–210). London: David Fulton.
Robertson, J. and Bakker, D.J. (2008) Model równowagi półkulowej i dysleksja [The balance model of reading and dyslexia]. In G. Reid and J. Wearmouth (eds) *Dysleksja. Teoria i praktyka* [*Dyslexia and Literacy. Theory and Practice*] (pp. 141–162). Gdańsk: Gdańskie Wydawnictwo Psychologiczne.
Rosenthal, J. (1970) A preliminary psycholinguistic study of children with learning disabilities. *Journal of Learning Disabilities* 3, 181–198.
Ryan, M. (1992) The social and emotional effects of dyslexia. *Education Digest* 57 (5), 68–71.
Saduś, Z. (2000) Analiza błędów ortograficznych popełnianych przez uczniów w starszym wieku szkolnym oraz sposoby ich przezwyciężania [The analysis of orthographic errors committed by older school children and ways of overcoming spelling problems]. In W. Turewicz (ed.) *Jak pomóc dziecku z dysortografią* [*How to Help a Child with Spelling Difficulties?*] (pp. 25–36). Zielona Góra: Ośrodek Doskonalenia Nauczycieli w Zielonej Górze.
Saduś, Z. (2003) *Jak pomóc uczniowi w nauce ortografii. Poradnik dla nauczycieli i rodziców* [*How to Help Students in Learning Orthography? A Guide for Teachers and Parents*]. Opole: Wydawnictwo Oświatowe 'Promyk'.
Saiegh-Haddad, E. (2007) Epilinguistic and metalinguistic phonological awareness may be subject to different constrains: Evidence from Hebrew. *First Language* 27, 385–405.
Savage, R. (2007) Cerebellar tasks do not distinguish between children with developmental dyslexia and children with intellectual disability. *Child Neuropsychology* 13, 389–407.
Sawa, B. (1999) *Jeżeli dziecko źle czyta i pisze* [*If a Child Reads and Spells Poorly*]. Warszawa: Wydawnictwa Szkolne i Pedagogiczne.
Schneider, E. (1999) *Multisensory Structured Metacognitive Instruction. An Approach to Teaching a Foreign Language to at-Risk Students*. Frankfurt am Main: Peter Lang.
Schneider, E. and Crombie, M. (2003) *Dyslexia and Foreign Language Learning*. London: David Fulton.
Seymour, P.H.K. (2005) Early reading development in European orthographies. In M.J. Snowling and C. Hulme (eds) *The Science of Reading: A Handbook* (pp. 296–315). Malden, MA: Blackwell.

Seymour, P.H.K., Aro, M. and Erskine, J.M. (2003) Foundation literacy acquisition in European orthographies. *British Journal of Psychology* 94, 143–174.

Shaw, R. (1999) The case for course substitutions as a reasonable accommodation for students with foreign language learning difficulties. *Journal of Learning Disabilities* 32, 320–328.

Shaywitz, B.A., Shaywitz, S.E., Blachman, B.A., Pugh, K.R., Fulbright, R.K., Skudlarski, R., Einar Mencl, W., Constable, R.T., Holahan, J.M., Marchione, K.E., Fletcher, J.M., Reid Lyon, G. and Gore, J.C. (2004) Development of left occipitotemporal systems for skilled reading in children after a phonologically-based intervention. *Biological Psychiatry* 55, 926–933.

Shaywitz, S.E. (1997) Dysleksja [Dyslexia]. *Świat Nauki* 1, 58–64.

Shaywitz, S.E., Shaywitz, B.A., Fulbright, R.K., Skudlarski, P., Mencl, W.E., Constable, R.T., Pugh, K.R., Holahan, J.M., Marchione, K.E., Fletcher, J.M., Lyon, G.R. and Gore, J.C. (2003) Neural systems for compensation and persistence: Young adult outcome of childhood reading disability. *Biological Psychiatry* 54, 25–33.

Shemesh, R. and Waller, S. (2000) *Teaching English Spelling*. Cambridge: Cambridge University Press.

Shovman, M.M. and Ahissar, M. (2006) Isolating the impact of visual perception on dyslexics' reading ability. *Vision Research* 46, 3514–3525.

Siegal, L.S. (1989) IQ is irrelevant to the definition of learning disabilities. *Journal of Learning Disabilities* 22, 469–78.

Silani, G., Frith, U., Demonet, J.F., Fazio, F., Perani, D., Price, C., Frith, C.D. and Paulesu, E. (2005) Brain abnormalities underlying altered activation in dyslexia: A voxel based morphometry study. *Brain* 128, 2453–2461.

Simos, P.G., Fletcher, J.M., Bergman, E., Breier, J.I., Foorman, B.R., Castillo, E.M., Fitzgerald, M. and Papanicolau, A.C. (2002) Dyslexia-specific brain activation profile becomes normal following successful remedial training. *Neurology* 58, 1203–1213.

Siok, W.T., Niu, Z., Jin, Z., Perfetti, C.A. and Tan, L.H. (2008) From the cover: A structural-functional basis for dyslexia in the cortex of Chinese readers. *PNAS* 105 (14), 5561–5566.

Skibińska, H. (2001) *Praca korekcyjno-kompensacyjna z dziećmi z trudnościami w czytaniu i pisaniu* [Correction-compensation Work with Children Encountering Reading and Spelling Difficulties]. Bydgoszcz: Wydawnictwo Uczelniane Akademii Bydgoskiej im. Kazimierza Wielkiego.

Slobin, D.I. (1971) *Psycholinguistics*. London: Foresman.

Smith, S. (2002) Considerations in the development of foreign language substitution policies at the postsecondary level for students with learning disabilities. *Association of Department of Foreign Languages (ADFL) Bulletin* 33, 61–67.

Smythe, I. and Everatt, J. (2000) Dyslexia diagnosis in different languages. In L. Peer and G. Reid (eds) *Multilingualism, Literacy and Dyslexia. A Challenge for Educators* (pp. 12–21). London: David Fulton.

Snowling, M. (1981) Phonemic defects in developmental dyslexia. *Psychological Research* 43, 219–234.

Snowling, M.J. (2000) *Dyslexia*. Oxford: Blackwell.

Snowling, M.J. (2001a) From language to reading and dyslexia. *Dyslexia* 7 (1), 37–46.

Snowling, M.J. (2001b) Developmental dyslexia. *Current Paediatrics* 11, 10–13.

Snowling, M.J. and Caravolas, M. (2007) Developmental dyslexia. In M.G. Gaskell (ed.) *The Oxford Handbook of Psycholinguistics* (pp. 667–683). Oxford: Oxford University Press.

References

Snowling, M.J. and Nation, K. (1997) Language, phonology and learning to read. In C. Hulme and M.J. Snowling (eds) *Dyslexia: Biology, Cognition and Intervention* (pp. 153–166). London: Whurr.

Snowling, M.J., Gallagher, A. and Frith, U. (2003) Family risk of dyslexia is continuous: Individual differences in the precursors of reading skill. *Child Development* 74, 358–373.

Snowling, M.J., Muter, V. and Carrol, J. (2007) Children at family risk of dyslexia: A follow-up in early adolescence. *Journal of Child Psychology and Psychiatry* 48 (6), 609–618.

Sochacka, K. (2004) *Rozwój umiejętności czytania* [*Reading Ability Development*]. Białystok: Trans Humana.

Sparks, R. (1995) Examining the Linguistic Coding Differences Hypothesis to explain individual differences in foreign language learning. *Annals of Dyslexia* 45, 187–214.

Sparks, R. (2001) Foreign language learning problems of students classified as learning disabled and non-learning disabled: Is there a difference? *Topics in Language Disorders* 21 (1), 38–54.

Sparks, R. (2006) Is there a 'disability' for learning a foreign language? *Journal of Learning Disabilities* 39 (6), 544–557.

Sparks, R. and Ganschow, L. (1991) Foreign language learning difficulties: Affective or native language aptitude differences? *Modern Language Journal* 75, 3–16.

Sparks, R. and Ganschow, L. (1993) The effects of multisensory structured language instruction on native language and foreign language aptitude skills of at-risk high school foreign language learners: A replication and follow-up study. *Annals of Dyslexia* 4, 194–216.

Sparks, R. and Ganschow, L. (1995) Parent perceptions in the screening for performance in foreign language courses. *Foreign Language Annals* 28, 371–391.

Sparks, R. and Ganschow, L. (1996) Teachers' perceptions of students' foreign language academic skills and affective characteristics. *Journal of Educational Research* 89, 172–185.

Sparks, R. and Javorsky, J. (1999) Students classified as learning disabled and the college foreign language requirement: Replication and comparison studies. *Journal of Learning Disabilities* 32, 332–349.

Sparks, R. and Miller, K.S. (2000) Teaching a foreign language using multisensory structured language techniques to at-risk learners: A review. *Dyslexia* 6, 124–132.

Sparks, R., Ganschow, L. and Pohlman, J. (1989) Linguistic coding deficits in foreign language learners. *Annals of Dyslexia* 39, 179–195.

Sparks, R., Ganschow, L., Kenneweg, S. and Miller, K. (1991) Use of an Orton-Gillingham approach to teach a foreign language to dyslexic/learning-disabled students: Explicit teaching of phonology in a second language. *Annals of Dyslexia* 41, 96–118.

Sparks, R., Ganschow, L., Javorsky, J., Pohlman, J. and Patton, J. (1992a) Test comparisons among students identified as high-risk, low-risk, and learning disabled in high school foreign language courses. *Modern Language Journal* 72, 142–159.

Sparks, R., Ganschow, L., Pohlman, J., Skinner, S. and Artzer, M. (1992b) The effects of multisensory structured language instruction on native language and foreign language aptitude skills of at-risk high school foreign language learners. *Annals of Dyslexia* 42, 25–53.

Sparks, R., Ganschow, L. and Javorsky, J. (1993) Perceptions of high- and low-risk students and students with learning disabilities about high-school foreign language courses. *Foreign Language Annals* 26, 491–510.

Sparks, R., Ganschow, L. and Javorsky, J. (1995a) I know one when I see one (or, I know one because I am one): A response to Mabbot. *Foreign Language Annals* 28 (4), 479–487.

Sparks, R., Ganschow, L. and Patton, J. (1995b) Prediction of performance in first-year foreign language courses: Connections between native and foreign language learning. *Journal of Educational Psychology* 87 (4), 638–655.

Sparks, R., Javorsky, J. and Ganschow, L. (1995c) Satiating the appetite of the sociologic sponge: A rejoinder to Mabbot. *Foreign Language Annals* 28 (4), 495–498.

Sparks, R., Ganschow, L., Fluharty, K. and Little, S. (1996) An exploratory study on the effects of Latin on the native language skills and foreign language aptitude of students with and without learning disabilities. *The Classical Journal* 91 (2), 165–184.

Sparks, R., Ganschow, L., Artzer, M. and Patton, J. (1997a) Foreign language proficiency of at-risk and not-at-risk learners over 2 years of foreign language instruction: A follow-up study. *Journal of Learning Disabilities* 30 (1), 92–98.

Sparks, R., Ganschow, L., Artzer, M., Siebenhar, D. and Plageman, M. (1997b) Anxiety and proficiency in a foreign language. *Perceptual and Motor Skills* 85, 559–562.

Sparks, R., Ganschow, L., Patton, J., Artzer, M., Siebenhar, D. and Plageman, M. (1997c) Prediction of foreign language proficiency. *Journal of Educational Psychology* 89 (3), 549–561.

Sparks, R., Artzer, M., Ganschow, L., Siebenhar, D., Plageman, M. and Patton, J. (1998a) Differences in native-language skills, foreign-language aptitude, and foreign-language grades among high-, average-, and low-proficiency foreign-language learners: Two studies. *Language Testing* 15 (2), 181–216.

Sparks, R., Artzer, M., Javorsky, J., Patton, J., Ganschow, L., Miller, K. and Hordubay, D. (1998b) Students classified as learning disabled and non-learning disabled: Two comparison studies of native language skill, foreign language aptitude, and foreign language proficiency. *Foreign Language Annals* 31 (4), 535–550.

Sparks, R., Artzer, M., Patton, J., Ganschow, L., Miller, K., Hordubay, D. and Walsh, G. (1998c) Benefits of multisensory structured instruction for at-risk foreign language learners: A comparison study of high school Spanish students. *Annals of Dyslexia* 48, 239–270.

Sparks, R., Philips, L. and Javorsky, J. (2002) Students classified as LD who received course substitutions for the college foreign language requirement: A replication study. *Journal of Learning Disabilities* 35 (6), 482–499, 538.

Sparks, R., Philips, L. and Javorsky, J. (2003) Students classified as LD who petitioned for or fulfilled the foreign language requirement – Are they different? A replication study. *Journal of Learning Disabilities* 36 (4), 348–362.

Sparks, R., Patton, J., Ganschow, L., Humbach, N. and Javorsky, J. (2006) Native language predictions of foreign language proficiency and foreign language aptitude. *Annals of Dyslexia* 56 (1), 129–160.

Sparks, R., Ganschow, L. and Patton, J. (2008a) L1 and L2 literacy, aptitude and affective variables as discriminators among high- and low-achieving L2 learners with special needs. In J. Kormos and E.H. Kontra (eds) *Language Learners with Special Needs* (pp. 11–35). Bristol: Multilingual Matters.

Sparks, R., Humbach, N. and Javorsky, J. (2008b) Individual and longitudinal differences among high- and low-achieving, LD and ADHD L2 learners. *Learning and Individual Differences* 8, 29–43.

Spencer, K. (2007) Predicting children's word-spelling difficulty for common English words from measures of orthographic transparency, phonemic and graphemic length and word frequency. *British Journal of Psychology* 98, 305–338.

Spencer, L.H. and Hanley, J.R. (2003) Effects of orthographic transparency on reading and phoneme awareness in children learning to read in Wales. *British Journal of Psychology* 94, 1–28.

Spionek, H. (1985) *Zaburzenia rozwoju uczniów a niepowodzenia szkolne* [*Developmental Disorders vs. Scholastic Failure*]. Warszawa: PWN.

Spolsky, B. (1989) *Conditions for Second Language Learning*. Oxford: Oxford University Press.

Stambolitzis, A. and Pumfrey, P. (2000) Text genre, miscue analysis, bilingualism and dyslexia: Teaching strategies with junior school pupils. In L. Peer and G. Reid (eds) *Multilingualism, Literacy and Dyslexia. A Challenge for Educators* (pp. 70–79). London: David Fulton.

Stanisz, A. (1998) *Przystępny kurs statystyki* [*An Easy Course in Statistics*]. Kraków: StatSoft.

Stanovich, K.E. (1980) Towards an interactive-compensatory model of individual differences in the development of reading fluency. *Reading Research Quarterly* 16, 32–71.

Stanovich, K.E. (1986) Matthew effects in reading: Some consequences of individual differences in the acquisition of literacy. *Reading Research Quarterly* 21, 360–407.

Stanovich, K.E. (1996) Towards a more inclusive definition of dyslexia. *Dyslexia* 2 (3), 154–166.

Stein, J.F. (2001) The magnocellular theory of developmental dyslexia. *Dyslexia* 7 (1), 12–36.

Stein, J.F. and Talcott, J.B. (1999) The magnocellular theory of dyslexia. *Dyslexia* 5 (2), 59–78.

Stein, J.F., Richardson, A.J. and Fawler, M.S. (2000a) Monocular occlusion can improve binocular control and reading in developmental dyslexics. *Brain* (1), 2–3.

Stein, J.F., Talcott, J.B. and Walsh, V. (2000b) Controversy about the visual magnocellular deficit in developmental dyslexics. *Trends in Cognitive Sciences* 4 (6), 209–211.

Stein, J.F., Talcott, J.B. and Witton, C. (2001) The sensorimotor basis of developmental dyslexia. In A.J. Fawcett (ed.) *Dyslexia. Theory and Good Practice* (pp. 65–88). London: Whurr.

Stoodley, C.J., Talcott, J.B., Carter, E.L., Witton, C. and Stein, J.F. (2000) Selective deficits of vibrotactile sensitivity in dyslexic readers. *Neuroscience Letters* 295, 13–16.

Stoodley, C.J., Fawcett, A.J., Nicolson, R.I. and Stein, J.F. (2006) Balancing and pointing tasks in dyslexic and control adults. *Dyslexia* 12, 276–288.

Szczerbiński, M. (2007) Dysleksja rozwojowa: próba definicji [Developmental dyslexia: An attempt towards defining the disorder]. In M. Kostka-Szymańska and G. Krasowicz-Kupis (eds) *Dysleksja. Problem znany czy nieznany?* [*Dyslexia. Familiar or Unfamiliar Problem?*] (pp. 48–70). Lublin: Wydawnictwo Uniwersytetu Marii-Skłodowskiej.

Szempruch, J. (1997) *Umiejętność czytania a osiągnięcia szkolne uczniów klas początkujących* [*Reading Ability vs. Educational Achievement of First-graders*]. Rzeszów: Wydawnictwo Wyższej Szkoły Pedagogicznej.

Szenkovits, G. and Ramus, F. (2005) Exploring dyslexics' phonological deficit I: Lexical vs. sub-lexical and input vs. output processes. *Dyslexia* 11, 253–268.
Szepietowska, E.M. (2002) *Badanie neuropsychologiczne. Procedura i ocena* [*Neuropsychological Assessment. Procedure and Evaluation*]. Lublin: Wydawnictwo Uniwersytetu Marii Curie-Skłodowskiej.
Talcott, J.B., Witton, C., McClean, M.F., Hansen, P.C., Rees, A., Green, G.G.R. and Stein, J.F. (1999) Can sensitivity to auditory frequency modulation predict children's phonological and reading skills? *NeuroReport* 10, 2045–2050.
Talcott, J.B., Hansen, P.C., Assoku, E.L. and Stein, J.F. (2000a) Visual motion sensitivity in dyslexia: Evidence for temporal and energy integration deficits. *Neuropsychologia* 38, 935–943.
Talcott, J.B., Witton, C., McClean, M.F., Hansen, P.C., Rees, A., Green, G.G.R. and Stein, J.F. (2000b) Dynamic sensory sensitivity and children's word decoding skills. *Proceedings of the National Academy of Science* 97 (6), 2952–2957.
Tallal, P. (1980) Auditory temporal perception, phonics and reading disabilities in dyslexic children. *Brain and Language* 9, 182–198.
Tallal, P., Miller, S.L., Bedi, G., Byma, G., Wang, X., Nagarajan, S., Schreiner, C., Jenkins, W.M. and Merzenich, M.M. (1996) Fast-element enhanced speech improves language comprehension in language-learning impaired children. *Science* 271, 81–84.
Temple, E. (2002) Brain mechanisms in normal and dyslexic readers. *Current Opinion in Neurobiology* 12, 178–183.
Temple, E., Poldrack, R.A., Salidis, J., Deutsch, G.K., Tallal, P., Merzenich, M.M. and Gabrieli, J.D. (2001) Disrupted neural responses to phonological and orthographic processing in dyslexic children: An fMRI study. *Neuroreport* 12, 299–307.
Thomson, M.E. and Watkins, E.J. (1990) *Dyslexia. A Teaching Handbook*. London: Whurr.
Thornbury, S. (1999) *How to Teach Grammar*. Harlow: Longman.
Tod, J. (2008) Indywidualne plany nauczania dla uczniów dyslektycznych [Individual educational plans and dyslexia]. In G. Reid and J. Wearmouth (eds) *Dysleksja. Teoria i praktyka* [*Dyslexia and Literacy. Theory and Practice*] (pp. 355–384). Gdańsk: Gdańskie Wydawnictwo Psychologiczne.
Tomaszewska, A. (2001) *Prawo do nauki dziecka z dysleksją rozwojową w świadomości nauczycieli* [*Teachers' Awareness of Dyslexic Children's Right to Learn*]. Kraków: Oficyna Wydawnicza 'Impuls'.
Treiman, R. and Kessler, B. (2007) Learning to read. In M.G. Gaskell (ed.) *The Oxford Handbook of Psycholinguistics* (pp. 657–666). Oxford: Oxford University Press.
Turner, M. (2003) Diagnoza dysleksji w Wielkiej Brytanii – przegląd testów [Assessment of dyslexia in Great Britain – review of tests]. In B. Kaja (ed.) *Diagnoza dysleksji* [*Dyslexia Assessment*] (pp. 36–49). Bydgoszcz: Wydawnictwo Akademii Bydgoskiej im. Kazimierza Wielkiego.
Uppstad, P.H. and Tønnessen, F.E. (2007) The notion of 'phonology' in dyslexia research: Cognitivism – and beyond. *Dyslexia* 13, 154–174.
Ur, P. (1988) *Grammar Practice Activities: A Practical Guide for Teachers*. Cambridge: Cambridge University Press.
Van der Leij, A. and Morfidi, E. (2006) Core deficit and variable differences in Dutch poor readers learning English. *Journal of Learning Disabilities* 39 (1), 74–90.
Vellutino, F.R. (1979) *Dyslexia: Theory and Research*. Cambridge, MA: MIT Press.

Vellutino, F.R., Scanlon, D.M. and Tanzman, M.S. (1998) The case for early intervention in diagnosing reading disability. *Journal of School Psychology* 36 (4), 367–394.
Vellutino, F.R., Fletcher, J.M., Snowling, M.J. and Scanlon, D.M. (2004) Specific reading disability (dyslexia): What have we learned in the past four decades? *Journal of Child Psychology and Psychiatry* 45 (1), 2–40.
Vogel, S.A. (1983) A qualitative analysis of morphological ability in learning and achieving children. *Journal of Learning Disabilities* 16, 416–420.
Vousden, J.I. (2008) Units of English spelling-to-sound mappings: A rational approach to reading instruction. *Applied Cognitive Psychology* 22, 247–272.
Vukovic, L.K. and Siegel, L.S. (2006) The double-deficit hypothesis: A comprehensive analysis of the evidence. *Journal of Learning Disabilities* 39 (1), 25–47.
Wagner, R., Francis, D.J. and Morris, R.D. (2005) Identifying English language learners with learning disabilities: Key challenges and possible approaches. *Learning Disabilities Research & Practice* 20 (1), 6–15.
Wearmouth, J. and Reid, G. (2008) Ocena i planowanie nauczania oraz nauki [Issues for assessment of planning of teaching and learning]. In G. Reid and J. Wearmouth (eds) *Dysleksja. Teoria i praktyka [Dyslexia and Literacy. Theory and Practice]* (pp. 211–234). Gdańsk: Gdańskie Wydawnictwo Psychologiczne.
White, S., Milne, E., Rosen, S., Hansen, P., Swettenham, J., Frith, U. and Ramus, F. (2006) The role of sensorimotor impairments in dyslexia: A multiple case study of dyslexic children. *Developmental Science* 9 (3), 237–255.
Whiteley, H.E., Smith, C.D. and Connors, L. (2007) Young children at risk of literacy difficulties: Factors predicting recovery from risk following phonologically based intervention. *Journal of Research in Reading* 30 (3), 249–269.
Wiig, E.H. and Semel, E.M. (1976) *Language Disabilities in Children and Adolescents*. Columbus, OH: Charles E. Merrill.
Wiig, E.H. and Semel, E.M. (1984) *Language Assessment and Intervention for the Learning Disabled* (2nd edn). Columbus, OH: Charles E. Merrill.
Wiig, E.H., Semel, E.M. and Crouse, M.B. (1973) The use of English morphology by high-risk and learning disabled children. *Journal of Learning Disabilities* 7, 457–465.
Wimmer, H. (1993) Characteristics of developmental dyslexia in a regular reading system. *Applied Psycholinguistics* 14, 1–33.
Wimmer, H., Landerl, K. and Schneider, W. (1994) The role of rime awareness in learning to read a regular orthography. *British Journal of Developmental Psychology* 12, 469–484.
Wise, J.C., Sevcik, R.A., Morris, R.D., Lovett, M.W. and Wolf, M. (2007) The growth of phonological awareness by children with reading disabilities: A result of semantic knowledge or knowledge of grapheme-phoneme correspondences? *Scientific Studies of Reading* 11 (2), 151–164.
Włodarski, Z. (1998) *Psychologia uczenia się [Psychology of Learning]*. Warszawa: Wydawnictwo Naukowe PWN.
Wolf, M. and Bowers, P.G. (1999) The double-deficit hypothesis for the developmental dyslexia. *Journal of Educational Psychology* 91, 415–438.
Wolf, M. and O'Brien, B. (2001) On issue of time, fluency, and intervention. In A.J. Fawcett (ed.) *Dyslexia. Theory and Good Practice* (pp. 124–140). London: Whurr.
Wolf, M., Vellutino, F. and Berko Gleason, J. (2005) Psycholingwistyczna analiza czytania [Psycholinguistic analysis of reading]. In J. Berko Gleanson and N. Bernstein Ratner *Psycholingwistyka [Psycholinguistics]* (pp. 439–476). Gdańsk: Gdańskie Wydawnictwo Psychologiczne.

Wszeborowska-Lipińska, B. (1996) Dysleksja a badanie rozwoju poziomu umysłowego [Dyslexia vs. assessment of the level of cognitive development]. *Psychologia Wychowawcza* 2, 126–133.

Zakrzewska, B. (1999) *Trudności w czytaniu i pisaniu. Modele ćwiczeń* [*Reading and Spelling Difficulties. Types of Exercises*]. Warszawa: Wydawnictwa Szkolne i Pedagogiczne Spółka Akcyjna.

Zelech, W. (1997) *Zaburzenia czytania i pisania u dzieci afatycznych, głuchych i dyslektycznych* [*Reading and Writing Disorders in Aphasic, Deaf and Dyslexic Children*]. Kraków: Wydawnictwo Naukowe Wyższej Szkoły Pedagogicznej.

Ziegler, J.C. and Goswami, U. (2005) Reading acquisition, developmental dyslexia, and skilled reading across languages: A psycholinguistic grain size theory. *Psychological Bulletin* 131, 3–29.

Ziegler, J.C. and Goswami, U. (2006) Becoming literate in different languages: Similar problems, different solutions. *Developmental Science* 9 (5), 426–453.

Ziegler, J., Perry, C., Ma-Wyatt, A., Ladner, D. and Schulte-Korne, G. (2003) Developmental dyslexia in different languages: Language-specific or universal? *Journal of Experimental Child Psychology* 86, 169–193.

Index

accommodations vi, ix, 4, 45, 73, 95, 102, 117, 121, 126, 131, 145, 146, 147, 184, 217, 226
accuracy 14, 21, 22, 24, 25, 28, 29, 39, 51, 55, 61, 82, 83, 85, 88, 89, 95, 96, 98, 103, 107, 109, 110, 116, 119, 193, 224
adding 87, 91, 162, 175, 207
alliteration 19, 87, 213
alphabetic principle 9, 13, 15, 44, 48, 101, 193
alphabetic stage 18, 19, 20
anatomical magnetic resonance imaging (aMFI) 39, 40
anxiety 66, 69, 75, 76, 98, 99, 112, 147, 213, 224, 228
articulation 12, 16, 62
attention span 54, 212
auditory perception 12, 91
auditory processing 34, 43, 64
automatisation viii, 18, 34, 47, 61, 62, 63, 87, 103, 116, 179, 181
automatisation deficit hypothesis 61, 62

balance 34, 52, 61, 87, 95, 121, 229
balance model of reading 18, 20, 118, 119, 152, 214, 225
bilingual v, vii, 30, 82, 83, 101, 106, 107, 108, 109, 113, 117, 118, 191, 194, 195, 214, 215, 223, 229
binocular instability 58, 120
blending 14, 45, 46, 87, 153, 156, 157, 161, 162, 168, 197, 198, 200, 201
bottom-up model/strategy 16, 17
brain function 20, 38, 39, 191
brain mechanism vii, 34, 35, 65, 152, 230
brain structure 37, 39, 40, 43, 63, 65, 190
cerebellar v, 42, 52, 61, 62, 63, 65, 113, 215, 223, 224, 225
cerebellar deficit hypothesis v, 42, 61, 62, 63, 65, 113
cerebellum 34, 42, 43, 52, 60, 61, 65, 215
colour coding 148, 149, 157, 168, 169, 180, 182
corpus callosum 41, 43, 211, 224

decoding abilities 104, 107, 117, 195
decoding difficulties 52, 104, 217
decoding skills 6, 36, 68, 104, 107, 117, 230
decoding strategies 19, 154

– single word decoding 7, 53, 86, 103
– word decoding 4, 7, 53, 55, 78, 85, 96, 103, 107, 108, 117, 192, 195, 230
deletions 29, 56, 87, 90, 162
diagnosis x, 2, 6, 8, 15, 32, 37, 68, 71, 72, 100, 101, 103, 105, 106, 109, 112, 120, 191, 194, 195, 211, 212, 220, 223, 226
dictation 88, 91, 103, 138, 174
digit span tasks 47, 103, 104
double-deficit hypothesis v, 54, 213, 231
dual route model of reading 23
dyseidetic 92, 113, 114
dysphonetic 92, 113, 114

educational accommodations vi, x, 73, 145
educational system vii, x, 27, 145, 146, 194, 196
emotional-motivational problems/ disorders v, 7, 12, 32, 89, 97, 122, 123
encoding 3, 4, 9, 10, 27, 85, 103, 104, 105, 136, 192
environment 4, 6, 8, 34, 36, 70, 81, 98, 100, 102, 106, 107, 110, 113, 116, 145, 150, 165, 190
eye movements 58, 59, 223

fluency 14, 20, 29, 30, 56, 96, 101, 112, 116, 217, 224, 229, 231
foreign language ability 77, 79, 132, 194
foreign language acquisition 67, 74, 75, 77, 194, 222
foreign language aptitude 66, 67, 71, 75, 76, 77, 78, 79, 80, 83, 84, 11, 128, 129, 130, 131, 132, 216, 227, 228
foreign language aptitude test 67, 71, 75, 76, 77, 129, 130, 132
foreign language competence 79, 194
foreign language course 66, 72, 74, 76, 77, 78, 79, 111, 128, 132, 133, 219, 227, 228
foreign language grade 76, 77, 78, 79, 228
foreign language learners
– at-risk foreign language learners 70, 114, 128, 129, 130, 131, 132, 228
– good foreign language learners 72, 78, 80, 128, 143
– LD foreign language learners 71, 76, 77
– poor foreign language learners 32, 68, 69, 72, 75, 77, 80, 133, 135, 194
foreign language learning v, vii, viii, x, 32,

233

66, 67, 68, 69, 70, 71, 72, 74, 75, 76, 77, 78, 80, 83, 84, 90, 127, 134, 194, 195, 214, 215, 216, 219, 222, 223, 224, 225
foreign language learning disability (FLLD) v, 70, 71, 216, 224
foreign language performance 111, 128, 129
foreign language proficiency viii, 75, 78, 80, 132, 194, 228
foreign language requirement vii, viii, 66, 194, 216, 227, 228
foreign language skill 76, 79, 133, 145
foreign language study vi, 84, 99, 111, 127, 130, 132, 146, 194, 216
foreign language teachers viii, ix, 76, 77, 79, 102, 128, 133, 195
foreign language teaching ix, 127, 128, 129, 131, 145, 213, 219, 221, 223, 224
functional magnetic resonance imaging (fMRI) 41, 57, 63, 64, 106, 225, 230

genes 6, 7, 34, 35, 36, 37, 63, 215, 216, 222, 224
grain size v, x, 13, 21, 24, 25, 26, 28, 50, 81, 84, 113, 114, 154, 213, 215, 232
grammar viii, 32, 69, 81, 87, 111, 133, 135, 149, 150, 179, 181, 182, 184, 185, 186, 188, 223, 225, 230
grapheme complexity 22
grapheme-phoneme conversion rules 19, 21, 24, 114, 134
grapheme-phoneme correspondences 14, 21, 24, 25, 48, 136, 231
grapheme-phoneme relations xi, 22, 46, 50, 90, 134, 154, 165

handwriting 62, 88, 92, 95, 138, 147, 206, 208, 209
heritability 35, 37

inclusion education/mainstreaming 145, 196
intelligence (IQ) 2, 4, 5, 6, 7, 8, 32, 63, 66, 67, 70, 73, 74, 75, 78, 79, 86, 96, 100, 103, 104, 135, 138, 215, 222, 226
interactive-compensatory model 17, 229
intervention xi, 9, , 31, 32, 37, 39, 49, 54, 56, 83, 89, 102, 104, 105, 106, 112, 115, 116, 117, 118, 119, 121, 122, 134, 142, 144, 146, 165, 179, 189, 193, 194, 195, 218, 219, 220, 221, 225, 226, 227, 231

language anxiety 75, 99
learning disorders ix, x, 2, 4, 52, 100
learning styles 66, 127
letter knowledge 13, 14, 103, 117, 153
letter-sound correspondences 13, 116, 125, 154, 196
letter-sound mapping 18, 29, 116, 193, 196
letter-sounds relations 19, 22

lexical/visual strategy 15, 49
linguistic coding differences hypothesis (LCDH) v, 68, 69, 71, 74, 78, 80, 82, 227
literacy acquisition x, 23, 37, 50, 86, 95, 98, 106, 115, 118, 193, 226
literacy difficulties 36, 89, 117, 231
literacy skills vii, ix, 37, 62, 97, 128
literacy training 50, 110
logographic stage 19
L-type dyslexia 20, 21, 118, 119

magnetic resonance imaging 39, 40, 63, 220, 225
magnocellular v, 34, 41, 52, 56, 57, 58, 59, 60, 61, 65, 120, 210, 216, 229
magnocellular deficit hypothesis v, 56, 65
mappings 16, 18, 19, 22, 23, 24, 25, 26, 28, 29, 36, 38, 39, 44, 46, 87, 90, 92, 101, 107, 116, 193, 196, 200, 231
memory 7, 11, 12, 13, 14, 19, 30, 32, 34, 43, 44, 47, 48, 50, 56, 58, 66, 67, 78, 83, 87, 92, 95, 96, 103, 104, 105, 107, 113, 114, 123, 126, 129, 130, 147, 148, 151, 214, 222
metacognitive 10, 124, 127, 133, 150, 195, 225
minimal brain damage (MBD) 39, 40
mnemonics 149, 150, 151
monolingual 39, 106, 108, 109, 113, 116, 118, 194, 195
morphemes 28, 93, 125, 175, 176, 178, 214
morphological awareness vi, 175, 214
motivation v, 7, 12, 32, 66, 68, 69, 74, 75, 76, 89, 97, 106, 121, 122, 123, 148, 151, 179, 182
motor skill 61, 62, 87, 92, 95, 105, 228
movable device xi, 148, 151, 157, 167, 168, 169, 170, 171, 176
multisensory approach viii, 124, 130
multisensory instruction viii, xi, 128, 133, 134, 143, 144, 145, 165, 223
multisensory methods viii, 124, 125
multisensory structured learning (MSL) v, vi, viii, 84, 122, 123, 124, 125, 126, 127, 128, 129, 130, 131, 132, 133, 134, 135, 137, 138, 142, 143, 144, 145
multisensory techniques 126, 151, 179

naming speed 13, 54, 55, 56, 107
native language abilities 73, 74, 76, 78, 80, 84, 128, 130, 131, 132
native language difficulties 69, 75, 83, 111, 216
native language learning vii, 67, 75, 76, 124
native language phonological measures 129, 132
native language skills vii, viii, 68, 69, 74, 75, 76, 77, 78, 79, 80, 111, 127, 129, 130, 131, 132, 133, 135, 145, 194, 216, 228
neuroimaging 38, 39, 64, 65, 112, 116, 217, 224

Index

non-word 26, 27, 29, 43, 47, 48, 49, 85, 87, 103
non-word repetition 47, 103

onset 13, 14, 16, 23, 24, 25, 31, 44, 45, 46, 50, 51, 62, 86, 97, 142, 154, 157, 158, 165, 192
orthographic awareness v, xi, 36, 165
orthographic depth v, x, 15, 21, 22, 23, 25, 27, 28, 38, 65, 84, 90, 101, 107, 110, 113, 114, 216, 220
orthographic neighbourhood 25, 26, 29, 221
orthographic processing 26, 70, 111, 194, 213, 230
orthographic stage 18, 19
orthography
– deep/opaque orthography 21, 22, 23, 27, 28, 30, 50, 82, 91, 112, 134
– transparent/shallow orthography 14, 22, 23, 24, 25, 26, 29, 30, 49, 50, 56, 82, 83, 101, 213, 214, 217
Orton-Gillingham (OG) 124, 126, 128, 225, 227

personality disorders 89, 97, 99, 135
phonemic awareness 14, 31, 44, 46, 47, 50, 69, 111, 121, 122, 153, 210, 229
phonics 44, 121, 124, 153, 154, 217, 230
phonological abilities 13, 14, 21, 36, 43, 54, 60, 63, 79, 223
phonological assessment battery 109, 113, 215
phonological awareness vi, 9, 13, 14, 23, 31, 43, 44, 45, 46, 47, 48, 52, 63, 67, 69, 80, 81, 83, 110, 112, 116, 125, 153, 154, 155, 193, 196, 218, 222, 224, 225, 231
phonological coding deficit hypothesis v, 43, 47, 48, 51, 84, 113, 218
phonological competence 31, 45
phonological decoding 15, 16, 36, 52, 82, 113
phonological deficit 8, 30, 32, 47, 50, 51, 52, 53, 55, 80, 101, 103, 110, 121, 193, 218, 221, 230
phonological development 36, 44, 49, 85, 87
phonological difficulties 47, 51, 64
phonological dyslexia 49, 52
phonological elements 10, 28, 44, 47, 50
phonological impairment 29, 51, 54, 101
phonological measures 56, 108, 109, 129, 132
phonological neighbourhood 49, 50
phonological/orthographic awareness 36
phonological/orthographic competence 128, 131
phonological/orthographic measures 130, 132
phonological/orthographic processing 70, 194
phonological/orthographic skills 77, 79, 82, 83, 143
phonological/orthographic system viii, 136, 137, 142, 194

phonological processing x, 4, 5, 7, 8, 9, 15, 30, 31, 32, 34, 37, 38, 40, 43, 47, 48, 49, 50, 51, 52, 53, 54, 55, 56, 60, 61, 63, 64, 65, 68, 69, 83, 84, 85, 86, 87, 93, 96, 101, 103, 104, 105, 107, 108, 114, 120, 129, 192, 193, 195
phonological representations 26, 48, 49, 50, 51, 54, 85, 87, 96, 193, 217, 218
phonological segments 24, 45
phonological skills 13, 30, 32, 50, 51, 56, 58, 60, 63, 81, 96, 109, 110, 120, 121, 129, 193, 194, 213, 217, 219
phonological/sublexical/indirect strategy 15, 16, 27, 49
phonological training 47, 115, 116, 117, 193, 196, 121
phonological units 10, 24, 45, 46, 81, 154
planum temporal 40, 41, 64, 106, 114, 218
pragmatics 10, 85, 103
pre-alphabetic stage 19
pre-literacy 13, 14, 37, 50
predictors x, 13, 14, 30, 47, 56, 69, 78, 79, 82, 111
pre-school 15, 35, 86, 89, 211, 219, 222
print processing 4, 6, 85, 104, 108, 124
pseudo-word 13, 16, 26, 48, 85, 96, 103, 107, 132, 195
psycholinguistic grain size theory 24, 25, 28, 213, 232
P-type dyslexia 20, 21, 118, 119, 210

rapid serial naming (RAN) 13, 47, 54, 55, 103
readiness for learning to read and spell 11, 12
reading ability 17, 27, 29, 31, 32, 43, 46, 53, 56, 93, 100, 101, 110, 116, 119, 120, 121, 192, 194, 196, 220, 226, 227, 229
reading development v, 1, 4, 13, 14, 15, 17, 18, 25, 29, 30, 35, 47, 51, 55, 65, 113, 152, 192, 193, 194, 213, 214, 217, 224, 225
reading difficulties 3, 8, 9, 23, 31, 46, 48, 51, 52, 53, 54, 55, 56, 59, 61, 81, 82, 85, 86, 89, 90, 97, 100, 101, 104, 108, 118, 122, 213, 218, 221
reading disorder 1, 2, 3, 4, 5, 17, 32, 35, 36, 38, 48, 56, 62, 100, 109, 190
reading errors 53, 90, 119, 217
reading impairment vii, 1, 6, 36, 38, 47, 48, 55, 57, 61, 86, 89, 102, 217
reading instruction 13, 15, 25, 26, 39, 44, 47, 48, 51, 87, 116, 117, 121, 126, 192, 225, 231
reading problem 2, 6, 8, 9, 30, 35, 38, 49, 52, 53, 62, 81, 86, 89, 97, 101, 107
reading skills 2, 7, 8, 10, 13, 14, 17, 18, 27, 32, 46, 47, 51, 52, 58, 83, 86, 96, 98, 107, 108, 117, 120, 127, 139, 141, 142, 143, 145, 192, 193, 213, 217, 227, 230
reading strategy v, 13, 15, 16, 24, 26, 27, 65, 90, 101, 113, 118

reading subskills 14, 67
restructuring 22, 49, 50
retrieval vii, 47, 48, 87, 93, 95, 96, 103, 147, 149, 151
rewriting 88, 91, 103, 151, 175
rhyme 12, 21, 34, 45, 46, 87, 119, 156, 157, 213, 217
right ear advantage (REA) 40, 64, 105, 106, 114
rime 13, 14, 16, 19, 23, 24, 25, 31, 44, 45, 46, 50, 62, 81, 154, 157, 158, 165, 231
risk for dyslexia 35, 37, 48, 86, 87, 88, 89, 112, 113, 122, 211

segmenting 14, 19, 24, 36, 44, 45, 48, 49, 50, 51, 81, 128, 153, 155, 156, 157, 161
self-esteem 97, 99, 102, 106, 112
self-perception 74, 75, 76, 97
semantics 5, 10, 13, 17, 20, 26, 48, 51, 53, 68, 69, 72, 75, 77, 79, 80, 81, 85, 88, 94, 103, 113, 130, 175, 231
sensorimotor impairment 52, 53, 121, 217, 229, 231
sequencing 7, 11, 15, 16, 18, 21, 36, 42, 45, 46, 47, 56, 87, 91, 95, 96, 106, 109, 120, 125, 126, 149, 153, 154, 193
short-term memory (STM) 7, 13, 30, 43, 47, 48, 129, 222
sound-symbol 66, 67, 70, 78, 127, 128
special educational needs (SEN) ix, 4, 145, 211
speech sounds 9, 40, 44, 48, 60, 64, 68, 103, 106, 113, 114, 193, 222
spelling ability 1, 14, 27, 85, 88, 103
spelling choices 11, 22, 49, 90, 133, 137, 149, 165, 207
spelling difficulties 3, 8, 34, 51, 62, 63, 89, 92, 98, 100, 105, 115, 192, 212, 217, 223, 224, 225, 226, 229, 232
spelling disorder vii, 1, 2, 3, 143, 219
spelling impairment 3, 48

spelling mistakes 90, 91, 92, 96, 150, 151, 208, 223
spelling patterns xi, 19, 29, 134, 137, 151, 154, 165, 166, 167, 169, 170, 172, 174, 193, 211
spelling problem vii, 100, 225
spelling skills viii, xi, 2, 10, 86, 90, 97, 113, 116, 121, 123, 128, 133, 134, 139, 140, 141, 142, 145, 165
spelling rules 136, 138, 144, 213
spelling-to-sound 22, 25, 231
substitutions 29, 73, 88, 90, 113, 153, 162, 163, 164, 226, 228
syllable 19, 24, 44, 45, 46, 50, 88, 91, 105, 154, 156, 165, 166, 167, 170, 218
symptoms v, x, 1, 5, 8, 32, 34, 47, 51, 53, 57, 85, 86, 88, 89, 90, 91, 93, 95, 96, 97, 98, 99, 100, 101, 103, 105, 112, 191, 192, 211, 224
– inconsistent spelling 91, 134, 207
– phonetic spelling 91, 207

teaching/instructional approach xi, 115, 124, 126, 191, 194, 195, 196
top-down model/strategy 16, 17
tracing 88, 125, 148, 149
treatment v, x, 39, 56, 105, 106, 109, 112, 115, 116, 117, 118, 119, 120, 121, 134, 137, 138, 146, 191, 195, 196, 210, 212, 220, 223, 225

verbalizing 149, 150, 151
visual motion sensitivity 57, 58, 60, 230
visual-motor co-ordination 87, 88, 105, 114
visual perception 12, 58, 104, 113, 168, 169, 217, 226
visual processing 17, 30, 53, 112, 151, 215
visual system 52, 56, 57, 58, 59, 60, 65

word family 152, 172, 177
word letter-length 22
word recognition 15, 17, 23, 24, 26, 27, 28, 31, 36, 64, 81, 83, 96, 107, 108, 116, 127, 132, 154, 193, 195, 213, 216